SEASONS OF MY LIFE

Rudolph F. Kapitan

RUMSCLAD PUBLISHING, Crown Point, Indiana
Printed by Messenger Press, Carthagena, Ohio

First Printing

On the Cover

The family photo was taken in 1998 on my wife Mary's 65th birthday. The last two of our grandchildren, Olivia Small and Maggie Metcalf, were born in 2001.

Olivia Small   Maggie Metcalf

In the background, to the left, is the St. Charles Seminary building in Carthagena, Ohio with an overview photo of me as a 20 year old seminarian.

To the right is the wedding picture of Mary Kasper Kapitan and the author, Rudolph F. Kapitan.

To Mayor Tom   11-7-19
Enjoy Dad's story
Mike

SEASONS OF MY LIFE

By Rudolph F. Kapitan

Published by:

    Rumsclad Publishing
    P.O. Box 1434
    Crown Point, Indiana 46308

Printed and bound in the United States of America

ISBN 0-9701515-2-7
Library of Congress Card Number

DEDICATION

I dedicate this book to my dear wife Mary.

As **Wife** she fulfilled her responsibilities with love and understanding.

As **Mother** she carried and gave birth to six beautiful children.

Through her values and convictions she continues to inspire us.

Through her sacrifices she motivates us in principled ways.

Acknowledgements

Thanks to my wife Mary (Kasper) Kapitan for the unselfish giving of her time. Many hours were taken from her to devote to the production of this book.

Thanks to my daughter Carol (Kapitan) Sanders for her inspiration in naming my first publication "Seasons Of My Childhood" and also this publication "Seasons Of My Life" and her photographic expertise.

Thanks to my children for their assistance in critiquing the pages as they related to their lives.

Thanks to my sister Mary Kapitan Germek for her assistance with the recipes from our mother's kitchen.

Thanks to seminary classmates and friends, especially to Rev. Dominic Gerlach, C.PP.S. and to Steve Almasy for assistance in critiquing the chapter on seminary life.

Thanks to Dr. James Lane of Indiana University for his gracious assistance in critiquing and proof reading this manuscript.

Thanks to Kathy Nuzzo and the staff of Via Marketing of Merrillville, Indiana for their design assistance.

Thanks to Randy Heitkamp of The Messenger Press for his assistance in the production of this book.

Thanks to all those, who in any way contributed to this story of my life.

CONTENTS

SEASONS

OF MY

LIFE

SEASONS OF MY LIFE

PROLOGUE

It was 1940, the beginning of a new decade, and this is where my book, Seasons of My Childhood, published earlier, ended. As this story unravels, Mom, Dad and seven of us children lived at 2115 New York Ave. Whiting, Indiana in a five room basement apartment. The eldest, John, was 17, Mary was 12, I was 10, Tillie 5, Ambrose 3 years old and the twins, Joey and Tony were 1. Dad was a strict disciplinarian and there was little, if anything, to be desired in our deportment. Our lives revolved around our Catholic religion and our Slovak ethnicity.

At this time, in Europe, Adolph Hitler had declared Austria, Hungary and Bulgaria as German protectorates. Earlier Hitler had invaded and occupied Czechoslovakia and Poland. The war in Europe had expanded as Nazi troops invaded Denmark, Norway, Sweden, Belgium, Luxembourg and the Netherlands. It wasn't long after that France fell to German troops

Italian troops, under the leadership of Benito Mussolini, "Il Duce," joined forces with the Nazis, as together they invaded Yugoslavia, Albania, Romania and Greece. The swastika flew over most of Europe including Latvia, Lithuania and Estonia.

Then Germany declared war on Great Britain and began daily bombing flights over England. Italy, an ally of Germany, followed suit and declared war on Great Britain. President Franklin D. Roosevelt condemned what the Germans and Italians were doing in Europe. Churchill pleaded for help from the U.S. Our president did not want the United States to get involved with the war. After all, we were just recovering from the depression. Our Gross National Product had doubled as our unemployment rate fell some 15%, to less than 10% unemployed. New products came to market. Among the new products was cellophane wrap. It was introduced as a domestic aid for simplifying certain kitchen tasks. Morton's Salt appeared on grocery shelves in disposable boxes. There was an expansion of canned goods. Electric refrigerators and gas stoves were becoming commonplace in the kitchens of America.

The songs we sang proclaimed the good times of our lives. Songs like "When You Wish Upon A Star," "You Are My Sunshine," "The Woodpecker Song," "Blueberry Hill," "The Breeze and I" and songs from Walt Disney's *Fantasia* and *Pinocchio*.

In the Orient, the Japanese were busy buying up all the scrap metal that our junk dealers could collect from unsuspecting Americans. Max Barton, our junk man, made weekly passes through our alleys with his horse drawn old gray buckboard wagon. "Rex O Lie" (rags old iron) he sang in his gravely base voice. Out to the alley we ran with our hands full of old rags and junk iron, three cents for a pound of rags and a nickel for a pound of rusty old iron.

Cargo ship after cargo ship sailed towards Japan with millions of tons of American scrap metal. Small changes began to appear across the country. President Roosevelt signed the first peacetime draft into law. Every American man aged 18 to 35 had to register with the draft board. Registering for the draft from our block on New York Avenue in Whiting were the Dado, Stecy and Kertis boys, together with John Sinal and Edwin Markut.

Even Joe Louis, the "heavyweight boxing champion of

the world," registered for the draft. As he did, the Chicago *Tribune* reported that he promised to fight one last fight before his induction into the army. I remember the fight very well. Mom had just finished breast feeding the twins, put them to bed (they slept in the same crib in the dining room) and had retired to the kitchen. There she was making homemade noodles for the next day's pot of beef soup. Dad, Johnny, Mary and I were in the living room with our ears attuned to our Philco table model radio. My brother Ambsie lay on the living room floor watching Tillie color the coloring book she had gotten from Santa. We were part of the millions who sat by their radios to listen to the "brown bomber's" last fight. Just as it had before, Gillette sponsored this fight. Joe Louis' contender was Buddy Baer, the younger brother of former heavyweight champion, Max Baer. Buddy Baer was a giant of a man, taller and heavier than Louis. He also had a longer reach than Louis.

The bell sounded the beginning of the first round and the fight began. "A right and a left jab by Louis and then an uppercut to Baer's chin." "A left jab to Louis' chin and then a right and a left." An excited announcer visualized, for the radio audience, all the jabs to the face, uppercuts to the chin and rights and lefts to the body. So it went for five rounds as we sat glued to the radio. Then, as if struck by a bolt of lightning, Joe Louis went staggering to the ropes. The thunderous blow landed by Baer opened a gash over Louis' left eye. "Blood is streaming down Louis' face," the announcer shouted. "Louis' left eye is covered by streaming blood as he staggers around." Baer was hovering over Louis as the ringside bell announced the end of round five. "Saved by the bell" shouted the exhausted ringside announcer.

The sixth round was uneventful as Louis and Baer exchanged blows. Then in the seventh round Joe Louis landed a smashing right to Baer's jaw, a blow that sent him crashing to the canvas. "One, two" began the ref's count. Dad, Johnny, Mary and I joined in the radio announcers count — "3,4,5,6,7,8,9,10 and you're OUT!"

"EXTRA, EXTRA read all about it," shouted newspaper carriers as they ran throughout the streets early the next morning, offering the special "extra edition." Putting two cents into my hand Dad said "*chod a kup papier*" (go and buy the paper). I ran out to get a copy of that extra.

Chapter I - The War Years

It was Sunday afternoon, Dec. 7th, 1941. Our radio program was interrupted. "The Japanese have just bombed Pearl Harbor. Thousands of American sailors and soldiers have been killed. Our fleet, anchored in Pearl Harbor, has been completely destroyed." I ran outside looking upwards towards the sky. In my child's mind I was looking for Japanese bombers. In a state of shock and utter disbelief I looked up and down New York Avenue for signs of war. I saw none and ran back into the house. President Franklin Delano Roosevelt had just made an announcement on the radio. He confirmed the fact that the Japanese had bombed Pearl Harbor in a sneak attack on our fleet. In a very somber voice he said "this day will live in infamy." The next day, December 8th, the United States declared war on Japan. Since Adolph Hitler's Germany and Benito Mussolini's Italy were allies of Japan, they declared war on the United States several days later.

In his Christmas holiday Fireside Chat, President Roosevelt announced that Jan. 1, 1942 was to be held as "National Prayer Day." That announcement set the tone for religious services throughout the Whiting churches. At Immaculate Conception, Fr. Lach, the pastor, announced that a Novena to Our Sorrowful Mother would be held every Friday evening. Fr. Bach conducted the Novena in English at 6:30 P.M. and Fr. Lach in Slovak at 7:30 P.M. It was standing room only for the Friday evening Novenas as parishioners and non-parishioners, like our family, packed the church. Tears flowed down many a cheek as the Friday night congregation lifted up their plaintiff voices in the concluding hymn.

"Dear Lady of Fatima, we come on bended knee
To beg your intercession, for peace and unity.
Dear Mary won't you show us, the right and shining way,
We pledge our love and offer you, a rosary each day."

Many worshippers stayed in their pews to sing the second verse:

"You promised at Fatima, each time that you appeared,
To help us if we pray to you, to banish war and fear.
Dear Lady of Fatima, we ask your guiding hand,
For grace and guidance here on earth, and protection for our land."

Prayer services were being held throughout our great country. There were no vocal atheists on the home front.

As weeks ran into months the signs of war began to appear, signs involving and changing all of our lives. Volunteers eagerly responded to the posters of Uncle Sam pointing his finger with the caption "**I WANT YOU**." Banks began selling War Bonds and the post offices began selling ten-cent "war bond stamps" as did the Hoosier Theater. The cardboard stamp holders contained 187 slots, which, when filled with ten cent stamps, plus a nickel, were cashed in for a Twenty Five Dollar War Bond. That made the purchase price of the War Bond $18.75. The matured value (in ten years) was the $25.00 face value.

Within the year rationing came into existence. No longer were we free to buy whatever we wanted. Red ration stamps were for meat. Blue ration stamps were for canned goods. The ration stamps received by each family depended on the number of persons in the family. There were also ration stamps for other consumer goods as shoes and gas. Silk stockings became non-existent as the silk went to making parachutes for the war. The gasoline rationing involved the issuance of A, B and C and E decal stickers. The amount of gas allowed for each car depended

OFFICIAL TABLE OF CONSUMER POINT VALUES FOR MEAT, FATS, FISH, AND CHEESE

No. 1—Effective March 29, 1943

BEEF

STEAKS	Points per lb.
Porterhouse	8
T-bone	8
Club	8
Rib—10-inch cut	7
Rib—7-inch cut	8
Sirloin	8
Sirloin—boneless	9
Round	8
Top Round	8
Bottom Round	8
Round Tip	8
Chuck or Shoulder	7
Flank	8

ROASTS	Points per lb.
Rib—standing (chine bone on) (10" cut)	7
Blade Rib—standing (chine bone on) (10" cut)	6
Rib—standing (chine bone on) (7" cut)	8
Blade Rib—standing (chine bone on) (7" cut)	7
Round Tip	7
Rump—bone in	7
Rump—boneless	8
Chuck or Shoulder—bone in	6
Chuck or Shoulder—boneless	7

STEWS AND OTHER CUTS	Points per lb.
Short Ribs	4
Plate—bone in	4
Plate—boneless	5
Brisket—bone in	4
Brisket—boneless	6
Flank Meat	5
Neck—bone in	5
Neck—boneless	6
Heel of Round boneless	8
Shank—bone in	4
Shank—boneless	6

HAMBURGER	Points per lb.
Beef ground from necks, flanks, shanks, briskets, plates, and miscellaneous beef trimmings and beef fat	5

BEEF

VARIETY MEATS	Points per lb.
Brains	3
Hearts	4
Kidneys	4
Livers	3
Sweetbreads	4
Tails (ex joints)	3
Tongues	6
Tripe	3

VEAL

STEAKS AND CHOPS	Points per lb.
Loin Chops	8
Rib Chops	7
Shoulder Chops	6
Round Steak (cutlets)	7
Sirloin Steak or Chops	7

ROASTS	Points per lb.
Rump and Sirloin—bone in	6
Rump and Sirloin—boneless	8
Leg	6
Shoulder—bone in	6
Shoulder—boneless	8

STEWS AND OTHER CUTS	Points per lb.
Breast—bone in	4
Breast—boneless	6
Flank Meat	5
Neck—bone in	5
Neck—boneless	4
Shank—bone in	5
Shank and Heel Meat—boneless	6
Ground Veal and Patties—veal ground from necks, flanks, shanks, breasts, and miscellaneous veal trimmings	6

VARIETY MEATS	Points per lb.
Brains	4
Kidneys	5
Livers	8
Sweetbreads	6
Tongues	6

LAMB—MUTTON

STEAKS AND CHOPS	Points per lb.
Loin Chops	8
Rib Chops	7
Leg Chops	7
Shoulder Chops—blade or arm chops	7

ROASTS	Points per lb.
Leg—whole or part	6
Sirloin Roast—bone in	6
Yoke, Rattle, or Triangle—bone in	5
Yoke, Rattle, or Triangle—boneless	7
Chuck or Shoulder, square cut—bone in	6
Chuck or Shoulder, square cut—boneless	8
Chuck or Shoulder, cross-cut—bone in	5

STEWS AND OTHER CUTS	Points per lb.
Breast and Flank	3
Neck—bone in	4
Neck—boneless	5
Shank—bone in	4
Lamb Patties—lamb ground from necks, flanks, shanks, breasts and miscellaneous lamb trimmings	6

VARIETY MEATS	Points per lb.
Brains	3
Hearts	3
Livers	6
Kidneys	3
Sweetbreads	4
Tongues	6

BACON

BACON	Points per lb.
Bacon—slab or piece, rind on	7
Bacon—slab or piece, rind off	8
Bacon—Canadian style, piece or sliced	11
Bacon—sliced, rind off	8
Bacon—rinds	1
Bacon—plate and jowl squares	5

PORK

STEAKS AND CHOPS	Points per lb.
Center Chops	8
End Chops	7
Loin—boneless, fresh and cured only	10
Tenderloin	10
Ham, sliced	8
Shoulder Chops and Steaks	7
Bellies, fresh and cured only	6

ROASTS	Points per lb.
Loin—whole, half, or end cuts	7
Loin—center cuts	8
Ham—whole or half	7
Ham—butt or shank end	7
Ham—boneless	9
Shoulder—shank half (picnic) bone in	6
Shoulder—shank half (picnic) boneless	8
Shoulder—butt half (Boston butt)—bone in	7
Shoulder—butt half (Boston butt)—boneless	8

OTHER PORK CUTS	Points per lb.
Spareribs	4
Neck and Backbones	2
Feet—bone in	1
Fat Backs and Clear Plates	4
Plates, regular	5
Jowls	5
Hocks and Knuckles	3
Leaf Fat	4

VARIETY MEATS	Points per lb.
Brains	2
Chitterlings	4
Hearts	3
Kidneys	2
Livers	5
Tongues	6
Ears	1
Tails	3
Snouts	2

READY-TO-EAT MEATS

COOKED, BOILED, BAKED, AND BARBECUED	Points per lb.
Dried Beef	12
Ham—bone in, whole or half	9
Ham—bone in, slices	11
Ham—butt or shank end	9
Ham—boneless, whole or half	10
Ham—boneless, slices	11
Picnic or Shoulder—bone in	8
Picnic or Shoulder—boneless	10
Bouillon Cubes, Beef Extract, and all other meat extracts and concentrates	7
Tongues	8
Spareribs	6
Pigs Feet—bone in	2

The point value of any other ready-to-eat meat item shall be determined by adding 2 points per pound to the point value per pound of the uncooked item from which it is prepared if it is sold whole, or 3 points per pound shall be added if it is cooked and sliced.

SAUSAGE

SAUSAGE	Points per lb.
Dry Sausage—Hard: Typical items are hard Salami, hard Cervelat, and Pepperoni	9
Semi-dry Sausage: Typical items are soft Salami, Thuringer, and Mortadella	8
Fresh, Cooked and Cooked Sausage:	
Group A: Typical items are Pork Sausage, Wieners, Bologna, Baked Loaves, and Liver Sausage	7
Group B: Typical items are Scrapple and Tamales. Souse and Head Cheese also included	4

MEATS (In tin or glass containers)	Points per lb.	MEATS (In tin or glass containers)	Points per lb.	FISH (In any hermetically sealed container)	Points per lb.	FATS AND OILS	Points per lb.
Brains	3	Pigs Feet, boned Cutlets	3	Bonito	7	Butter*	8
Bulk Sausage	7	Potted and Deviled Meats	4	Caviar	7	Lard*	5
Chili Con Carne	3	Sausage in Oil	4	Crabmeat	7	Shortening*	5
Deviled Ham	6	Tamales	2	Fish Roe	7	Margarine	5
Dried Beef	12	Tongue, Beef	7	Mackerel	7	Salad and Cooking Oils (1 pint = 1 pound)	6
Hams and Picnics (whole or half)	10	Tongue, Lamb	7	Salmon	7		
Luncheon Meat	7	Tongue, Pork	6	Sardines	7		
Meat Loaf	7	Tongue, Veal	7	Sea Herring	7		
Meat Spreads	6	Vienna Sausage	7	Tuna	7		
Pigs Feet, bone in	2	All Other	7	Yellow Tail	7		
				All Other	7		

CHEESES*

Rationed cheeses include natural cheeses and products containing 30 percent or more by weight of natural cheese.

Examples of rationed cheeses:		CHEESES*	
Cheddar (American)		Greek (all hard varieties)	All 8
Swiss		Process Cheese	
Brick		Cheese Foods	
Münster	All 8		
Limburger		Some cheeses are not rationed. The important examples are: Cream Cheese, Neufchatel, Cottage, Camembert, Liederkranz, Brie, Blue.	
Club			
Gouda		(For a complete list of cheeses not rationed, see the Regulations.)	
Edam			
Smoked			
Italian (all hard varieties)			

*Except purchases in bulk units containing more than five (5) pounds (not subdivided into units of 5 pounds or less.) For such purchases see Official Table of Trade Point Values.

U S GOVERNMENT PRINTING OFFICE 817306

Point values that consumers will pay beginning next Monday morning, March 29, for meats, cheeses, fats and oils, and canned fish are shown on the accompanying "Official Table of Consumer Point Values" released by the Office of Price Administration.

Examination of this table, which every seller of the newly-rationed foods will be required to display in his store, discloses that the meats and fats rations are relatively more liberal than the rations of processed foods.

---

on the sticker pasted in the lower left-hand corner of the front windshield. Even paper matchbooks disappeared from stores. We bought wooden "kitchen matches" from Bubala's grocery store located on the corner of 121st Street and White Oak Avenue. They came in a five cent 2" x 6" rectangular cardboard box, faced on one edge with a sandpaper striking surface. Sugar disappeared from the A&P and Kroger shelves. In the beginning, as regular grocery customers, Benny Bubala saw to it that we had enough sugar, especially when Mom was canning.

Application Blank For Canning Sugar

OPA Form No. R-315

UNITED STATES OF AMERICA
Office of Price Administration

SPECIAL PURPOSE APPLICATION
for
Sugar Purchase Certificate

NOT TO BE FILLED IN BY APPLICANT

Local Rationing Board No._____

County _____ State _____

Date _____

IMPORTANT

This form is to be used in applying for a Sugar Purchase Certificate necessitated by a special purpose such as home canning. Applicant must present this application along with War Ration Books of each member of family unit to local OPA War Price and Rationing Board. If application is mailed to local OPA War Price and Rationing Board, a stamped and addressed return envelope must be mailed in with application, along with the War Ration Books of each member of the family unit.

1. Name of applicant_____War Ration Book No._____

2. Address _____
   Number   Street   City   County   State

3. Names of the other Individuals in the Family Unit, and Serial No. of War Ration Book held by each:

   Name _____   War Ration Book No. _____
   Name _____   War Ration Book No. _____
   Name _____   War Ration Book No. _____
   Name _____   War Ration Book No. _____
   Name _____   War Ration Book No. _____
   Name _____   War Ration Book No. _____
   Name _____   War Ration Book No. _____

4. Number of quarts of fruit of all kinds canned in year 1941 _____

5. Amount of sugar already obtained in 1942 on previous applications for home canning _____lbs.

6. Amount of canning sugar still unused out of previous canning allotments _____lbs.

7. Number of quarts of fruit canned with sugar already obtained on previous applications in 1942 _____lbs.

8. Number of quarts of fruit now in possession of Family Unit, or individual applying _____

9. Number of quarts of fruit to be canned between date of this application and December 31, 1942 _____

10. Number of pounds of sugar for which application is made _____ lbs. (IMPORTANT: Applicant is entitled to receive only one pound of sugar for each four quarts of finished canned fruits or fruit juices for home consumption.)

11. Number of additional pounds of sugar needed for preserves, jams, jellies or fruit butters? _____lbs. (IMPORTANT: Only one pound of sugar per person per year is allowed for this purpose. If allotment has already been made on previous application in 1942, no further allotment can be made until 1943.)

12. If no War Ration Books were issued, how many pounds of sugar did family unit have on May 4, 1942? _____lbs.

13. Registered at _____
    (Name of school, building, or other address.)

NOTE: Presentation of incorrect facts on this application represents a violation of Rationing Order No. 3 which is a crime punishable by a fine of not more than $10,000.00, or imprisonment of not more than one year, or both.

APPLICATION AND CERTIFICATION

I HEREBY make application for the issuance of a Sugar Purchase Certificate authorizing the acceptance of delivery of sugar in such amount as may be allotted on the basis of statements made herein, and certify and represent to the Office of Price Administration, an agency of the United States, that I am the _____(applicant, agent of applicant, or representative of applying organization); that the facts herein stated are true; and that I am authorized to make the statements herein.

Signature _____
(IMPORTANT—Application must be signed.)

Date _____   Acting for _____

CERTIFICATION OF ISSUING OFFICER

I CERTIFY that I have issued to the person above the following Sugar Purchase Certificate on the basis of the information submitted.

Effective date _____   Signature _____

Serial Number of Certificate issued_____ Weight value _____ lbs.

SPECIAL FOR REGION III

Aluminum kitchen utensils began to be replaced by PLASTIC, a new substance. Plastic also replaced rubber. Rubber and aluminum had gone off to war, as did the green on Lucky Strike cigarette packs. The color of the new "war production" Lucky Strike cigarette packets was changed to white. Our coins changed. The copper used in penny production went to war. The new war cent was made of a zinc steel composition. The nickel in the five-cent piece went to war and was replaced with silver.

A federal agency was established to fix and set prices on goods and on rents. A blue ribbon panel of industrialists was chosen to govern the Office of Price Administration, or the OPA. as it was called. The federal government also formed a "War Production Board." The War Production Board dictated what companies would produce, how much and at what price.

Air raid wardens were chosen for every block in town. They wore steel helmets and carried flashlights and pump canisters of water. Mr. Andrew Fedorko was the air raid warden for our 2100 block of New York Avenue. The air raid wardens were responsible to see to it that every light in every house and all streetlights were turned off when the air raid siren was sounded. If we wanted to continue listening to the radio when the air raid sounded, we pulled down all the window shades in the house, turned off all the lights and sat in the darkness listening to the radio until the "all clear" sounded.

Before long most every child in Whiting knew the words to all the service songs. They were played over and over again on the radio. My sister Mary played them on her harmonica. We felt very patriotic as we sang "Anchors Aweigh" the Navy song, or the Marine song "From the Halls of Montezuma," or the Air Force song "Off We Go into the Wild Blue Yonder" or the

STATE OF INDIANA

AIR RAID INSTRUCTIONS

WHEN YOU HEAR Steady note of siren or whistle for 2 minutes. — AIR RAID IS PROBABLE — (1) All building, home, store and street lights black out. Keep radio on. (2) Pedestrians and vehicle movement permitted. (3) Prepare to seek shelter. Civilian Defense forces mobilize.

WHEN YOU HEAR Warbling note of siren for 2 minutes, or. Choppy blasts of steam whistle for 2 minutes. — RAIDERS ARE OVERHEAD — (1) All lights blacked out. Keep radio on. (2) Vehicles stop, discharge passengers. (3) Everybody take cover.

WHEN YOU HEAR Steady note of siren or whistle for 2 minutes. — RAIDERS MAY RETURN — (1) Building, home, store and street lights stay out. Keep radio on. (2) Pedestrians may leave shelter. (3) Resume pedestrian and vehicular movements.

"ALL CLEAR" Street lights go on, no-tification by wardens, police, etc., or possible radio announcements. — RAIDERS HAVE PASSED — (1) Resume all normal activities. All lights may go on.

REMAIN CALM. WALK, DO NOT RUN. OBEY INSTRUCTIONS OF POLICE AND AIR RAID WARDENS.

(DO NOT USE TELEPHONE)

INDIANA STATE DEFENSE COUNCIL

Effective March 15, 1943   Clarence A. Jackson, Director

Army "Caisson" song, a song my Dad learned in WWI. It was a song he taught my Mom to sing. Songs that we sang along with the military ones were "You Made Me Love You," "Don't Sit Under The Apple Tree," "Why Don't You Do Right" and a favorite of mine, Vaughn Monroe's "Racing With the Moon." Another wartime favorite, a tribute to our airmen, was "Coming In On a Wing and a Prayer."

Bricklayers and carpenters erected "Honor Roll" memorials in honor of those serving in the armed forces. These memorials were erected on vacant lots throughout the city. The memorial on our block was erected in the empty lot of the north east corner of New York and Steiber Street. The names of all Soldiers, Sailors, Marines, Airmen, Coast Guardsmen, WACS and WAVES were imprinted in a glass enclosed framework for all to see. A forty-eight star United States flag waved proudly atop the twenty five-foot tall flag pole of the memorial. Ladies of our block planted flowers at the site. Mrs. Kovach, Sinal, Gesik, Nemish, Markut, Dado, Stecy, Kertis were among those ladies. The memorial was dedicated on Sunday Nov. 21, 1943. Here is a copy of that memorial service.

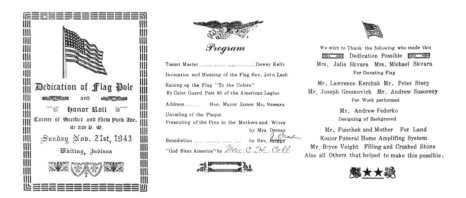

The photograph of the memorial shown is one from the next block on West Fred St.

East Fred St. Memorial Dedication

Proudly displayed in many front room windows, hanging by a gold embroidered cord, were 6" x 12" banners of white silk cloth edged in red with a red star in the center. The star signified that a serviceman or service woman from that house was serving in the war. If there were more than one person in the service additional stars were sewed onto the banner. There were homes that displayed two, three and even more stars. The Hruskocy house on Indianapolis Boulevard proudly displayed SIX stars for their sons Andrew, Thomas, Stephen, John, Frank and Milton. Mr. & Mrs. Joe Kujawa were another "six star Whiting family."

"Victory Gardens" could be found in many Whiting "back yards." Ours was a 10' x 20' plot. We considered it a patriotic duty to "pitch-in" and help conserve precious energy by producing vegetables. Early in the spring Dad "turned over" spade full after spade full of that fertile humus in our "back yard." Mom mounded the area into four by five-foot sections. Nickel packets of seeds were purchased at Woolworth's five and dime store. We planted radishes, peas, onions, kohlrabi, leaf lettuce, parsley, tomatoes and cucumbers. There was no room for vine crops like melons and pumpkins; they took up too much growing area. The vegetables not grown in our Victory Garden were purchased from Bill Scheeringa, the *pitlar* (farmer).

Now is the time to
PLANT A
VICTORY GARDEN

Make your spare time count for Victory!

Planting a Victory Garden is not only patriotic ... but it's thrifty and healthful too.

PATRIOTIC because food fights for freedom. The food grown in your own garden saves transportation, packing and labor.

THRIFTY because you save points.

HEALTHFUL because you get exercise, sunshine and fresh air and your family will thrive on the tasty vegetables you grow.

If you grew a Victory Garden last year, why not try to manage a bigger one this year?

THIS SPACE CONTRIBUTED TO THE NATION'S ALL-OUT WAR EFFORT BY NORTHERN INDIANA PUBLIC SERVICE COMPANY

Call to Victory Gardeners

"Aa-uga Aa-uga" came the sound from farmer Bill's dark green two-ton stake truck loaded with fresh vegetables from his Highland farm. Housewives dressed in flowery aprons and babushkas hurried to the farm truck parked at the curb. With just three cars on our entire block, the farmer had his choice of parking spots. On Saturdays the *pitlar's* truck was loaded with crates full of chickens, usually hens whose egg laying days had come to an end.

"Puck, puck, puck" came the sound from under the bushel basket on the floor in the corner of our kitchen. Mom placed a heavy Sears & Roebuck catalogue on top of the bushel basket to keep her hand-picked chicken confined until butchering time. A sheet of newspaper had been placed under the bushel to catch the chicken droppings. These precious droppings were used to fertilize our "victory garden." At our president's exhortation and request we made use of everything. It was part of our patriotic duty to "Use it up, Wear it out, Make it do or Do without!"

Weekly baths were taken every Saturday evening. It was after that ritual that Dad performed another Saturday ritual. Grabbing the chicken from under the bushel basket in the kitchen, he folded the chicken's wings and walked the few steps to the bathroom. There, standing above the toilet bowl he placed the chicken between his legs and cut off the head. A pot of water was brought to a boil on our new gas stove. The boiling water was poured over the butchered chicken to loosen the feathers. We ran for the living room as the "foul" smell filled the kitchen. Feathers that were not plucked out were singed off over the flames of our gas stove. The "burnt feather" smell coupled with the "boiled feather" smell permeated every nook and cranny of our ten by twelve-foot kitchen.

Early the next morning Mom stuffed the chicken with her special stuffing made of home made bread, bacon bits, eggs and spices. Placing the stuffed chicken into a pot of water she added kohlrabi, tomatoes, onions, carrots and parsley, all freshly picked from our garden. Several hours later we observed that the pot of water had been transformed into a golden yellow liquid. Removing the stuffed chicken from the soup pot, Mom placed it into a large pan to brown. While the chicken was browning we filled our bowls with the delicious chicken soup and added Mom's homemade noodles. We didn't have to be told to eat. We ate! Not only did we have the most delicious chicken soup but also the broasted chicken, smothered with creamy dill sauce, was out of this world.

Chapter II - TRAGEDY HITS

IN WHITING (A home town tragedy)

On a bright sunshiny morning in the summer of 1942 some 80 eighth grade graduates of St. John the Baptist Catholic School assembled in front of the church. It was the long awaited eighth-grade picnic day. Zavesky's red Diamond T. truck and Celenica's truck came to a smooth stop in front of the church. The trucks glistened in the early morning sunlight as eager children climbed aboard, boys in Celenica's truck and girls in Zavesky's truck. It was to be an invigorating forty-mile ride in those open-air trucks to Michigan City's Washington Park. On the outskirts of Gary, the truck carrying the boys had a flat tire. As the boys sat on the grassy knoll, George Mateja decided to send his homing pigeons home now rather than waiting to do so in Michigan City as he had originally planned. He opened the pigeon cage and attached a message to the homing pigeons that read: "Dear Mom we're almost there. I love you." The birds winged their way back to their home base in Whiting as the truck, carrying its precious cargo, continued its way toward Michigan City.

As Celenica's truck approached the South Shore tracks on the edge of Michigan City, a South Shore train struck it. Thirteen year old George Mateja was killed instantly while Anthony Pavliscak, age 15, whose leg was severed, lay dying on the blood stained tracks. Anthony was taken to the hospital where he died shortly thereafter. Mike Celenica, the truck owner, and Mike Solomon, the truck driver, lay dying in the mangled cab of that doomed truck. Other boys lay bleeding and injured along the tracks. Among those taken to local hospitals, treated and released, were fourteen year olds Anthony Pardinek, George Saliga,

14

Eugene Kasper, John Vargo, John Vrabely, John Zondor and Thomas Zondor.

The homing pigeons released earlier by George Mateja were homeward bound and so was his immortal soul as it winged its way heavenward. Large black funeral wreaths appeared on the front porch of George Mateja's home and on the front porch of Anthony Pavliscak's home. Both boys were "laid out" in the living room of their homes for their three-day wakes. They were dressed in their graduation suits.

High up in St. John's church tower, the bells tolled as the funeral processions winded their way to a church overflowing with grieving family, classmates, relatives and friends. With tears in his eyes, Fr. John Kostik, our pastor, dressed in black funeral vestments, stood at the entrance of the church as he welcomed the deceased for their final funeral rites. The somber strains of "*Dies ire, dies illa*" resounded throughout the massive cathedral-like church. Never before had there been so much grieving in the city of Whiting. The boys were laid to rest at St. John's cemetery in Hammond.

IN THE PACIFIC – (A wartime tragedy)

A national disaster occurred in the same year as the Whiting disaster. On Friday, November 13th 1942, the sinking of the USS Juneau, a newly commissioned light cruiser, proved to be the greatest family disaster in naval history. Newspaper headlines broke the tragic news: "Five Sullivan Brothers Die Together."

It was in January of 1942, just days after the bombing of Pearl Harbor, that George, Joseph (Red), Madison (Matt), Francis (Frank) and Albert (Al) Sullivan marched into the Waterloo, Iowa Navy recruiting center and made their request to the recruiting officer. They would voluntarily enlist if he promised to let them stay together. Otherwise they would wait their turn to be drafted. Their request was denied. It was contrary to Navy policy to assign five brothers to the same ship. The five Sullivan brothers sent letters of protest to the Navy Department in Washington. At long last the Navy Department agreed to let the four unmarried boys stay together. Al, the youngest, whose wife had just given birth to the first Sullivan grandchild, was exempt and would not be taken. After much writing, Al's joy knew no bounds when he was told that he was accepted. The Navy decided to break yet another rule. All five would be assigned to the same ship! They were assigned to the newly commissioned USS Juneau, a light cruiser.

It was just months after being commissioned that the flotilla, of which the USS Juneau was a part of, that a Japanese submarine was encountered in the battle for Guadalcanal. Although the sub aimed at a much larger ship, the Juneau sailed into the path of the oncoming torpedo and was sunk. It happened on Friday Nov. 13, 1942. Most of the sailors went down with the ship into the depths of the Pacific. George Sullivan, the oldest of the five Sullivan brothers, got away in a raft with several other sailors. He scanned the ocean waves hoping to catch sight of his four brothers. For hours he shouted out their names until he could shout no more. Dreadful hours rolled by and George received no response. How could he? Unbeknownst to him, his four brothers had gone down with the ship. George was hallucinating as he jumped off the life raft into shark infested waters to look for his brothers. After all, he was the eldest and had promised his Mom that he would look after his younger brothers. His mates on the raft attempted to call him back to the raft. It was to no avail. As George churned the waters in search of his drowned brothers, sharks flailed around him. As they began their attack George screamed for help!. On the nearby raft his mates looked on in horror as George disappeared into the blood stained ocean. Only ten sailors who were on board the Juneau, survived. Several years later, a movie was produced to recall the heroism of the Sullivan Brothers. Even today, I can hear Al, the youngest, calling after his brothers "Hey, wait for me!"

Chapter III - GRADE SCHOOL GRADUATION

The next year was a much happier one for me as a member of the class of 1943. 42 boys were to graduate from St. John the Baptist Catholic School. Oh yes, 40 girls were also part of the graduation class, classmates with whom we were not allowed to associate. During all our eight years boys and girls were kept separate in the classroom, in the playground, in church and at all school functions. There was a strict policy at St. John's that kept the boys and girls separate. Although we were in the same graduation class, we didn't know them and they didn't know us. Note that some of the boys who were the more spiffy dressers in our class wore "spats" to partially cover their shoes.

In preparation for our graduation, our eighth-grade teacher, Sister Xavier, smiled as she gave us written instructions as to what we should wear. She was dressed in black from head to toe with a crisp starched linen headgear that covered all but her face. A symbol of ultimate authority, she ruled with a gentle but firm hand. Unlike our second grade teacher, Sister Saint Lawrence, she did not believe in using the ruler for anything other than what it was intended for.

The dress instructions called for us to wear dark blue graduation suits. Although boy's suits were available in town, they were cheaper in "Jew Town." On the following Sunday Dad and I headed for the bargain of bargains stores in "Jew Town." With a wax coated white paper bag stuffed in my pocket, the two of us caught the early streetcar on 119th St. It would take approximately two-hours for the jerky ride to 12th and Maxwell in Chicago. As

Class of 1943 Graduation St. John the Baptist School, Whiting, In.
(me in row 1, fourth from right)

19

we transferred to the third and final streetcar, the conductor punched a hole in the yellow and red transfer paper to signify the end of transfers for us. The streetcar bell dinged and donged as the motorman jerked the streetcar away from its last stop. At that moment I knew that I shouldn't have had that extra piece of breakfast Polish sausage. My head was spinning and I needed relief. Out came the wax-coated paper bag! Whew, I felt better as I heard the conductor announce that our next stop would be "12th & Maxwell."

The sights and sounds of that place were familiar. I had been here twice before, once for my Communion suit and then, several years later, for my Confirmation suit. Crowds of people milled around outdoor stands loaded with clothing and merchandise of every kind. It was a bargain hunter's paradise. My stomach churned as the smell of grilled meats and onions filled the air. Smoke billowed from strategically placed outdoor grills loaded with sausages and onions.

It wasn't long until Max Epstein's store came into view. Max rolled up the long sleeves of his shirt and wrapped his left arm over Dad's shoulder as he said "*Ako sa mate moj dobry priatel?*" (How are you my good friend?) The majority of the "Jew Town" merchants knew Slovak. I noticed that Max's hair had grayed some since the last time we were here. His dark horn-rimmed glasses seemed to accentuate the graying brown hair.

Max moved over to a rack full of dark blue boy's suits. The brightly colored cardboard sign above the rack said, "Gabardine boy's suits ONLY $11.50 — two pair of pants!" In one swooping motion Max had retrieved one of the suits and was buttoning the coat for me. "Vat a fine fit" he said as he tugged here and pulled there. Dad nodded his approval, and, as he did with every suit we ever bought on Maxwell Street, Dad pulled a strand of material from the pant bottom and lit a match to it. Dad knew whether or not the material was good by the way it burned. "Vel, doz it pass yurr test?" asked Max. "*HEJ*" (yes) Dad said, "*ale nie pre jedenast i pol dollarou* (but not for $11.50.)" Dad knew how to "jew" Max down, he had done it before. He offered nine dollars and Max countered. As they argued back and forth, Max began wiping his brow. When that happened, Dad knew, as in the past, that his final offer of $9.75 would stand. It was when we began walking towards the exit that Max shouted, "Oki-doke., O.K. Vait!"

With package in hand we walked victoriously towards the corner of 12th and Maxwell Streets to await the streetcar that would take us and the bargain winning, dark blue graduation suit, back to Whiting.

Chapter IV - THE EFFECTS OF WAR BECOME MORE EVIDENT

The following Sunday evening, Walter Winchell began his news broadcast with his special opening. Tapping on a Morse code bar, dot dot da rat dot, he began, "Good evening Mr. And Mrs. America and all the ships at see." "In Detroit," he said, "as in the past year, there will be no new car production. As a matter of fact we have seen the last of new cars for the duration, no new Fords or Chevys or any other new cars as long as the war lasts."

Instead of private passenger cars, thousands of jeeps and army trucks began rolling off the converted auto production lines in Detroit. Local industry had also converted to war production. Inland Steel Company of Indiana Harbor began producing steel for the frames, fenders and bumpers of army trucks, jeeps and ambulances. Production of plates for Liberty ships, troop transports and oil tankers was in high gear at all our local steel mills. Inland's "Tin Mill" supplied the tin plate for, among other things, tin cans to hold soldier's foodstuffs. Inland's steel also helped make helmets, artillery shells and bomb casings for our fighting troops. Our area steel mills produced landing mat steel and war entanglement pots. The coke byproducts of our steel mills were used in the production of tons of explosives and also for life saving sulfa drugs. Our region had become a Machine of War as it continued to gear up for war production. Our radios began playing some lilting war time melodies one of which was, "When the Storm Clouds Gather Far Across The Sea." Then, to lighten our mood, novelty songs were introduced, the likes of which were: "Chickery Chick Chilla, Chilla,"

"One Meatball," "Mairzy Doaats," "Tutti Frutti," "Jeepers Creepers" and Tex William's "Smoke, Smoke, Smoke that Cigarette."

Truckload after truckload of steel for ship construction and armor plates for tanks rolled off the production lines of U.S. Steel in Gary. Not far away in Willow Run, Michigan, a suburb of Detroit, aircraft production was in full swing. Airplane bombers were being built each and every day of the week in one of the largest war production buildings in the country. The building had just been built for the exclusive production of warplanes. It was over a half mile long and about a quarter mile wide. Both men and women manned the massive production lines in that building. The assembly line was busy twenty-four hours each and everyday, seven days a week. Steel from local mills and other raw materials from around the Midwest were fed into one end of that three and one half million square foot war production building, and, at the other end, fully airworthy bombers taxied out. As ladies became part of the work force, songs in their honor became popular. One was "Rosie The Riveter." We reveled in songs which Spike Jones composed. One such song, "Der Fuehrer's Face," was a favorite of mine. Other songs inspired by the war were "Pistol Packin Mama," "Praise the Lord and Pass the Ammunition," "Bell Bottom Trousers" and "Remember Pearl Harbor."

In Hammond, railroad boxcar production was halted at the Pullman Standard plant located on 165th street. Tank after armored tank rolled out of that factory. It was a common sight to see hundreds of 28 ton Sherman tanks lining the drive into that factory. The Junior Toy Company of Hammond stopped making wagons and bicycles and began production of "bomb heads." Here, as in Detroit and

23

around the nation, three shifts of men and women worked around the clock. Our nation had pulled together in the greatest production effort in the history of mankind.

At the Standard Oil Company of Whiting more than half of the oil company's production was for the war effort. Railroad tank cars filled with hundreds of barrels of aviation gasoline were shipped out on a daily basis. Workers at the candle factory and at the barrelhouse worked around the clock, seven days a week. Grease from the Whiting refinery lubricated the heavy war machinery on land and the guns at sea. Women working at the grease works, labeled barrels packed with grease stenciling them for "U.S. Army" and other barrels for "U.S. Navy." Toulene, a basic element in the manufacture of TNT, came off the production line on a daily basis. Enough Toulene was produced at the Whiting plant for over a half million tons of bombs, such was the production at our local oil refinery.

Deep inside the Whiting plant, in a secluded area, there were several highly restricted office complexes. It was there that, unbeknownst to most everyone in Whiting, Standard Oil company researchers were working on an extremely secret project known as the "Manhattan Project," a project for the development of the *ATOMIC BOMB*. Day after day scientists and researchers worked long into the night seeking to uncover atomic secrets. It was through their efforts and determination that a new chapter in history was written.

SOME WARTIME PASTIMES

Taverns flourished outside the gates of this massive oil company. It was there that, after a long day's work, weary refinery workers refreshed themselves. There were three such taverns on the corner of Schrage and 121st Street; Klen's, Novotny's and Runick's. Local and world problems were also solved at Bucsanyi's, Spebar's and other taverns on the Far East end of 119th Street. Serving workers exiting the refineries on the Boulevard side were Stanish's tavern, Dusty's Place, Mary Price's and Benetich's taverns. Workers riding their bicycles homeward paused at many a local tavern, totally unconcerned about riding while inebriated. There were as many taverns in Whiting as there were grocery stores; and that's a lot of watering holes!

A variety of recreational activities were available at the Community Center, not only for children but also for grown ups. There was an Olympic sized swimming pool, a billiard and poolroom, basketball courts, volleyball courts, indoor tract, a weight lifting room, a bowling alley and an auditorium. Located in about the center of town, the Community Center complex was in walking distance for most everyone, a very important factor due to gasoline rationing.

The most significant form of recreation for the adults was the twelve lane bowling alley. From seven to midnight, all week long, the twelve bowling alleys located on the first floor were a beehive of activity for weary production workers. Team after team competed in match games. Pinsetters were assigned to set pins by Mr. Hardy Keilman, the bowling alley manager, and a stern taskmaster. His gray hair was thin and he wore horn-rimmed glasses. Hardy was a dapper dresser and smoker of fine cigars. His trousers were held several inches above his waistline by sporty suspenders that, on occasion, matched his bow tie. Assisting Hardy was Mr. Al Koch, a much more affable and congenial taskmaster.

Generally I arrived at the bowling alley shortly after six. If early enough, I would be assigned an alley for a double match game. That meant setting pins for thirty lines of bowling. At 10 cents a line, the pay for approximately five hours of pin setting was $3.00. A year earlier, as a newspaper boy, delivering papers for Mr. John Chrustowski, it took a week of delivering some two hundred newspapers each evening to earn that kind of money. If I was lucky and got to set pins each weekday evening plus "open bowling" on weekends, I could earn $18.00 to $20.00 in one week! That was enough to pay the rent for one month on our two bedroom, five room flat at 2115 New York Avenue.

After some practice shots, the teams were ready for their match games. An opening bell sounded. Black and multi colored 16 pound bowling balls came whirling down each of the twelve highly polished lanes. I sat on a ledge in the pit of alley #5, legs held high, as the ball and pins came crashing into the "pit." It was a strike. In the pit were ten felled pins and the sixteen-pound ball. Jumping down off the ledge I returned the ball, and, picking up three pins in the right hand and two in the left, I flung five pins into the setting rack in one sweeping motion. Repeating this motion, all ten pins rested in the rack ready for setting. It took two hands to pull the rack down and the pins were set for the next bowler. Some fussy bowlers called for a "re-set" if they didn't like the way the pins stood. That always made for more work. To alleviate the monotony I would often whistle a tune that was new to the Saturday "Hit Parade" radio program. As I stood in the confining bowling alley "pit," one such very appropriate tune was "Don't Fence Me In." I whistled and hummed that catchy melody over and over again.

The record for pins set in a one-week span was held by Tom Jancosek. Tom and his brother George had a corner on alleys five, six, seven and eight. Tom was a regular pinsetter on alley's seven or eight. On many evenings he set "double alley, double match game," sixty lines in a night of match game play. He was one lucky guy to be on the good side of Hardy. Setting double alley, double match game every night, Monday to Friday, earned Tom 300 lines. He set another 50 lines during open bowling on Saturday and Sunday. Tom's pay for one week of pin setting was over eighty dollars! His younger brother George held the record for the second most lines set in one week. Those Jancosek brothers were the envy of many a pinsetter.

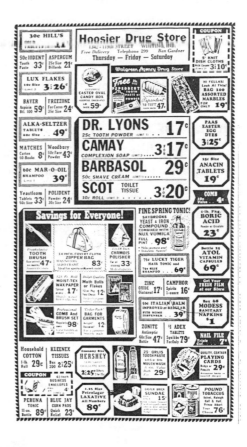

Chapter V - SUMMER AND FALL OF 1943

We were losing the war in the Pacific. The Japanese had captured Corregidor and then the Philippines and controlled the seas and skies of the entire South Pacific. We sat glued to our Philco table model radio listening to President Roosevelt's Fireside Chats. With the fall of the Philippines, the President confirmed that the Japanese had cut off about 90% of the nations critical rubber supply. The President concluded by saying, "We are going to see to it that there is enough rubber to build the planes to bomb Tokyo and Berlin——enough rubber to win the war." As the president concluded his fireside chat a popular tune began to be played. It was "When the Lights Go On Again." President Roosevelt urged us to search our basements, attics and garages for scrap rubber products and to take them to the nearest gasoline filling station. Standard Oil volunteered its gasoline filling stations as collection depots. Loyal citizens responded by taking wagon full after wagon full of scrap rubber products to Harry Gold's station on the corner of Indianapolis Boulevard and 121st St. "A penny a pound" announced a large red and white sign in the window of the gas station building. Large trucks

from East Chicago rumbled by to haul the scrap rubber to awaiting freight cars at Indiana Harbor Railroad yards. As those trucks labored by, we send them off singing "Tarawa-Boom de Aye, Tarawa Boom de Aye...." Truckload after truckload came rumbling into the railroad freight yards from all over northwest Indiana. The response to President Roosevelt's plea was overwhelming. There was no question about the strong patriotic spirit of the European immigrants who called Northwest Indiana their home.

A SUMMER JOB

During the summer of 1943 I began working at Stanek's tailor and dry cleaning shop. Mr. Stanek, born in Bobrovec, Czechoslovakia, was a countryman of my parents and a godfather to my twin brothers Joey and Tony. He knew of our financial plight which was due to my dad's military service connected disability, and offered me a good day's pay for a good day's work. I was happy to oblige. He didn't do his own dry cleaning but farmed it out. He did, however, do the clothing pressings. As an expert tailor, he did the tailoring for several of the local men's clothing shops. One of the premier men's clothiers was "Winsberg's" operated by Mayo and Hershel Winsberg. Mr. Stanek needed help with all the tailoring work brought to his shop. I learned how to shorten trousers and let out or take in the trouser waist. While Mr. Stanek was pressing, I was tailoring. Each afternoon after all the pressing was done; a sweaty Mr. Stanek walked over to McHale's tap for a cold beer or two. I took care of the shop while he was gone. Once in a while, when he stayed a bit longer, I got an unexpected tip from that jolly Bobrovcan.

HIGH SCHOOL

In September of 1943 I began my high school studies at Immaculate Conception High School in Whiting. Fr. Lach, the pastor of Immaculate Conception Parish, had opened a Slovak high school several years earlier. It was the only two-year Slovak high school in the state of Indiana. Being a dedicated Slovak, Dad insisted that all Slovaks support such a worthwhile endeavor. I had no choice but to spend my first two years in a Slovak high school taught by the Sisters of Sts. Cyril & Methodius. Being in class with girls was a new and interesting experience for me. I began brushing my teeth with "Teel" and "Ipana," the new tooth pastes in order to avoid "Beee-Ooooh." The class was relatively small compared to St. Johns. With highly polished shoes and neatly pressed trousers I attended the freshman dance in the school library. Sister Clotilda, our first year high school teacher, saw to it that each boy and girl had a partner for most every dance. That small library room was filled with polka sounds and the sounds of the big time bands as Sister Clotilda spun record after record on the school's Victrola. . *The Beer Barrel Polka* and "*Hej, Ona Debela*" Polka were dancing favorites. We hummed and even sang the words of those Polka tunes as we shuffled those newly found dancing feet of ours. On the jumpy side were "Acc-cent-tchu-ate the Positive" and "I've Got A Gal In Kalamazoo." Mood music was highlighted by "People Will Say We're In Love" and "I Love You For Sentimental Reasons." I found my first dance to be an exhilarating experience!

During this high school year I not only worked at Stanek's but also at Harry Gold's Standard station on weekends. With coin changer attached to my belt I serviced customers at the gas pumps. Although gasoline was fifteen cents a gallon, there were restrictions depending on whether you had an "A" "B" or "C" sticker attached to your windshield. For example, the "A" stickered cars (cars driven for personal use and pleasure) were allowed 5 gallons per week. The "B" books contained 16 coupons for 5 gallons each or 80 gallons for a three-month period. Doctors and other professionals received the C stickers which were less restrictive. The "E" sticker allowed for unlimited gas and was issued to fire and police departments and the clergy.

There was no "fill 'er up" during those war years. For a dollar and a 5-gallon "B" coupon you got 5 gallons at a total pump price of seventy-five cents. That's where the belt changer came in handy. Instead of running into the station building for the quarter change, I simply depressed the quarter lever on the changer and out came two bits. For that seventy-five cent gasoline purchase we cleaned the customer's windshield and checked the oil level and also the battery water. If the battery needed water we filled it for free from a "special battery water container." Little did the customers know that the special battery water container was filled with water straight from the bathroom sink tap. If the customer wanted the tire pressure checked, we did that, dispensing free air where needed. Harry Gold insisted that we perform according to the advertisements that his gasoline filling station was one where full service was always given.

MOVING

The two-bedroom apartment at 2115 New York Ave. was getting small for us. It had been several years since twins Joey and Tony outgrew their crib. Mom and Dad slept in the "living room" bedroom while Tillie and Mary had the "dining room" bedroom. John, the oldest, had gone to a seminary to study for the priesthood. Our uncle, Father Ambrose Kapitan, made all the arrangements for his enrollment at St. Vincent's Seminary in Latrobe,

Pennsylvania. That left the four of us boys sleeping on two davenports, one davenport in the living room and the other in the dining room. Each evening the davenports were opened and the living and dining rooms became our bedrooms for the night.

One morning in late December of 1943 while Mom attended Mass at I C church, Mrs. Beda approached Mom with the news that one of her three bedroom apartments was being vacated. She had heard about our cramped quarters. With the temperature at freezing she wanted us to take it the day the other people moved out. The rent would be sixteen dollars a month, two dollars more than we were now paying. Mom and Dad walked over to see it immediately. It was only two blocks from where we were living. They liked it and rented it. The next day Mary and I ran over to 1456 Fred St. to peek through the windows. Wow, what a nice looking apartment and the rooms were large and airy. We were going to move on the Sunday after Christmas. What about our beautiful double needle balsam fir Christmas tree? We never took down our tree until after January 6th, the Feast of the Three Kings. We decided that the tree would have to be moved. Our Christmas season could not end early. We pondered the question: "How do you move a decorated Christmas tree?"

Here is how we did that. We removed all the ornaments and disassembled the Bethlehem set. We made sure the lights were secure to the branches. It was snowing and the wind howled as Mary and I, trudging through the snow, carried the seven-foot tree, stand and all, laden with lights and silver, to our new apartment. Tillie, Joey and Tony followed carrying the Bethlehem set - the manger and statues. Ambsie followed picking up strands of silver tinsel as they fell from the tree to the snow-covered sidewalks.

Huffing and puffing we arrived at our new apartment with Christmas tree in tow. We stood the Christmas tree up in the corner of our living room and Ambsie rehung the silver tinsel strands. We didn't dare plug the lights in until the tree dried up from the melted snow. That evening we sat on our new living room floor, rejoicing over our successful Christmas tree transfer and singing Christmas Carols. We sang "White Christmas," a new Christmas song entry that year made famous by Bing Crosby. Mom and Dad joined us as we sang Slovak Christmas Carols "*Dnesny Den sa Radujme,*" (Today We Rejoice) and "*Do Hory Do Lesa Valasi*" (To the Hills and Dales Come Shepherds). We were overjoyed and comforted by the fact that we were moved into our new apartment and that our transported Christmas tree glistened in all its pre Christmas majesty. All was well as we sat around our tree on that first evening in our new apartment.

Chapter VI - 1945 —
A MEANINGFUL YEAR

On April 12, 1945, just two weeks before Germany's surrender our President, Franklin D. Roosevelt died. Taking office as president in 1933, he was the only president I had known. History recognizes him as the most influential president of the twentieth century. He was buried in his beloved Hyde Park Rose Garden. Vice President, Harry S. Truman, a Missouri farm boy and a no-nonsense ("the buck stops here") politician, succeeded FDR.

V E DAY

On May 8th, 1945 the newspaper headlines read "V. E. Day!" The war in Europe was over. An unconditional surrender was signed in bombed out Berlin. At home, thousands flocked to the streets. School children joined in the celebration as all schools were let out early. Standard Oil horns blasted loud and clear for a full two minutes. Church bells throughout Whiting rang out in joy. The oil and steel cargo ships on Lake Michigan and in the ports all sounded repeated blasts of their horns. On 119th Street streetcars stopped in their tracks as people flocked to the streets shouting and hugging each other. It was a never to be forgotten moment. That evening we sat glued to the radio as President Truman announced that "The allied armies, through sacrifice and devotion and with God's help have triumphed." As he continued, he asked us not to slacken but to remain diligent in our wartime sacrifices so that the war in the Pacific could come to a quick end.

WORKING AT THE MILL

During the summer of 1945 Inland Steel Co. continued to place "help wanted" ads in the newspapers. Sixteen-year-olds were welcomed to apply, and apply I did. I was told at the employment office that I needed a work permit from the school system in East Chicago. The lady who issued the work permits from the East Chicago public School system advised that it would be necessary to bring along either a birth certificate or a baptismal certificate. I wouldn't be sixteen until August of that year and the summer opportunity for employment at the steel mill would be just about gone. I didn't want to tamper with either of my original documents so I got a duplicate baptismal certificate from Fr. Lefko, assistant pastor at St. Johns. It said I was born in August of 1929 and baptized in 1929. So, in June of 1945 I was 15 and not 16 years old. I solved my problem by purchasing a bottle of ink eradicator from the dime store. After much practice I carefully changed the 9 of 1929 to an 8. I was now SIXTEEN!

Armed with my altered baptismal certificate I arrived at the East Chicago City Hall-Dept of Education and was ushered into Miss Dudley's office. She issued all the work permits for the school board. I trembled a bit as she motioned for me to sit at her desk. Dressed in a somber gray colored outfit, she was stern looking with her hair up in a large, no-nonsense bun. She reminded me of a lady jail warden I had seen in a scary movie at the Hoosier Theater. "Why do you want to work?" she asked sternly. I told her about my Dad who couldn't work because he was mustard gassed in the First World War and about all of us six kids living in a six room flat. She held the baptismal certificate to an overhead light, looked at me and asked if I changed the birth date. She knew that the crude "ink eradicator job" was visible when exposed to a bright light. I cleared my throat, took a deep breath and said, "No, I had not changed it!" She looked at me over her glasses and said, "I'm issuing the work permit only because of your family's need and I expect you to behave yourself as a productive sixteen year old young man." "Thank you, Thank you!" I said in as joyful a voice as I could muster up, and out the door I went with my work permit. I was the happiest kid in the whole world.

Next day I punched the time clock at Inland Steel's gate #2. I was assigned to work in the tin mill. I reported to Mr. Dobrota and Mr. Hammond my foremen. They sent me to the factory shoe store for a pair of metatarsals, steel toed work boots. When I returned to the tin mill I was given a pair of heavy duty canvas work gloves and a pair of hand held shears.   Mr. Dobrota gave me a "hand signal" instruction sheet, instructions for the overhead craneman. He also handed me a paper with a long list of numbers. They corresponded to numbers on the 20,000-pound coils of tin plate. At $1.02 per hour, I was introduced to steel production as a crane hooker for that day.   At my command, coil after numbered coil was hoisted up and onto ramps leading to the "tandem mill," the "rolling mill" or to the "flying shears." My responsibility was to keep the ramps to those mills and the four flying shear ramps full of tin plate rolls.

During that summer I advanced to higher paying jobs as a tractor operator at $1.06 per hour and $1.08 per hour as a second helper on the flying shears. Working the three shifts (8 to 4, 4 to 12 and 12 to 8) provided new experiences for me. Never before had I eaten lunch at 4:00 AM, and what a lunch it was. Four sandwiches, two bolshevik on rye, two honey-loaf on home made bread and a "Banana Twinkie" cake for dessert. I washed everything down with a quart of chocolate milk. As if all that food wasn't enough,

I usually finished my lunch with a juicy piece of fresh fruit. During the midnight shift I ate my lunch sitting near mill window openings looking out over Lake Michigan. I watched as the sun began dispelling the darkness of night. It was a breathtaking experience as a large reddish orange globe crept out of the dark blue waters of Lake Michigan giving birth to a new day.

Dad rode the bus with me to the steel mill on my first payday. My first two-week check was for $85.65. I was one proud fifteen-year-old (sixteen according to my baptismal certificate) as I endorsed that check and gave it to my Dad. That was enough money for five months rent with some left over for bus fare and quarts of chocolate milk. Several weeks later my paycheck, with some scheduled overtime, was over a hundred dollars! I could hardly believe that I was making as much money as most grown ups, including my Dad.

Harry Gold had a junker car for sale at his filling station on the corner of 121st Street and Indianapolis Boulevard. It was a nifty blue Chevrolet coupe. What a sixteenth birthday present that would be for me. Since I had worked at his filling station the summer before, he reduced the price from sixty dollars to fifty. Even so, I could not afford it. My parents needed the money more than I needed a car. Dad pointed out that a car needed gas and oil and insurance and battery and tire replacements, etc. Dad said that I would be working for the car and nothing more. I guess he was right so I continued to ride the bus to work.

THE BIG HOUSE

One day as I exited the bus on Michigan & Guthrie, Ron Guard, a fellow tin mill worker, was waiting on the corner for the light to turn. He asked if I liked excitement. "Sure," I said as we walked along. "Follow me, we've got about fifteen minutes before punching in," he said. We approached an empty storefront on Michigan Avenue. Opening the front door on the side of the empty building, we walked up a tall flight of stairs. The building looked abandoned. I got nervous as I began to wonder what we were doing walking up that tall, dimly lit flight of stairs. All of a sudden, right there in front of us was a huge well-lit gambling hall. I couldn't believe what I saw! Men with green visors were dealing cards at tables loaded with patrons. Roulette wheels whirled around and dice flew on crap tables as skimpily clad cigarette girls paraded around. In sultry voices they sang out "cigars, cigarettes, cigars, cigarettes." I stood there with open mouth, taking all this in while Ron went over to a dice table. All of a sudden all eyes seemed peeled on me as a burley unshaven man yelled, "Get that kid outa here." Before I knew it, two men grabbed me by the arms and escorted me out the door.

Later that day, while at work, Ron laughed as I confessed that I knew nothing about that gambling hall. "It's the **BIG HOUSE**" he said. Then I realized why people talked about the importance of a certain neon sign attached to the north side of Peter's tavern on the south end of Whiting. Peter's concrete block building sat on the corner of 129th Street and Indianapolis Boulevard. The sign was the all-clear signal for big time gambling in East Chicago. When that neon sign was lit, gamblers from Chicago knew the Big House was open.

Laboring at the steel mill was serious work. There was no time for play, or was there? One day Joe and Ed, operators at the continuous annealing line, stopped me as I loaded coils onto the ramp leading to the line. "Hey Rudy," Joe said, "I just made a bet with Ed that I could guess your weight. Will you be a sport and let me try?" I saw no reason why I shouldn't go along with those two fine gentlemen so I said "Okay." "To guess your weight I've got to pick you up," said Joe. So I stood behind him as he put his two hands up near his shoulders. He took my two hands and lifted me up onto his back. My backside was exposed. Once I was lifted off the ground Ed wound up and swatted my rear end with a wooden paddle. That swat left a large red paddle imprint on my rear end, a swat to be remembered forever. Ed and Joe doubled over with laughter as I walked away cussing under my breath.

Several days later, I told one of the older mill workers about that humiliating experience. A suggestion was made as to how I could get even with Joe and Ed. I wasn't the first kid that they made a fool of. It was suggested that I take a fire extinguisher onto the roof and douse them. I located an open window just above Joe and Ed's annealing line and headed for the north steps leading to the roof.

Once in position at the open window on the roof, I emptied the fire extinguisher onto the two below as they squirmed around covering their heads trying to avoid the spray. At that moment I saw Mr. Dobrota, our foreman, head for the south steps leading to the roof. I dropped the fire extinguisher and ran to the north set of steps as Mr. Dobrota climbed the south set of stairs to apprehend me. I was one happy kid that I outfoxed the foreman and "got even" with those two culprits. Many mill workers were overjoyed as word got around that part of the mill that someone had doused those two culprits with a fire extinguisher.

V J DAY

It was on August 6, 1945, exactly 3 months after V E Day that an American superfortress, called the *Enola Gay* flew toward Japan carrying an atomic bomb. In 60 seconds, Hiroshima, an important Japanese army base city was destroyed and 80,000 people died. Reports from the crew of the *Enola Gay* were printed in the papers. They read, "A giant ball of fire rose as from the bowels of the earth. Then a pillow of purple fire rose 10,000 feet high. Then there came shooting out of the top of the pillar of fire a giant mushroom that increased the height of the pillar a total of 45,000 feet."

Our ears were attuned to the radio as President Truman announced that the atomic bomb harnessed the basic power of the universe. "What has been done is the greatest achievement of organized science in history. If the Japanese do not now accept our terms, they may expect a rain of ruin from the air, the likes of which has never been seen on earth." Three days later, hearing nothing from the Japanese another bomb was dropped on Nagasaki. The Japanese surrendered the very next day. As on V E Day, horns on vessels in Lake Michigan joined the blasts of the Standard Oil Company's horns to announce "V J Day." The war in the Pacific was over and thousands of American lives had been saved thanks to the dedication and ingenuity of all those who worked on the Atomic bomb. As mentioned before, substantial contributions regarding that effort came from Standard Oil researchers who worked in those highly restricted office complexes on that secret Manhattan Project.

Summer was ending and so were the mill jobs worked by high school students. If we couldn't work the three shifts, around the clock, we were out of a job when school started. Mr. Hammond, my foreman, liked my work ethic and wanted me to stay. There were two forklift operator jobs open in the sorting room of the tin mill on a steady 3 to 11 PM shift. One was mine, he said, if I could be on the sorting room floor by 3:00 PM each weekday. My last class at Catholic Central High School[1] was "Home Room" at 2: PM. Since I was on the "A" honor roll, the principal allowed me to skip "home room." Mr. Hammond took care of the transfer to the sorting room for me. School began and I continued to work at Inland Steel Company

When school started and the mill "let go" all the high school students, I began my daily assignment of driving a forklift tractor in the sorting room. During the day shift, ladies dressed in light green dresses with white cuffs stood behind long rows of tables sorting stacks of tin plate. They sorted lift after lift of tin plate on tables hundreds of feet long. Two of us had the responsibility of clearing off all the tables in the sorting room. Ray, another high school student, who transferred to the sorting room, as did I, had the responsibility of clearing off all the tables together with me. Each pile of sorted tin plate had been sorted into four

[1] Today's Bishop Noll HS

piles - "good plate," "waste-waste," "cobbles" and "culls." Ray and I cleared off the tables and delivered the lifts of "good plate" to a designated storage freight area for delivery to customers in the United States. The "waste-waste," "cobbles," and "culls" were taken to an area where they were loaded onto boxcars for shipment on secondary barges bound for Thailand and other Far Eastern countries. After all the tables were cleared of the sorted plate, Ray and I stacked fresh lifts of tin plate on the tables for the next day's sorting.

Generally, at about seven PM, the two of us were able to take at least a half-hour off for our evening meal. My lunch was in the brown bag that Mom had packed for me earlier that morning just before I left for school. At that time a canteen truck would pull up to the sorting room with soup, coffee and milk. My daily order was a quart of chocolate milk, which I drank as I emptied that brown bag of four sandwiches and a dessert cake. Usually, by about ten PM, the two of us forklift operators had all the tables cleared and fresh lifts set up for the next day. Off to the showers we went. At times I even had time to do homework. A mill bus took us to the clock house where we waited until 11:00 PM to punch out. I then hurried to the corner of Michigan & Guthrie, about a mile from the "clock house," where I caught the bus for Whiting. It was about midnight by the time I got home.

The next morning, brown bag and books in hand, I walked over to the corner of Schrage and Steiber. With Al Janik, a classmate of mine, I waited for the seven o'clock bus to take us to "Four-Corners" in East Chicago. It was about a mile walk from that corner to Catholic Central High School. We usually arrived in time for the first class that began at 8:00 AM. I stored my brown lunch bag in my locker and retrieved it at 2:00 PM as I headed for "Four Corners" to catch a bus bound for Inland Steel.

School and work, and more school and work! This continued well into my third year of high school. Then, one day I was notified that a veteran who had just returned from the war was to get my job. Well, why not? After all, he went to war to protect our freedoms, and, having done that, wanted his job back. I considered myself fortunate to have worked at the mill as long as I did. I emptied my locker and said a fond farewell to a work place that had provided rewarding experiences for a teen-aged boy.

Chapter VII - THE FIRST POST WAR YEAR

Veterans were returning home. President Truman ordered that we "decontrol as fast as we can!" Within a short time wage and price controls ended. Meat shortages disappeared and scarce canned goods reappeared at grocery stores in Whiting and throughout the nation. Stacks of new tires appeared at gas stations, including Harry Gold's in Whiting. Newspapers began carrying advertisings for shoes which were no longer rationed. In Detroit new automobile production began in earnest. The postwar "good times" were about to begin. "Damn the Cost" became a national slogan, as leisure industries cropped up in many parts of our country.

A cartoon called "Meet Joe" gave credence to the postwar economic optimism. The words went something like this: "Hi folks, Joe's the king because he can buy more with his wages than any other worker on the globe. He's no smarter than workers in other countries. Sure, being an American is great, but how could you be superior to any foreigner when you or your folks might be any of a dozen races or religions? So, if you're no superman. It must be the American way of doing things that makes you the luckiest guy in the world."

Big business and big labor began cooperating as never before. Our nation's productivity increased and so did worker's wages. A new era of prosperity had begun. The G I Bill allowed veterans to purchase homes through the FHA at discounted interest rates. It was an era which saw the creation of suburbs and all that went along with those new suburban homes— cars and roads and cheap gasoline. Thousands of discount stores appeared and began selling appliances for all those new homes. Euphoria reigned.

During that summer my Dad hired me as a "power lawn mower" operator at the Whiting Park. Dad was the foreman at the park, a job he had gotten earlier that year from Andrew S. Kovacik, the newly elected mayor of Whiting. Dad had played some politics during the election and helped Mr. Kovacik win the mayoral slot. One evening, after the new mayor's victory party, Dad came home "tipsy." It was the first time in my life that I saw Dad in that state. Mom scolded us for laughing as Dad, out of the clear blue, he sang one of his favorite Slovak songs "*Ja parobeck z Kapušian*" (I'm a bachelor from Kapucian). She suggested that we remove his shoes and stop laughing. We did so and Mom walked Dad to the bedroom where she helped him into bed.

My first day of work as a park worker was on a Friday. I walked to the Whiting Park with Dad. As we walked along, the topic of our conversation was the "victory celebration" at which Dad got tipsy. Dad confessed that he had one celebration drink too many and said that would never happen again, and it didn't. At noon we sat down at Dad's usual spot as we waited for one of the kids to bring our hot lunches from home. Along came the eight year old twins Joey and Tony carrying the hot lunch, which Mom had prepared for Dad. They also brought my lunch—three grilled cheese sandwiches with lettuce and tomato and a lunch pie. Because it was Friday, a meatless day for Catholics, Dad's meal was a creamed hot lettuce soup topped with sliced hard boiled eggs, one of Dad's favorite meatless noon day meals.

We walked over to one of four wooden glider swings, painted a "Whiting Park green," to enjoy our lunch dessert.

Waves crashed onto the shoreline boulders just across the street. Lake Michigan was producing a symphony of sound as an endless stream of waves pounded against the shoreline. As usual Dad shared his lunch cake with the twins, a thank you for bringing his hot lunch. I shared my Dolly Madison strawberry pie with Joey and Tony as my way of saying thank you for bringing those delicious "hot off the grill" cheese sandwiches. While Dad and I relaxed on the glider swing, the twins ran over to the 15-foot high metal slide located in the center of the playground. Typical eight-year-olds, they ran from slide to swing; from swing to teeter-totter; from teeter-totter to merry-go-round, until, finally exhausted, they climbed back onto the glider swing and onto Dad's lap. There they rested until it was time to return home. Along with the empty enameled pail and empty coffee thermos, they carried with them pleasant memories as they made the one mile return trip home.

Chapter VIII - MAKING A CHOICE

On a day near the end of that 1946 summer, Joe Tomko, a grade school classmate, came to the park on a mission from Fr. Lefko. He spotted me behind the huge gas-powered mower and signaled for me to stop. "Father Lefko wants to see you after work," he said. When I asked "Why," he said that he didn't know why, just that Father wanted to see me.

As I stood nervously at Fr. Lefko's desk in the St. John rectory after work that day, Father asked if I wanted to study for the priesthood. I said yes, just as I had many times during my grade school days at St. John's. "But how do I do that," I asked, "since my parents cannot pay for such an education?." "Don't worry about the finances," he said, "they will be taken care of in the same way they were taken care of for me when I went to study for the priesthood." Father said that seminarians in the Society of the Precious Blood were educated without any cost to family. "If you are accepted," he said, "it will be necessary to make a complete commitment." "Seminarians" he said, "remain at the seminary all year long except for a ten-day vacation in the summer." I began to fidget as I thought about giving up everything, including the family I held near and dear. No more holidays at home with Mom and Dad and brothers and sisters. No more Christmas or Easter celebrations; no more Whiting Fourth of Julys or birthday celebrations. Father Lefko must have read my mind. "Rudy," he said, "it's not like you will never see your parents or brothers or sisters. Once a month there is a visiting Sunday. Your family will be able to visit you all afternoon on that day." To further dispel my doubts, he talked about the scholastic program at the seminary of the

47

Society of the Precious Blood. "The first three years of high school are spent at Brunnerdale seminary in Canton, Ohio. Then the last year of high school and first two years of college are spent at St. Joe's in Rensselaer. Since you have finished three years of high school just like the students coming from Brunnerdale seminary, you will fit right in. All your classmates will be new at St. Joe's just the same as you. Once you have finished your studies at St. Joe's, you will spend six years at St. Charles, the major seminary in Carthagena, Ohio. There you will study philosophy for two years and theology for four years." I stood there in a daze not knowing if I wanted to make that kind of a commitment. "Take until tomorrow to decide," Father Lefko said, "and talk it over with your parents."

Without reservation, Mom and Dad encouraged me to take the step. It would be a blessing beyond compare - another son studying for the holy priesthood! Earlier that year my older brother John decided to quit his studies for the priesthood. His leaving the seminary was a disaster for my parents. They were overcome with grief and their hearts ached! Given this opportunity to have a second son study for the priesthood was a blessing. They promised that they would support my decision in any way they could. The next day, prepared to make the commitment, I went to the Rectory. Father Lefko smiled as he accepted my decision. It was set. Father Brenkus our pastor would take me to St. Joe on the day after Labor Day.

As I left St. John's rectory that day, I decided to take a leisurely stroll down 119th Street, the main street of my youth. The sights and sounds of that center of town would no longer be available to me; I was leaving Whiting. So come with me as we take that wistful stroll down memory lane.

48

Chapter IX - A STROLL DOWN MAIN STREET

As we begin, we walk past St. John's Cathedral-like church with its steeple rising some 190 feet into the sky. It is my family's church serving the Slovak community. We look to the right as we cross 119th street viewing the usual beehive of activity at Poppen's Service Station. As we look to the left, we see that there are no cars coming so we cross the street and there, just ahead, is Frenchik's candy store. Mrs. Frenchik, wearing a colorful apron, is standing behind the large glass cases filled with every kind of childhood delight. We linger for a while taking in the pleasurable sights and smells of this candy store. In one of the enclosed glass cases are "Mary Janes" filled with a creamy peanut butter filling; black "Dots-in-a box," "Holloway suckers," "Boston Baked Beans," lemon drops, root beer barrels, "red hots," evergreen mint leafs, little wax bottles filled with orange, strawberry, lemon and lime colored water. In the next case are "Walnettos," a white rectangular shaped chewy carmel loaded with chunks of walnuts. There are different colored "jaw breakers," crystal white "rock candy" on a string, "guess whats," "circus nuts" (those delicious banana flavored lady fingers), pink and white "Snaps" in a box, "Necco Wafers" (the kind we played communion with) boxes of candy-cigarettes, (the kind we walked down the street during the cold of winter pretending we were smoking as we blew "smoke" from our mouths). On the bottom glass shelf are packets of bubble gum containing a tiny folded paper with a miniature cartoon. Inviting are the neatly arranged stacks of gum packets containing Indian cards and Baseball cards. Black Jack gum is available in single stick form. That is the gum with which we covered our front teeth to make them look as though they were rotten.

Across the street from Frenchik's is Swarthout Chevrolet. On display in what was a new car show room before the war are used cars made to look like new. There is a 1941 Chevrolet model "Master DeLuxe Station Wagon" with wood paneling. Positioned next to the station wagon is a look-like new, dark blue, 6 cylinder, 1941 Master sport sedan. The price of the Chevrolet sedan was just reduced $50.00 and is now only $495.00. Since there are no new models, the used cars are hard to get and are really holding their value.

As we continue eastward, we come to Rudy Wunder's Rudolf's House of Beauty. It is located next to Condes Grocery where Mr. & Mrs. Condes together with their oldest sons, Sam, George and Pete offered choice meats, produce and groceries. Chris, the youngest Condes son, is washing the large store windows.

On the showroom floor of Schlatter Ford, next to Condes, are several good looking Fords. In pristine condition are a sleek, black, super DeLuxe Convertible, and a dark green model 022A, four-door sedan. They were both sold as new off the same showroom floor before the war began. We pause a while, and with nose pressed up against the windowpane, we give these reconditioned beauties the once over.

Looking across the street we see Banana Bill standing at his fruit stand with umbrella in hand as if protecting his produce stand. We hurry by because Banana Bill didn't like kids. No wonder, we love to tease him as he shook that umbrella at us. Crossing over Atchison Avenue, from the Hammond side to the Whiting side, we stand at the entrance to the Igloo Ice Cream Shoppe, the corner store of the three-story Illiana Hotel Building. Pictured in the windows, around an igloo of frosty iced-snow cubes, are large sized, delicious looking, double dipped ice cream cones.

A few giant steps forward and just past the main entrance to the hotel we pass the Hob Nob Restaurant located on the first floor of the Illiana Hotel Building. The counter stools are half-empty and, no wonder, it's between lunch and dinnertime.

Just ahead looms the tallest building in Whiting, the stately stone constructed six story Central State Bank Building. Getting a haircut at Leo Grothouse's barbershop located on the first floor is Mr. Dominic P. Sevald, one of the building's owners. Mr. Jim Griffin, owner of the Ben Franklin Press, has just emerged from his newspaper print shop located in the basement of the Central State Bank Building. If we listen closely, we can hear the purring and clicking sounds coming from the printing presses below as they print out copy after copy of the *Whiting Times*. At the main entrance to the building is a sign advertising a 1% interest payment on all new savings accounts at Liberty Savings & Loan. Joe and Ben Chilla help their prominent father Mr. Joseph Chilla run that Savings and Loan.

Friendly Ed Brandman waves at us from his pharmacy windows fronting on the Boulevard side of the bank building. The windows on the upper floors are gold lettered with names of the doctors occupying its offices. This building contains a veritable "who's who" of Whiting's professionals. Some of the doctors are Peter Stecy, his brother John Stecy, Doctors Smith, Silvian, Doll, Kopcha, Ferry, Rudser and Reed. Some of the dentists are Drs. Kosior, Cabot and Taggart. Haney's pharmacy is located on the second floor along with the offices of Chiropractor

Leo Nuerenberg. The Whiting Robertsdale Chamber of Commerce offices are located on the third floor as is the Whiting Credit Bureau. Among those occupying the fourth floor are lawyers Charles Perel, and John Fetterhoff. The Charles Gainer Insurance agency is on the fifth floor. The entire sixth floor is occupied by the "Whiting Clinic." What a treat to ride the attendant operated elevator when going to see the doctor or dentist or to get shots at the clinic.

A shift was just changing for the policeman patrolling the corner. Emil Walsko was being relieved by patrolman Lawrence Vidovich all dressed up in his spiffy jodhpurs. The traffic light changes and policeman Vidovich blows his trusty whistle, a whistle he loves to blow.

Looking northward, on the corner of 119th and the Blvd, is the IGA store. My cousin George Pieters lives in an upstairs apartment of that insul-sided, frame building with his mother and sisters. Across the street is a donut shop, which fries up the most delicious fresh potato doughnuts each morning. Then comes Abe Mills Auto Supply store and Corman Plumbing and Jim Bayus' Radio Shop. As a streetcar comes clanging southward turning east on 119th St, a mild wind blows in from the north, permeating the air with a burnt corn smell, the unmistakable Amaizo smell. Looking southward, down the boulevard, Oberlander's Laundry comes into view. The newly constructed Hungarian Reformed church building stands prominently near Ondrejko's Photography shop. Mr. Ondrejko is the official photographer for most Whiting schools. A famous saying of his, before snapping a picture, is "look at the burdie!"

Next to Ondrejko's is Ciesar's Chrysler Plymouth dealership. In the distance we get a glimpse of Poracky's grocery store located just across the Blvd. from Jancosek's grocery and Kollar's candy store. Further down the Blvd. are Ed Kosior's Funeral Home, Johnny Mojzik's quality meats and Mr. John Dudzik's clothing and shoe store. Kolina's Tavern fronts a three-story brick apartment complex on the corner of West Fred and the Blvd. Almost beyond our sight and rising into the sky is the St. Adalbert's church steeple. St. Als is the parish church for the Polish people. Across the street from the church is Wojcik's White Star grocery and Harry Gold's Standard Service Station. As we walk across the Blvd. towards the main part of town, the streetcar heading southward has just turned eastward following the streetcar tracks onto 119th St.

As we crossed the boulevard, the Amaizo smells that saturated the air are now partially overcome by the sweet smells of grilled onions and hamburgers at the White Castle on the corner of Cleveland and 119th. Our White Castle is the only one in all of Northern Indiana and the only White Castle for miles around. People come from all around to buy them by the sackfull. All day long twenty-four hamburgers, smothered in minced onions, are being grilled all at the same time. What a feast for the eyes and for our noses and, if we are lucky and have a nickel, a real feast for our mouths.

On the other corner of Cleveland, across from the White Castle, is Owen's Funeral Home. Immediately next door is Baran's new funeral home. Baran's has just moved there from their Schrage Ave. funeral parlor.

As we walk past Frank Harangody's Standard Gas Station we approach Lipay's lady's clothing store and Burton's clothing where boy's slacks are on sale for 79 cents, polo shirts for 29 cents and children's pajamas for 39 cents. Abe Finkelstein and his son Marvin own and operate the next store, Whiting Shade & Awning. Upstairs, on the second floor, Dr. Harry Barton drills, fills and pulls teeth.

Across the street, signs in the A&P windows announce their sale items. Two 1 pound bags of EIGHT O'CLOCK coffee for 39 cents, pork loin roast 29 cents, fifteen pounds of Idaho Russet potatoes for 45 cents, a 25 pound bag of Saunnfield flour is 75 cents, a 46 ounce package of Sno Sheen cake mix is 22 cents and two cakes of Swan Soap are sale priced for a dime.

On the northeast corner of Central Ave. is the Indiana Plumbing & Heating Supply and across from the Central Ave. crossing on the south side of 119th St. is an empty lot owned by Ciesars. Fifteen wooden steps descend from the sidewalk to the lot below. The lot is fenced all along the edge of the sidewalk with 3" pipe railings, painted a "Whiting green." Men are delicately perched on the top pipe railing pretending that they are watching the streetcars go by. We know better, they are watching the ladies go by, checking to see if the seams on their silk stockings are straight.

Mike Scandal, a crippled, sly looking man with a perpetual smile, specializes in "girlie" magazines in his small frame store next to Ciesar's empty lot. Next to Scandals is Dave Tolchinsky's Rexall Drugs. Dave has one of the best soda fountains in town. Paul Demkovich works the soda fountain whipping up delectable green rivers, root beer floats, cherry cokes and any flavor of malt or milkshake you could dream of. Pop owns the taxi stand next door and Jim McHale cheers up many weary and thirsty Whitingites at his tavern. If you need an attorney, the law offices of Gilbert Brindley are just above McHale's tavern.

Across the street, next to Indiana Plumbing & Supply is Neil Price's Firestone store. Nipsco (Northern Indiana Public Service Co.) offices are located next door. Mary Pawelko and Emma Kostolnik do a remarkable job in assisting Nipsco customers. Gas and electric appliances are also sold at the office including those new gas hot water heaters.

Further eastward, on that side of the street, are Lewin and Wolfe's store for men and Agnes Freel's millinery. The American Trust & Savings Bank is on the west corner of LaPorte Ave. Vice President John Sholopsky and Assistant Cashier Frank Kowalski assist Mr. Kozacik, the bank president. The Bank is also offering 1% interest not only on passbook savings accounts but also on Christmas Club accounts. Located on the second floor of the bank building are the law offices of Andrew Kozacik, the offices of Doctors Louis T. Kudele and Aubrey Sceersy and the beauty parlor of Billie Joyce. Continuing on the south side of 119th St. we cross over Community Court and, looking southward we see the church building of the First Church of Christ Scientist and the huge Community Center building, a gift donated to the City of Whiting by the Standard Oil Co. This massive brick building with a slate roof has an Olympic sized swimming pool; a thirteen-lane bowling alley managed by Hardy Keilman and his able assistant Mr. Al Koch. Andy Yanas mans the front desk. There is an auditorium, a fully equipped billiard and poolroom and two basketball courts, one for boys and a smaller one for girls. The boy's basketball court has an overhead indoor track. There is a handball court and a weight room and there are also various meeting rooms.

As we cross over Community Court, the Slovensky Dom, a three-story brick structure, rises ahead of us.

Johnson's Shoe Repair shop is located in the corner of that building right next to John Roman's restaurant and the first floor clubrooms of the Slovak Club. An ice truck parked in front of the Slovensky Dom is unloading large blocks of ice for the Turkish Star & Crescent dinner to be held that night. Osman Joseph, a well respected Turk, owner and operator of a café located at the corner of Fischrupp and Schrage, is helping unload food from a truck for tonight's Turkish dinner. Up on the third floor is where a Janošik movie was shown several times a year. Janošik was the "Slovak Robin Hood;" he did in Slovakia what Robin Hood did in England. At the conclusion of the movie, this past Sunday, our Slovak spirits were elevated to the point that all of us, young and old, stood up and sang "Hej Slovaci'" the Slovak national anthem.

As we continue, we note that, in the small hall of Slovak Dom, right behind Johnny's shoe repair shop, Helen Kocan is presiding over a Branch 81 Ženska Jednota meeting. Ann Hruskovich and Sophie Gresko are seated at the entrance of the meeting hall collecting the 10 cents monthly membership dues.

Looking northward across the LaPorte street crossing, Sacred Heart Church, the parish church for the Irish community, stands majestically in the distance.

The Capitol Theatre is located in the Obresk building and is next door to the Slovak Dom. On each side of the theater ticket booth are glass-encased panels announcing the movies playing today and the stars in the movies. Ten cents is the admission for the triple feature. "The Lost Wagon Train" starring Sunset Carson is the main feature. This all talking movie is an intriguing account about the disappearance of a 160 pioneer wagon train.

Across the street, on the east corner of Laporte Ave., is

Josephine's Dress Shop. Brown's Women's Apparel, owned and operated by Leo Brown, is next door. Getting back to the south side of 119th St. is Sherman's Hardware. Just next door is "The Main," a tobacco and cigar store. Cardboard cigarette posters in the windows proclaim that "Luckies are kind to your throat." The Chesterfield poster states that, "While my Chesterfield was burning my heart was burning too." The third poster, an Old Gold poster says, "Old Golds, not a cough in a carload." The talk about town is that this joint does more than sell tobacco. There is more to the building than the tobacco storefront!

Just next door is the newly built Woolworth's building. The old Murad restaurant building was demolished to make way for this new, modern dime store. Among the hundreds of items advertised to sell for 10 cents are anklets, neckties and Turkish towels. All the cookies including cream filled sandwich cookies, chocolate, vanilla and strawberry Sugar Wafers, are on sale for ten cents a pound. At the soda fountain banana splits, fresh tulip sundaes and chocolate fudge "Mondays" are being offered for 10 cents. Creamy Nut Fudge is sliced right before your eyes from thick loaves of nut-filled goodness. Hundreds of items are being offered for five cents, including hair nets, hankies, safety pins, bobby combs, hair curlers, pants hangers, dish cloths, vegetable brushes, clothes sprinklers and shelf paper.

Across the street the marquee of the Hoosier Theatre announces its main feature "On The Good Ship Lollypop" starring Shirley Temple. The second feature is "Boys Town" starring Mickey Rooney and Pat O'Brien. Coming on Saturday will be the first in the series of "Fu Man Chu." The "Bank Night Prize," according to the marquee is up to $300.00.

Looking south, as we stand on the corner of Clarke St., we see the Western Union office located behind Ben Gardner's Hoosier Drug Store, a Walgreen Agency. Coming into view is the Methodist Church building, and just across the street is Joe Stanek's tailor shop. Further on down is Mr. Benus' confectionery and St. Mary's Byzantine Catholic Church, the parish church for the Slovak Byzantine people.

Looking across to the north side of 119th St. we can see Jimmy Glenn's shoe store. That is where the Sisters of Providence teaching at St. John's and Sacred Heart schools buy all their shoes. Jim even gives them free clickers with their shoe purchases. In the building next to Glenn's shoes, Hershel and Mayo Winsberg present quality men's clothing. Located next door is Mrs. Kinel's lingerie shop. Mrs. Kinel is John Chrustowski's sister.

On the corner of Sheridan Ave. is the Whiting Flower shop owned and operated by the Stawitcke family. Colorful floral arrangements are offered by the Stawitckes all year long. Coming back to the south side of the street and located next to Ben Gardner's drug store is R & S Shoe store owned and operated by Otto and Florence Schmidt. Florence is Emma Kostolnik's sister and active with her husband in many of Whiting's community affairs. Otto's dedication as a premier organizer of Whiting's "Fourth of July Parades" was evident by the success of those parades in Whiting.

Aronberg & Kissen Jewelers is located in the next building. Displayed in the window of this glass and black marble like front is a sparkling seventeen jewel golden Bulova wristwatch, the kind I got as a confirmation present from my Godfather, Mr. Lawrence Kerchak.

Taking a few giant steps forward we come to a white

picket fence fronting Netz's candy and ice cream shop. The specialty is their rich and creamy double dip ice cream cones. Despite his bad hand, the owner quickly fills soda fountain and candy orders. Neal Postraw owns and operates the dress shop next door.

The next store on our way is Seifer's Furniture store managed by Bill Brandman, Ed Brandman's brother. Seifer's is the only store with a freight elevator going up to its' spacious showrooms and warehouse. On display, behind the huge glass windowpanes of the first floor, is a $39.95 dresser on sale for only $18.95. Displayed as an extra special is a seven-piece dining room set for only $24.50. An $89.50, freestanding, floor model Philco radio is sale priced at $57.50.

Gordon's furniture is right next door and also has a sale going on. Unfinished drop-leaf tables are on sale for $1.19. A porcelain kitchen table is priced at $3.95. Zavesky's red Diamond T moving truck is parked at the curb. Joe Zavesky is loading furniture purchased by one of his customers from Gordon's.

Looking back and across the street is Nick's Pool Hall owned and operated by Mr. Spiros. The K of C Building with its club rooms is next door.

John Chrustowski owner of Whiting News is advertising the relatively new Parker Brothers board game "Monopoly." John's brother Stanley is his able assistant. "Dutch" Serafin is tossing bundles of papers onto a shoot directed into the basement of the newspaper store building. The papers are being unloaded from the Chicago Herald American truck.

Back on the south side of the street we come upon the J.J. Newberry five and dime store. At the entrance is a large black and silver metal "stand up" scale-weighing machine. For a penny it even spits out a card with your fortune on it! As we look through the glass doors we see glass bins filled with every kind of chocolate and hard tack candy. Row upon row of counters comes into sight. Displayed on those counters are toys, houseware and kitchenware, clothing and garden supplies. Most anything is available at this five and dime store including refreshments. Situated at the other entrance are a soda fountain and a food counter serving up delicious hamburgers, hot dogs, popcorn, pop and ice cream.

Joseph P. Sullivan, City Attorney, has his offices on the second floor of Max Shlack's barber shop building. There are about thirty steps and a couple of landings to get to Mr. Sullivan's second floor offices. Bea is Attorney Sullivan's able secretary.

Before we continue eastward, we pause to admire the red, white and blue twirling barber pole on the sidewalk in front of Schlack's barbershop. Across the street is the McNamara Brothers meat and grocery market. The McNamara brothers sell quality meats and "everything to eat" proclaims the window banner in the store front window. Mayor James T. McNamara owns the store with his brothers. McNamaras are offering a pound of butter or a dozen of eggs for 21 cents. Swift's famous Calla Hams are 12 cents a pound; seedless Sunkist oranges are selling for 25 cents a dozen. The Miner & Dunn restaurant next door is located on the west corner of Oliver just across the street from the Whiting primary school building. Back on the south side is Riffers clothing. Dr. Goldstein's offices are located on the second floor of Riffer's building. Coming from the store front located next door we hear the whirling and buzzing and clanging sounds from the shoe grinding and polishing machines that shake the wooden floors and counter of Alex Terny's shoe repair shop.

Our senses continue to be rewarded as we approach Hot Dog Louies. The delectable, mouth-watering smells of the hot dog joint permeate the air around us. The shop is about 8 feet wide and 35 feet long and is the smallest hot dog joint around. Standing behind the counter, in white aprons and hats, are Louie and his cousin George. As usual they are arguing about something. The argument begins in English and ends in Greek.

We skip along past a couple of houses and are at Jack Wargo's insurance and license bureau. Jack is also the Whiting Park Commissioner for Mayor Jim McNamara. The street commissioner is Mr. Spurrier. Gambini's, a hang out for high school kids, is located next to Wargos, and the Elite Bakery is located in the next storefront. Eli Yuhas, the owner, is a look alike to Abraham Lincoln. He is selling day old cream horns "3 for 10 cents."

The Armory Building across the street is the headquarters for the National Guard. Back on this side of the street, next to Gambinis, is Krogers. In the window we see colorful store advertisement. Lard is advertised as 3 pounds for 13 cents; Wilson's salami is priced at 19 cents a pound and veal breast (pocket for stuffing) is selling for 19 cents a pound.

Vic Orr's radio shop and Stillwell's furniture sit next to each other. Displayed in the window of Stillwell's is a three-piece bedroom set for $9.85. The three pieces are a walnut finished steel bed, a link spring and a four-inch thick cotton mattress. Central Drugs owned and operated by pharmacists Matt Frankowski and Mr. Pekorik, is on the southwest corner of New York Ave. Mr. Frankowski stands about four feet tall and is very crippled. Just recently he moved his pharmacy from the rear of the Bank of Whiting building to this new location. The second floor of the Central Drug store building is occupied by Attorneys Green and Powers. Gold lettering on the door leading to the second floor tells us that.

Across the street, the State Bank of Whiting, referred to as the Standard Oil Company's bank, is ably directed by President W. R. Smith and assisted by Vice Presidents G. Paul Smith and Carl Binhammer. Mr. Steve Sabol, the vault and head teller, occupies the first cage. Ann Rusina and George Vater have just hired in as tellers. On the second floor of the State Bank building are the offices of Attorneys O. Ahlgren, and Tom Cerajewski. Looking southward at the New York Avenue crossing, Gurevitz's grocery comes into view as does Gardner's clothing store. Sam's barber shop, Hlebasko's tavern, Mazanek's grocery and Vacendak's poultry store.

As we cross over New York Avenue we can see Walter Schrage, president of the Bank of Whiting, sitting at the front desk. Charles O'Drobinak, the bank vice-president is standing in front of cage one, which is Joe Froelich's cage. Joe has his trusty green visor positioned on his head. Black garters hold up the long sleeves of his stripped shirt. Dr. Clementine Frankowski's offices are located on the second floor as are the offices of Dr. Michael Rafacz and attorneys James McCarthy, Dewey Kelley and Walter Smith.

Across the street a forty-eight star American flag waves proudly over the Whiting Post Office building. Mr. Laverne Fortin is the postmaster assisted by Urie Moore. As we continue eastward and just next to the Bank of Whiting building is Saylor's Dutch Boy paint store where interior and exterior oil paints are available for $1.20 a gallon. Oasis Liquors occupy the next storefront.

The Whiting Recreation Parlor and Billiards, owned and operated by the three Davis brothers, is located in the next building. Not only are there pool and billiard tables but, more importantly for many of us, is the fact that there is a ticker tape that cranks out a ribbon of white paper filled with sporting information. Sporting scores come over that ticker tape as they happen. On the wall, next to the ticker tape, is a large black chalkboard. One of the Davis brothers calls out the ball scores off the tape and another brother chalks them in onto the blackboard for all to see.

As we continue we pass Kaplan's Whiting Plumbing and Heating, followed by Spurrier's Hardware and the National Tea store. At the National Tea spare ribs are being offered for 15 cents a pound, rye or raisin bread is priced at 7 cents a loaf and a 10 pound bag of pure cane sugar is selling for 47 cents.

Clink Collins, Whiting's police chief, is just coming out of Joe Dernay's dry cleaning and tailor shop. Displayed in the tailor shop windows are bolts of suit material from which Mr. Dernay expertly tailors "custom made" suits. Apart from his tailor shop, Dernay is involved in Whiting politics as a Councilman-at-large. Hal Stice operates the jewelry store next door while the Elk's clubrooms are just across the street. Located in that same block are the Standard Food Mart, Robert and George Pate lawyers, Russell Wilkinson's restaurant, John Murad's restaurant, Ally Hassan grocers, the Star Hotel and Kemal Ahmet's restaurant.

Just ahead is Fred Beisal's building, a complete department store selling everything from soup to nuts. Men's suits are on sale for $10.00 and sanforized slacks are on sale for $1.12. On display in the large store windows are unpainted kitchen utility cabinets for $1.89

and studio couches for $8.95. A Mel Ott genuine horsehide baseball mitt is selling for $1.35.

The Whiting Moose clubrooms are located across the street from Beisal. Next to Beisal is Kiraly's Radio Center where most every model of radio is in stock. The large floor models begin at $47.50 while the table models sell for as low as $15.95.

Zelenke's tavern, a favorite stop of many Whiting shoppers is right next door to Kiralys. Liver sandwiches and those meaty Bolshevik sandwiches are offered for free along with a 25 cent frosty glass of beer. Sitting at the end of the bar is a glass container filled with pickled hard-boiled eggs floating in beet juice, introduced by the previous bar owner Andrew Kalapach.

Across the street a new sanctuary had been built for Whiting's Baptist community. Standing at the White Oak Ave. crossing, we look southward. Coming into immediate view is the brick, two-story Fire and Police station building, located on the corner of Fischrupp. Adolph Zweig, the fire chief, is standing on the corner. Whiting's two jail cells are located right behind the main police counter of the police station. As you enter the police station, any locked up prisoners come into sight immediately. Whiting City Hall is located on the second floor of the fire and police station building. Further in the distance we see the Immaculate Conception Church and school complex which serves the Slovak community in that part of town. The Jewish Synagogue is across the street from the church. It serves as the place of worship for many of Whiting's merchants and doctors.

As we cross over White Oak Ave. we come to Kozacik's hardware store where Pete Kayes offers his hardware and paints. Advertised in the main window are sink and lavatory faucets priced at $1.25. Coal and garden shovels, picks and axes are all sold here, as are electrical and plumbing supplies. Every imaginable kind of nut and bolt, screw and nail are stored in hundreds of wooden compartments mounted on walls going all the way up to the 14' ceilings of this establishment. "Universal" leaded paints are priced at $1.49 a gallon. The sign in the window says that you could choose from sixteen different colors.

The Venetian Grill is next door followed by George Cholyte's barbershop, the perfect place for a two-bit shave and a hair cut. Nardi's cigar store occupies the next storefront. Card games and all kinds of bookings go on here. From their Fischrupp Avenue firehouse, Whiting firemen send kids to Nardi's to buy ice cream sandwiches for them. Joe Kasper, is one of those firemen and his daughter Mary is one of the kids who runs errands for the firemen.[1] For her services as a runner she usually gets a quarter, enough money to buy five ice cream bars. Lucky Mary! Across the street from Nardis is Jack Wargo's Standard service station.

The four-storied Standard Hotel on the south west corner of Schrage and 119th St. offers reasonably priced rooms by the day, week or month. On this corner the streetcar tracks turn southward just past the Standard Hotel. Looking southward we view the sprawling Whiting Lumber & Coal Co. Just across the street is Baloff's Sugar Bowl Confectionary situated on the south east corner of Schrage and 119th St. and Shocaroff's Sundries on the north east corner. Baloff and Shocaroff are brother-in-laws who came to this country from Bulgaria.

The Pennsylvania and New York Central train tracks cross over 119th street right behind Baloff's and Shocaroff's. As we squint our eyes peering towards that

[1] Today Mary is my wife

last block of 119th street, the steeple of St. Peter & Paul Church rises in the distance. It serves the Croatian community in Whiting. Just across the tracks are Hansen's Buick sales, Mike Buscanyi's Roosevelt Café, Sramek's tavern and Hajduch's grocery. Hajduch had just taken over the grocery store from his brother-in-law Joseph Grenchik who was going into banking. The last building to be viewed is Haluska's Trucking. Our stroll down the main street of my youth ends. The sun is setting as I head homeward following the southbound streetcar tracks. May each of us keep in mind that as long as we have memories, yesterday will always remain.

Chapter X - SEMINARY LIFE

St. Joseph's College, Rensselaer, In.

On the appointed day Fr. Gabriel Brenkus, C.PP.S., the pastor at St. John's, pulled up in front of our house in his big, black Chrysler. Ambsie and the twins carried all my earthly possessions, two suitcases full, to the car. I said some tearful good-byes and we were headed southward. I was leaving my parents, brothers, sisters and the comforts of my humble home. It was the most somber moment of all my teen years.

I was in a melancholy mood as we began the two-hour trip to Rensselaer, Indiana. Father Brenkus told me about the day he entered the seminary and that lightened my mood. His good-byes were said at the Monon train station in Hammond where he boarded the train headed for Rensselaer. There was no private passenger car to transport him to the seminary. A melancholy train whistle sounded as he waved his tearful good-byes to his family. The sound of that whistle remained with him as it chugged along headed for Rensselaer.

The verdant green of the Indiana landscape unfolded before us — cornfields, bean fields and green grazing pastures. The grazing cows were professional said Father Brenkus; they were *OUT- STANDING* in their field. We both chuckled. Father Brenkus was trying to add a little levity to diffuse the seriousness of the situation. Huge-dome like clouds drifted lazily in the azure sky. My imagination ran rampant inviting me to form objects from those white billowing clouds. There I saw the shape of a fish and of a sheep, of a dog, an eagle, a sea horse, a snow crab and a swan. Separated from all the rest was a fluffy cloud floating along all by itself. That cloud resembled a bearded old man. Was that God the Father hovering above, pointing the way to the seminary?

Wooden posts, bearing Burma shave signs, popped out of the fields along the roadway. Reading them made the time go faster:

"Brother Speeders - Let's Rehearse - All Together- Good Morning Nurse. BURMA SHAVE," said the first of many signs.

The next set of signs said: "Passing School Zone - Take It Slow - Let Poor Little - Shaver Grow – BURMA SHAVE." Followed by: "Don't Lose Your Head - To Gain A Minute - You Need Your Head - Your Brains are in it - BURMA SHAVE."

"Spring has sprung- The grass has riz - WHERE last year's - Careless driver is - BURMA SHAVE"

Proper distance - To him was luck - They pulled him out - Of some guy's trunk - BURMA SHAVE"

"Cattle crossing - Means go slow - That old bull - Is some - Cow's beau - BURMA SHAVE"

We drove into the impressive stone entrance of Saint Joseph's College, gracefully arched with tall, majestic maples, past the circular

Entrance St. Joseph College, Rensselaer, In.

water pond and spraying fountain towards the three-story brick and stone administration building. I had remembered the impressiveness of the St. Joe's campus from our annual "Altar Boy Picnics." Father parked his car in front of the seminarian's Xavier Hall just past the twin towers of the chapel.

Father Brenkus introduced me to Father Marcellus Dreiling, the hall prefect. Robert Conway, the "house boss," showed me to the basement locker room where a locker had been assigned to me. He watched as I unpacked my suitcases. From there we went to the first floor study hall where a desk had been assigned to me, then on to the third floor

St. Joe's Administration Bldg. and "Twin Tower" Chapel

Seminarian's Xavier Hall

dormitory room. My bed was the second one in the third row, right near the "john." At the tailor shop I was introduced to Brother Conrad Lemanski. He took measurements for a cassock. Several days later the cassock was ready. A Roman collar with a black stripe in the center and a waist cincture completed the daily attire for all classes, for study hall and all chapel functions.

Now that I had been introduced to the surroundings of Xavier Hall, Robert Conway

Author, age 17 in my first cassock

handed me a very important type-written sheet of paper. He encouraged me to sit down, read and memorize it. It was a "Rookie Pledge" and went something like this. "I am a rookie, a silly little rookie, I think I am big but I'm only a rookie, I pledge allegiance to my rookie master...."

After my first evening meal, upperclassman John Klopke, had me hopping around the Xaviar Hall recreation room straddling a chair saying "hi-ho Silver I'm the Lone Ranger." I didn't know anybody and I felt like a fool! I thought "Is this why I came to the seminary, to make a fool of myself?" The next day the twenty-seven of us rookies blindfolded and barefooted, walked along single file with our right hand resting on the shoulder of the classmate in front of us. We were walked through a sticker patch and told we were walking on broken glass. We were paddled if we didn't keep up. Then, still blindfolded, we were led to the St. Joe's pond in front of the "Ad" building. There we were told that we were going to be thrown into deep water. The Rookie Master shouted "Please tell us if you can't swim. The water is very deep and we don't want you to drown." An upper classman jumped into the water, making a loud splash. The blindfold was taken off each of us rookies, one by one. We saw what was happening and were told to keep quiet. The next rookie name was called out. "Throw him in," shouted the upper classmen.

On the last night of the initiation Fritz was chosen from the rest and given an impossible task. He was commanded to recite the Stations of the Cross by heart. Fritz unbelievably did it! The upper classmen were in awe and you could have heard a pin drop when he finished. After several days the initiation came to an end with a grand welcoming party. It was then that the behavior of the upper classmen returned to normal. They couldn't be

70

more helpful in assisting us to adjust to our new schedule. Our class had just entered phase two of early seminary life at St. Joe's.

Our daily schedule began at 5:30 AM. We were roused by a loud bell, which rang throughout the building. In total silence we proceeded to ready ourselves for the new day. Dressed in a Roman collar with black stripe and cassock worn over shirt & trousers, we hurried to the chapel in silence for the 6:00 AM morning prayers and mediation. The Community Low Mass was celebrated at 6:30 AM. All the while, private Masses were celebrated by priest faculty members at the eight side altars. There was a little signal light and bell located on the left door leading from the sacristy into the sanctuary. When that bell rang, it signaled for the "next in line" server to come to the sacristy. One of the priests was ready to say Mass and needed a server. We answered that bell regardless of the time left for Community services. There were times when breakfast was eaten alone and in haste because of serving for a late Mass.

Breakfast served at 7:00 was always eaten in silence at tables set for eight in the Community refectory. Seating was according to precedence, which meant sitting in the same chair for every meal and surrounded by the same classmates for all meals, like it or not. There was about a half-hour of "free time" after breakfast till 8:00 AM. We were "free" to talk, free to make our beds and the bed of a priest for whom we were appointed to be a chamberlain. During my two college years at St. Joe, I was a "chamberlain" for Fr. Sylvester Hartman. I made his bed, brought fresh water to his room every morning and cleaned the room every Saturday afternoon. Fr. Hartman was a saintly old priest who looked especially funny when his wig

Fr. Hartman

sat on his head backwards. Although he laughed right along with us in the classroom, he would attempt to calm the situation by saying, "Psssst, go on boys," rubbing one hand over the palm of the other as he attempted to return order to the classroom. He was our Logic and Greek professor. All of our classes began with the sign of the cross which was said in Greek: "*En to onomati, tou Patros, kai tou Hyiou, kai tou Hagiou Pneumatos, Amen.*" Then came the recitation of the Our Father "*Pater hemon, ho en tois ouranois, Hagiastheto to onoma sou, eltheto he basileia sou, genetheto to thelema sou, hos en ourano, kai epi tes ges....*" Then we recited the Hail Mary in Greek: "*Charie, Maria, kecharitomene, ho Kyrios meta sou, eulogemene su en gynasin, kai eulogemenos ho karpos tou koilias sou,. Jesous....*" We were ready for another hour of instructions from Fr. Sylvester Hartman. With a "pony" (English translation) strategically placed in our bible printed in the Greek language, we were not at a loss to translate the Greek bible passages when called upon to do so. Fr. Hartman was well pleased with our distinct ability at translating those Greek bible passages. We did stammer and feign to struggle from time to time in order to make our translating sound more authentic. It was not uncommon for classmates to whisper "ride 'em cowboy" as we translated from our "pony." All in all, that saintly old priest was convinced that he had done a great job in teaching us Greek.

Even at his advanced age, Fr. Hartman was outstanding in his ability to teach Logic, the study of valid reasoning. Our textbook was one written by that saintly old priest. He had a unique ability to make Aristotelian concepts interesting. One of immutable truths structured in Logic class was the "esoteric square of opposition." We learned the theses embodied in that square very well. The following is a diagram of that SQUARE.

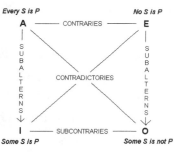

Esoteric Square of Opposition

The theses embodied in the above square are:

Every "S is P" and Some "S is not P" are contradictories

No "S is P" and Some "S is P" are contradictories

Every "S is P" and No "S is P" are contraries

Some "S is P" and "Some S is not P" are subcontraries

Some "S is P" is a subaltern of "Every S is P"

Some "S is not P" is a subaltern of "No S is P."

The above square provided a foundation for the entire study of valid reasoning!

Another of our notable professors was Fr. Ildephonse Rapp. Fr. Rapp was a very unique, robust elderly priest whose specialty was elocution. He taught the speech classes to both the lay students and the seminarians. He was a disciplined individual who expressed himself very eloquently. He strove to teach us by example and that he did quite well. We wrote and memorized all our speeches for his class. Apart from our recitation he gave extra points for dramatics and proper use of hand gestures.

Dressed in cassock, cape and biretta (head covering), he began his day with a brisk "*spaziergang*" (walk) around the campus. His specially handcrafted walking cane was strictly for show. He arched the walking stick keeping pace with his gingerly walk. Father's private celebration of morning Mass was at the first "side altar." Most of us seminarians fidgeted while serving Mass for Father Rapp.

He was meticulous in the pronunciation of each and every word of the entire Mass. His Mass began with, "*In No-mi-ne Pa-tris et Fi-li-i et Spi-ri-tus Sanc-ti* (In the name of the Father and of the Son and of the Holy Ghost.) He articulated each and every syllable. As a result, his Mass took quite a bit longer to celebrate then that of other priests.

Fr. Rapp

Once a year, on his birthday, Father Rapp climbed the Saint Joe's water tower. We watched in awe as he moved upward some 140 feet. It was a hard climb and he paused for a rest at each of the crossbeams. Reaching the top, he would wave to those of us below as we marveled at this septuagenarian standing proudly on the circular platform atop the water tower. He always took along a pair of binoculars to view the grounds far below as he stood victoriously on that platform. He focused his binoculars in every direction gazing on the breathtaking views of the surrounds. After one of those ascents Fr. Rapp's superiors advised him that he would be forbidden to climb the water tower on his 75th birthday. So, on June the 15th, the day before his 75th birthday, he climbed the water tower for the last time. That was his last ascent and although he obeyed his superiors, he outfoxed them. Technically he observed the order forbidding the climb once he reached his 75th birthday.

Dressed in cassock and collar we attended some classes with the secular college students. We called them "seckies" and they called us "mongies (short for monks)." There were four-50 minute classes each morning, beginning on the hour at 8, 9, 10 and 11. The ten minutes between classes was time for a quick "fag" (cigarette). Survey courses in all the natural sciences were exciting and educational. There were twelve-week survey courses in Astronomy, Biology, Botany, Physics, Earth Science (Geology) and Advanced Mathematical Theorem. The thinking was that a priest should be minimally versed in as many areas as possible. It was a grueling course of study, with much classroom time and so very little study time.

Each day's lunch, in the refectory, began with prayers. The Rector prayed *"Benedicite"* (Praise the Lord) and we responded *"Benedicite"* (Praise the Lord). The rector: *"Edent pauperes"* (the poor shall eat). The seminarians: *"Et saturabuntur, et laudabunt Dominum qui requirunt eum; vivent corda eorum in saeculum saeculi"* (And have their fill, and they shall praise the Lord that seek Him; their soul shall live forever.) *Gloria Patri* (Glory be to the Father) and *Kyrie* etc. after which the Lector (reader) said *"Iube, domne, benedicere"* (Please, Father, give the blessing) The rector responded *"Ad coenam vitae aeternae perducat nos Rex aeternae gloriae"* (May the King of eternal glory make us partakers of His heavenly banquet) The student Lector would conclude the prayers before meals with *"Deus caritas est, et qui manet in caritas, in Deo manet et Deus in eo"* (God is charity, and he that abides in charity, abides in God, and God in him). To which we responded: Amen. At long last we sat down to eat. If we were not hungry before we began to pray we sure were by the time the prayers were finished.

We ate in silence, while the student Lector, standing on a raised lecturn, read from a designated inspirational book during the meal. Each of us took turns in reading at meals. As the meal ended the Rector tapped a bell, the reader stopped reading from the inspirational book and announced the necrology (deceased community members death anniversary date), and the martyrology with all those unpronounceable names. We concluded with a litany of prayers all said in Latin and exited the refectory in silence. On special feast days like Christmas or Easter, and other major Community holidays table readings were dispensed with and talking at table was allowed.

Once outside we were free to talk as we prepared for our work assignments. A priest Procurator for the college assigned the tasks to be performed by the seminarians. A student "work boss" executed those work orders by assigning us to the tasks at hand. Although we were not paid for our work, we did receive credit on the Procurator's books at the rate of 10 cent an hour. The credits were used to defray our educational expenses. Each of us was generally assigned to work in the house gang, the laundry, the tailor shop, the farm gang, the paint shop, the carpenter shop or wherever the procurator needed us. The work period was till 2:00 each day.

During my second year at St. Joe, I worked in the carpenter shop. One day a classmate came into the shop. He was not authorized to be there. Despite the posted operational warning signs he turned on the joiner-plainer, took a small block of wood and inserted it into the machine. Within seconds his hand was pulled into the joiner along with that small block of wood. Blood squirted as flesh and bones became exposed. We prayed all night that his fingers would not have to be amputated. After months of recuperation Jim's hand healed to the point where he was allowed to continue his studies for the priesthood. Lucky for him, since missing fingers were an impediment to ordination.

After the daily 90 minute work period, we were free to recreate for two hours until four. There were about sixty of us seminarians who enjoyed the amenities of the

76

Seminarians converse before class

recreation room at Xavier Hall. There was a pool table, card tables, piano, and, of course, a radio. The first one to the radio got to tune in his favorite radio station. The card games we played were bridge, pinochle or euchre. In the corner was a table set up for checkers or chess. There were no magazines or newspapers to distract us. Secular papers were not allowed in Xavier Hall.

Rec room scene - Spitzig, Walters, Gatza, Zogran, Dueweke

The first of two fifty-minute afternoon classes began at 4:00. There were no afternoon classes on Wednesdays and Saturdays. On those

Study Hall

afternoons we worked at our assigned jobs from 1:00 until 5:00 PM. The dinner bell sounded at 6:00 PM each evening. Dressed in our cassocks and black-striped Roman collars, we proceeded to the refectory, a large room directly under the church sacristy. We said our "prayers before meals" (similar to those at noon) in Latin and sat down in silence. As at noon a student stood on an elevated lectern and read from an inspirational book during the meal. There was a short break after dinner until 7:00 PM at which time we strolled over to the chapel for evening prayers and benediction of the Blessed Sacrament. The last free period of the day was right after "chapel" from about 7:30 until 8:00 PM. The 8:00 PM bell sounded the beginning of the "*silentium altum*," the high silence, during which there was to be absolutely no talking. At 8:00 PM we marched into the studyhall to our pre assigned desks for a well-needed two-hour study period. With twenty-two credit hours per semester, those two hours were hardly enough to complete the assigned homework and reports. The *silentium altum* was observed until after breakfast the next day. Discipline!!

On school days our free time included a half-hour after breakfast, 10 minutes between classes, two hours in the afternoon and one hour in the evening. Many a day the "free time" was used for study assignments and homework.

During a typical school year week there were thirty two hours of class room study and seventeen hours of work. Two hours each evening, including Saturday and Sunday, were spent in study hall. Silence was observed during those fourteen weekly hours of study time. Not including Sundays we were free to recreate for about twenty-seven hours each week. It was a strongly disciplined regimen

Precious Blood Sisters, assigned to work at the college, prepared the meals for the professors and for all the students both secular and religious. The Sisters also washed the dishes and did all the laundry, which included not only the dining room laundry but also all the personal laundry of the seminarians, brothers and priests. They were the unsung heroes who toiled day in and day out for the benefit of the entire college which included some fifty priests, twenty brothers and over sixty seminarians.

During our two years at St. Joe, there were no electives. The emphasis was on the humanities, especially classical Latin and New Testament Greek. To acquaint us with the sciences and with college math, we took those "twelve week" survey courses as previously outlined. We carried an unbelievable twenty-four credit hours per semester! The course of study was very demanding, to say the least.

Fr. Marcellus Dreiling, C.PP.S., was our prefect. He was a man of Teutonic discipline. His brow furrowed at the slightest displeasure or provocation and so we called him the "brow." We towed the line for him. As our math professor he also demanded excellence from us in that discipline. Most of us were at a loss when, at the end of our "twelve week" college math survey course, he required a term paper from us. He furnished a list of mathematical theories on which to write. I chose to write on the "exponential theory." Although I understood very little about what I wrote, Fr. Dreiling graded more on "effort" than on anything else. I was thoroughly surprised that my grade for that math term paper, a paper replete with "quotes," was a "B."

During this time the Chicago Bears under George "Papa" Halas came to St. Joe's campus for their summer camp. Father Dreiling gave permission for us to watch some of the practices during our free times. Excitement was at a peak as we watched the Chicago Bear football greats practice. Among the more notable players was Sid

Luckman the Bears first string quarterback, Max "Bull Dog" Turner the center and George McAfee, the running back. The team stayed at Drexel Hall located at the far eastern end of the campus. It was a tranquil setting away from the main campus. As such it was the perfect hall for the Bears relaxation and rejuvenation. How well I remember cleaning those Drexel Hall rooms and making the beds for the Bear football players. The foot powder "Desenex" was in frequent use. We brushed that foot powder off many a bed sheet prior to making up the bed. Since we were allowed to clean Drexel Hall only when the players were at morning practice, we were unable to get any autographs.

My first year at St. Joseph's came to a quick end as some twenty-two of us seminarians graduated from St. Joe's Academy. Five of our class had left during that year. Father Henry Lucks C.PP.S., the president, presided over one of the final 1947 Academy commencements. World War II had come to an end. Veterans were returning to the campus and St. Joe's was returning to the full time college it was before the war.

Our summer schedule was about to begin. As during the school year we arose at 5:30 A.M. In silence we readied ourselves for chapel. Morning prayers began promptly at six. The leader began: "Let us place ourselves in the presence of God....God sees me....God hears me....God will be my judge.... We concluded the morning prayers with:

"Life is short and death is sure,
the hour of death remains obscure.
A soul you have an only one.
If that be lost all hope is gone.
Waste not your time, while time shall last,
For after death 'tis ever past.

The all seeing God your Judge will be,
Or heaven or hell your destiny.
All earthly things will fleet away,
Eternity shall ever stay!"
What a profound reflection at the break of each day.

After the Community Mass, unless we were serving Mass for a late rising priest, we marched into the refectory two by two where we took breakfast in silence.   Our workday began shortly after 8:00.   At noon, lunch was taken again in silence as we listened to inspirational readings.   As for every meal, we wore our cassock and collar. There was time for a smoke after lunch, and then, back to our assigned tasks until 5:00 PM.   The summer season gave us time to make all the necessary building repairs and improvements and "clean-ups" as directed by the Community's procurator.   Those of us seminarians working in the crafts took care of all that. The farm gang members worked the farms and mowed the lawns. Again our meager ten cent hourly earnings were credited towards the cost of our education.

The summer schedule after supper was much the same as during the school year.   We enjoyed an hour or so of recreation followed by evening prayers and Benediction of the Blessed Sacrament.   After chapel we proceeded to the study hall where, dressed in our cassocks, we studied in silence until 10:00 PM. There was no air conditioning. With some thirty seminarians in each study hall it became quite oppressive during those two-hour summer study periods.   Generally, sleep came very easily after a long day of work.

It was during my second summer, while working on the farm gang that the rupture repair of my childhood broke through. It happened on a hot summer day while tossing bales of hay onto a wagon. Two of us student seminarians walked alongside the bailer as it spit out golden brown, rectangular, what seemed like 100 pound, dusty bales of hay. We hoisted the bales onto the hay wagon. As the pile of bales became higher it was more strenuous to hoist them upward. With one of those heaves I felt the same pain as I did as a child jumping off of Gesik's garage roof while playing "reli-vi yo." Shivers ran up and down my spine as I recalled the trauma of an earlier rupture.

Several days later Fr. Carl Nieset, our Assistant Prefect, made arrangements for the hernia operation. My parents could not afford to pay for the surgery. As a result the hospital and the surgeon were chosen by my religious superiors. I had mixed emotions as Fr. Nieset drove me to the hospital in Lafayette. Dr. Ikins, (a butcher) did the hernia repair at that Lafayette hospital. My stay at the hospital was made bearable by the attentiveness of all those nurses who took care of me during my hospital stay. They were angels of mercy all dressed in white, treating me like royalty. After all, I was the only seminarian in the entire hospital and they told me that I was cute. Boy did they inflate my ego! WOW! I was whistling some happy tunes – "June Is Busting Out All Over" and another favorite of mine, "It's A Grand Night For Singing."

I didn't lift any more bales of hay for the rest of that summer. As a matter of fact I was on "light duty" until my scheduled ten-day vacation. Each summer we were allowed ten days of vacation time to spend with family. We were also allowed two traveling days. Those seminarians whose homes were west of the Mississippi were allowed an additional traveling day.

Many of us took walks out to the pits or to the grotto during evening recreation periods. During one of those walks, a classmate of mine, a "late vocation" (he had served in the navy during the war) and I were walking along. All of a sudden he asked if he could kiss me. I couldn't believe what I heard! "Kiss me," I said! "Yes," he said, "let me kiss you." I thought he was kidding, but he wasn't. "Absolutely not," I said. He began pleading, and I continued to say "**NO**" and "**NO**" and "**NO**!!" He asked if he could at least hold my hand. Again I said "*absolutely not*!" I hurried my pace towards safety — Xavier Hall and the company of other seminarians who were sitting around outside. There I breathed a sigh of relief. What an altogether abhorrent request coming from one seminarian to another! That evening, after some deliberation, I decided to report the incident to my spiritual director, Fr. Sylvester Hartman. The next morning that classmate was gone. His locker was empty and his personal belongings were all gone. He had been "*shipped out*!" There were never any other incidents similar to that during all of my seminary days

All year long, including summer, the first Sunday of each month was *Silent Sunday*, set aside for prayer and meditation. It was also called "Death Sunday" a day in which we were to properly prepare for a "happy" death. A priest spiritual director was assigned to preach and to lead us in meditation on that Sunday. The prayer schedule was more intense than on an ordinary Sunday. The silence of the day was uninterrupted at Xavier Hall until mid afternoon. We did have our "fizzers" (jokesters and cut-ups) who, at times, because of their antics, caused some uproarious laughter, laughter that, "God forbid!" broke up the deadening silence around Xavier Hall.

Most of us looked forward to the third Sunday of the month. It was "Visiting Sunday," a day when parents, brothers and sisters were allowed to visit. Visiting hours were from 1:00 to 5:00 PM in the afternoon. The seminarians who came from distant states rarely had visitors. So, later that Visiting Sunday evening, as we sat in the "rec" room, "goodie" packages from home were shared, especially with those who had no visitors. My "goodie" package, without fail, included Mom's scrumptious *"orechovnik"* (walnut) and *"djelovnik"* (strawberry jelly) squares. As a kid I remember that Mom only baked those nut squares and jelly squares for very special occasions; like Christening, First Holy Communion day and for Confirmation day. So, "Visiting Sunday" was always a very special treat for me.

It was on one of those "Visiting" Sundays referred to above, that my younger brother Ambsie brought a copy of the local newspaper from back home. The headlines read: "Whiting Oilers Take the State Football Championship." We were not allowed newspapers so I knew nothing of what was happening back home. The 1948 Whiting High School team had done our little city proud. They put Whiting on the map. It was the first ever Whiting State Championship. To top it off that spirited team went undefeated that year. The victorious team rode in style atop Whiting's fire trucks.[1] Ray Gallivan was one justifiably proud coach as he led his team in that torchlight parade. The entire city came out to revel in the victory as they cheered the parading football team. John Vetroczky with over 60 points, was the team high scorer for the season. Other high scorers were Jack Walters, Phil Mateja, Bob Gacsko, George Tobias, Neil Boyle, Ray Linko, Al Derbis, Rich "Zeke" Pramuk, Bob Desatnick and Joe Miller. Butch Kovalcik and Dick Dvorscak lead the defense. The newspaper article went on to praise all those players on both offense and defense who helped their team to victory.

[1] Little did I know that Captain Joseph G. Kasper, the driver of one of those fire trucks would some day be my father-in-law!

It was the team spirit of each and every member of that State Football Championship team that contributed to such a stunning season.

Some of those team members made significant contributions in later life. One is Bob Desatnick, who continues to make a significant contribution in his area of expertise "The Human Resource." Bob has taught courses in European and State side Universities. Recognized as a leader in his field, Bob has published eight books and hundreds of trade journal articles. He has served as International Vice President for McDonald Corp. and for Chase Manhattan

No School Tomorrow In Whiting! Students Honor State Champs

BY JIM SKUPAKISS
(Times Sports Writer)

NOVEMBER 23 - 1948

"No school Wednesday."

That's the announcement from the office of Principal E.L.Riordan of Whiting High.

An assembly honoring the state champion Oiler gridders and the coaching staff was scheduled for this afternoon.

The holiday will give Whiting students a five-day vacation through Monday. Thursday and Friday are annual off-days for the observance of Thanksgiving.

Here's advance warning for anybody who thinks that the Western Division will forever dominate the NIHSC football playoff.

South Bend Central is "loaded" for next year. Coach Bob Jones will have his chance for revenge in 1949 with much outstanding returnees as Backs Wayman Redding,Arvester Fleming and Jack Morrical and Linemen Dick and Don Barnhart,Entee Shine and Lou Zacrosky.

There won't be many Whiting regulars returning. There'll be Guard Jim Curtin and Halfback Gene Urbanik,and that's all.

Add quote from Coach Jones: "If Redding and Shine weren't hampered by leg injuries,we'd have put up a better battle. But you can't take credit away from a solid tailback like Whiting."

The Oiler victory gave the Western sector an 11-6 margin in the title series,and kept the crown on this side of the conference for the fourth straight year. South Bend Washington's 19-7 win over Hammond Clark in 1944 came just before East Chicago Roosevelt swept to three consecutive titles.

It was Jack Walters and not Johnny Vetrousky who received official credit for the last Oiler touchdown. Vetrousky carried the ball to within inches of the goal line on the short plunge out then fumbled,and Walters recovered in the striped zone. Only a few spectators,on the Whiting side of the field,saw what actually happened.

Center Al Kovalcik was named Whiting's honorary captain for the championship season and Jim Curtin was chosen 1949 captain in an election conducted after the game.

The Whiting pass defense and offense operated at peak efficiency against Central.

Four Oiler aerials were intercepted at crucial stages, two by Phil Mateja and one each by Kovalcik and Vetrousky. And Mateja's passes found nade-to-order targets in Al Derbis and Boo Gacsko. Derbis caught one for 19 yards, while Gacsko hauled down three throws for 66 yards. One of his catches,good for 26 yards, set up the subsequent heave for 37 yards that scored the first Oiler touchdown.

Memories of the 1933 Whiting-Central playoff were recalled by Steve Fowdy,Oiler end in that tussle who is now a coach at Whiting. That was the game the Oilers lost 14-13 when a "perfect" placekick that would have tied the score bounced off the crossbar. Vinnie Oliver was Whiting's star oack and Pete Kovachic manned the center post in the bitter struggle.

Coach Gallivan appeared on the sidelines attired in navy watch cap and jacket Saturday instead of his usual brown snap brim hat and coat. He was so excited before the game that he forgot to follow his usual tradition of reading admirers' telegrams to the team. He posted them on the gym bulletin board when he "found" them in his pocket after the win.

There was plenty of confusion following Whiting's initial touchdown in the waning seconds of the first half. Gacsko snagged Mateja's toss in the coffin corner before scooting into the end zone and when the ball was placed on the two-yard stripe most onlookers figured he had stepped out of bounds after the catch. However,all officials had given the O.K. sign to Referee Stan Dubis,who then correctly signaled the score from his position at midfield. Coach Gallivan, who didn't see Dubis,rushed in a substitute with a running play and the surprised Oilers followed orders and ran for the extra point instead of placekicking. When the gridders started walking back for the kickoff,everybody thought it was the end of the half. Only a hasty explanation by officials to the public address announcer clarified the situation for the confused crowd.

Nearly 1,500 Central fans attended the game and more than 400 made the trip by special train. They were mighty loud in their cheering,too, although not as happy as Oiler partisans.

Oilers Share State Crown With Reitz Of Evansville

NOVEMBER 25 - 1948
By Kurt Prudenthal

INDIANAPOLIS—(UP)—The mythical Indiana state football championship,for three years sole property of East Chicago Roosevelt,was split in two today,with both Evansville Reitz and Whiting claiming equal right to the imaginary grid honor.

Reitz' claim came from its victory in one of the two major Indiana prep grid games Thursday. The Reitz Panthers defeated their city foe, Memorial,14 to 0. In the other grid headliner, Terre Haute Wiley scored a mild upset of Terre Haute Garfield,14 to 13.

Both Reitz and Whiting closed their seasons with perfect records of 10 wins. The Reitz record was a bit more impressive. The 14-0 win they had been held to two touchdowns. It was also their smallest winning margin of the year.

Whiting didn't pile up as many points in amassing its victory string,but they scored five shutouts in the tough Northern Indiana conference. And Coach Ray Gallivan's Oilers left no doubt,when they left the field after each game,as to which team had been victor.

The Reitz win gave them,in addition to their portion of the state crown,the Pocket City championship,and the Southern Indiana conference crown, the latter for the second straight year.

Touchdowns by Pete Fisher and Tommy Wilson, plus two conversions by Malcolm Cook proved the Reitz margin in their win over Memorial. Memorial got as far as the Reitz 16-yard line on only one occasion,in the third quarter,and that threat was ended by a fumble.

Only two Indiana High school football powers repeated as conference champions in the seven major Hoosier prep grid loops,a United Press survey showed.

The repeaters were Evansville Reitz,in the Southern Indiana Athletic conference,and Terre Haute Wiley,in the West Central loop.

Lafayette Jefferson split the North Central championship with New Castle,and Auburn and Warsaw divided honors in the Northeastern conference. The Jeffmen and Auburn were the top-notchers of their respective conferences last year.

New champions included Elwood,Columbus,and Whiting. The Elwood Panthers displaced Plymouth's Rockies in the Central loop; the Columbus Bulldogs won the South Central crown held for the past two seasons by Franklin's Grizzly Cubs, and the Whiting Oilers were tops in the Northern Indiana association,a distinction held for the three previous years by East Chicago Roosevelt.

OILERS WIN FOOTBALL CHAMPIONSHIP !

By defeating South Bend Central Saturday night the Oilers completed their first undefeated and untied schedule and also won their first NIHSC Championship. They definitely put themselves in line for at a least a piece of the "mythical State Championship" title. If Evansville Reitz the other contender for the State title fails to defeat Evansville Memorial in their Thanksgiving day classic the Oilers may lay undisputed claim to the title of Indiana's best high school football team.

Front Row: Vetrocsay, Nastay, Blaster, Ross, Horna, Kalnas, Carter, De Barye, Mordus, and Fortner.
Second Row: Walters, Mateja, Kovalcik, Desatnick, Dvorcak, Urbane, Tobias, Davenport, Derbis, and Ford.
Third Row: Linko, Gadsko, Blascher, Varendas, Curtin, Dulla, Miller, Boyle, Wilson, Prasisk.

Whiting High School's championship football team were the guests of the W. H. S. A. A. at a victory banquet held last Wednesday at Phil Smidts, with their Coach Ray Gallivan and his assistant coaches Pete Kovachik and Honico. Members of the Board of Education were also present

Bank and has served on the Boards of various major corporations. His client list is a veritable "who's who" of Finance, Industry and Commerce. Robert L. Desatnick is currently the President of "Creative Human Resource Consultants" with offices in Chicago.

Studies at St. Joe's are completed

Our class, having earned over 80 college credit hours, had completed two years of intensive college study at St. Joe's. It was time for the twenty-three of us (we had gained several "late vocation" classmates during the past two years) to move on. St. Charles Seminary, the major seminary of the Precious Blood Community located in Carthagena, Ohio, was beckoning. In August of 1949 our class departed from St. Joe. We packed all of our earthly belongings; we were headed homeward for our ten day summer vacation, and then on to the "Major Seminary" at Carthagena, Ohio.

Chapter XI - St. Charles Seminary, Carthagena, Ohio

Towards the end of that brief ten-day vacation I received a letter from Very Reverend Lionel E. Pire, C.PP.S., rector of St. Charles Seminary. "You are not to come to the seminary until further notice. The seminary has been quarantined. Seminarian John Bican has contracted polio. You and your class members will be notified when the quarantine is lifted." This was a first. Never before had any ten-day summer vacation ever been extended.

Several days later a letter arrived from Fr. Pire. Our class was ordered to arrive on Sept 4, 1949. The quarantine was short lived. Our ten-day summer vacation had been extended by some six days. I was happy about the vacation extension but sad that it came because of John Bican's polio and sad that this brilliant young man was forced to discontinue his studies for the priesthood.

Life at St. Charles Seminary, Carthagena, Ohio

St. Charles Seminary grounds

Fr. John Blasick, a newly ordained assistant at St. John's, drove me to the seminary. The two hundred and some mile trip, along U. S. Rt. # 30, crossed over some of the most productive Mid-Western farmland. It was at 4:30 PM on that sunny September day that I first caught glimpse of the majestic seminary dome rising out of the fertile Ohio farmland. This was the "Motherhouse" of the Precious Blood Community in the United States. Set back a quarter mile from the highway, the massiveness of this Romanesque structure was at once most impressive. The façade was broken by a flight of granite steps leading to a large projecting portico. Corinthian columns and arches rose harmoniously upward to the cornice of the octagonal tower ornamented with stone minarets and gargoyles.

Main entrance

Crowning the tower was a large gold-leafed cross visible for miles around. Behind the main building there also rose upward a tall power house smokestack. Because of that stack the local farmers in the surrounds referred to the seminary intriguingly as the "Priest Factory."

A warm welcome awaited the twenty-three of our class arriving from different parts of the country. We were assigned lockers in the basement locker room, desks in the second floor study hall and beds in the north or south dormitory rooms on the third floor. The precedence followed was the same as at St. Joe, and remained that way throughout seminary life. We sat next to the same classmate in chapel, at table, in the study hall and in the classroom. We occupied lockers next to each other and beds next to each other in the dorm. Like it or not, the only variation happened when a classmate left. Then we all advanced one chair in the "refectory" (dining room) one desk in the studyhall, one locker, one bed in the dorm and one pew spot in the chapel.

The First year at St. Charles Seminary

As "major seminarians" we were given white roman collars without the black stripe of minor seminary days. Our daily classroom, refectory and chapel dress were the cassock and roman collar. Our headgear was the "priestly" biretta. (The biretta was a stiff square headgear with three projections and a tassel in the center.) How proud we were as visitors mistakenly called us "father!" We walked around the

Author in cassock, Roman collar & biretta - a major seminarian's outfit

grounds parading as "baby priests." We were to be the ordination class of 1955!

Not long after my arrival at the major seminary I decided to keep notes in the form of a diary. Some of my entries, although brief and to the point, were made in code. They were made in the Slovak language using characters of the Greek alphabet. So, I

My class on arrival at major sem in Sept. of 1949. 1st row: D. Ritzler, W. Miller, R. Woytych, L. Wildenhaus, H. Miller; 2nd row: J. McKay, J. Froelich, J. Herber, C. Wise, J. Dueweke; 3rd row: J. Martin, R. Gatza, R. Kapitan, J. Wohlwend, J. Egan; 4th row: L. Brown, M. Lizza, J. Dexter, B. Meiring; 5th row: J. Zogran, D. Shea, C. Farabaugh, R. Schiml.

wrote the Slovak words in Greek. The code idea came to me as I remembered that the Navajo Indians, serving with the Marines in the Pacific, during World War II, had their own code. They spoke in the Navajo language. The Japanese were befuddled and could not break the code of the Navajo code talkers.

During our first meeting with the boss, Fr. Lionel E. Pire, the "Major Seminary Rector," we were given our

Fr. Pire

classroom schedules and work assignments. Some of us had additional responsibilities as chamberlains for the priests in residence. As chamberlain for Fr. Ambrose Heiman, Metaphysics and Philosophy Professor, it was my duty to make his bed and deliver cold water to his room each morning. On Saturdays I cleaned his room without complaints. It was a privilege. After all he was the seminary Metaphysics and Philosophy brain. We were to become Philosophers under his tutelage.

During our first year, most of us were assigned to the "house-gang." With large, whirling, electric buffers we kept the terrazzo floors in the halls on all three floors, scrubbed and highly polished. Those powerful buffers would whip some of the smaller guys right across the floor! They really got a work out! There were three bathrooms on the third floor for seminarian use. We humorously referred to them as the "jigs." Each had a row of sinks, urinals, commodes and shower stalls, enough for the hundred and some of us students. The house gang kept them sparkling clean and did all the housekeeping in the recreation rooms, library, study halls, dorms and throughout the 371-foot structure flanked on the north and south sides by two 140 foot long wings. The chapel of the Assumption was kept sparkling clean.

Being a self-sufficient community, work assignments and opportunities abounded. There was the farm gang, garden gang, power house gang, lawn gang, the butcher shop, laundry distribution, barber shop, carpenter shop, paint shop, book bindery and printing shop and even a grave yard gang. We had our own five-bed Infirmary with a Brother in charge who was referred to as our "Infirmarian."

We raised our own cows and steers, hogs and chickens. We did our own butchering and sausage making. We raised all the feed for the farm animals. We bailed hay. We made silage for the animals and wine for our rare consumption. Altar wine was made in strict observance of all Canon Law prescriptions. Brother Walter was the official "lil-ol-wine-maker," and an excellent one at that. Surrounded by over five hundred acres of fertile Ohio farmland, there was enough work for all of us.

Besides the vineyard, we had an apple orchard, raspberry and strawberry patches and a walnut grove. We raised our own sweet corn, green beans, pickles, beets, onions, tomatoes, cabbage, celery, carrots, rhubarb, and every imaginable vegetable. One of my first work assignments was to join the farm gang in harvesting row upon row of potatoes, acres of those well-formed spuds. When harvest time came, all the various "gangs" pitched in and anyone else who was available. Those pesky sandburs (stickers) complicated the potato harvesting.

It wasn't all work and no play. During the Labor Day weekend we celebrated an annual "Field Day." Our meals were taken outside. Tables were set up in the walnut grove. Sporting events and races were held. Deacons competed against the priests and brothers; senior

Lang, ???, Bender, Cavanaugh, Gatza, Kapitan

McNicholas, Reimondo, Cody, Kalmanek, Friedrichsen, Dumminger, Grothjan, Alt, Hunnefeld

Almasy

Relay Race team champs - Gatza, Nagele, Grever, Reinhart

White, Duewke, ???, J. Wohlwend, Bolan, Spitzig, Nagele, Wellman, Ballmann, R. Conway, Van Horn, Meiring

Adelman, Joyce, T. DeBrosse, Schultheis, ??, Kapitan

classmen against "primies" (us yearlings). There was stick balancing, potato races, long distance throw, relay racing and a host of other events. At nightfall we retired to the now opened "rec" rooms. They had been closed since the polio scare. The festivities continued and beer was served; card games were played and songs were sung. The grand finale always was *SCHNITZEL BANK*. The schnitzel bank board was set up. With pointer in hand, the leader (the one who had consumed the most beer), began: *"Ist das nicht ein Schneitzel Bank?"* And we answered in loud response: *"Ja, das ist ein schneitzel bank"*

Pointing to the next image on the board the leader sang out *"ist das nich ein Kurz und Lang?"* We responded *"Ja das ist ein Kurz und Lang! Kurz und Lang, Schnitzel Bank. O de schoon ein under wand, ja das ist ein Schnitzel Bank!"*

Pointing to *"Hin und Her,"* the leader sang the question: *"Ist dast nicht ein Hin und Her?"* We responded in loud acclamation *"Ja das ist ein Hin und Her! Hin und Her, Kurz und Lang, Schnitzel Bank! O de schoon ein under wand, ja das ist ein Schnitzel Bank!"*

Pointing to the next image the leader asked *"Ist das nich?"* and, between sips of beer, we responded *"Ja das ist ein."* With each response the previous image names were added. We filled our beer steins as we came to the last of seventeen images. Meanwhile the leader asked, *"Ist das nicht ein Gefahrliches Ding?"* We responded: *"Ja das ist ein Gefahrliches Ding!"* Then, taking one deep breath, we attemped to hastily sing the name of each of the seventeen images being rapidly pointed to by the leader. Community bonding always took a giant leap forward during this annual fun filled day.

The "schmaltz" room was a smaller rec. room where silence usually prevailed as we sat listening to "long haired" music. Chess and checker games were played to a soothing background of classical music. It was in this room that appreciation for classical music was developed and nurtured. An extensive library of classical records and librettos were available. Many of us spent quiet, enjoyable hours learning to appreciate the music of the masters.

Located at the other end of the basement corridor was the "stamp room." Stamps were supplied by Catholic School children from throughout the Country. Most Catholic schools in the United States were members of the "Catholic Students Mission Crusade." As seminarians we were members of the Gasper Mission Society, an adjunct of the CSMC. We sorted the stamps into U. S. and foreign countries. We assigned values and presented them for sale throughout the country. The sale proceeds were used "for the missions."

Steve Almasy, a second theologian, was in charge of the "foreign desk." As newcomers, we were invited to join the stamp club. His nationality was Slovak and so was mine. Since the majority of seminarians were Germans, it was refreshing to be part of a program with another Slovak. So I joined Steve in the "foreign department." Apart from the camaraderie, it was also interesting and geographically educational. Steve Almasy saw to it that a fun time was had. Many recreational hours were spent in this room helping fund missionary efforts. At times our rector Fr. Pire came into the stamp room and ordered us out to "get some fresh air."

The first floor's main entrances lead directly to the Assumption chapel. This floor also housed the Library, the Infirmary, Study Hall, the priest's recreation room and some of the priest's private rooms. The second floor housed priest rooms and classrooms. North and South dorms were located on the third floor as were the private rooms of upper classmates. Usually one of the 8' x 12' student rooms became available as we progressed into our second and third year of study. It was indeed a happy day when a room became available for me toward the end of my second year. Privacy, at long last! I moved all my belongings from the study hall and dorm and some of my "locker" belongings into my "private room," a cubicle in reality. The room was of a size to accommodate my bed, a chair, desk, bookcase and an upright closet. There was an outside window and a transom above the door to provide for some air movement. That transom was especially effective during the hot and stuffy summer days and nights. Since we were not allowed in each other's rooms, a lot of "door hanging" went on as we conferred with each other regarding our studies. Each year on ordination day "deacon row," located on the south end of the third floor, emptied. On that happy day we all advanced rooms southward on that third floor. The closer your room came to "deacon row," the closer you were to ordination.

It was in October, just a month after I arrived, that I witnessed my first funeral for a deceased priest member. Fr. Maximillian Walz, famed for his book on the Precious Blood, "Why Is Thy Apparel Red?" had died. His body was placed for viewing in the parlor just off the main seminary entrance. With shovels in hand the graveyard gang went to work digging the grave for the deceased in the community cemetery, located just to the south of the seminary building. Vespers for the dead were chanted as priests gathered around for their final farewell. Our Provincial Father Seraphin W. Oberhauser celebrated the Solemn Requiem High Mass. The somberness of the occasion was accented not only by the Gregorian Chant and Office of the Dead but also by the black pall covering the casket and the black vestments worn by the three priest celebrants. Over sixty priests dressed in cassock, surplus and biretta proceeded in procession chanting in solemn Gregorian Chant: *"Miserere mei Deus, secundum magnam misericoriam tuam...."*(Have mercy on me, oh Lord, mercy according to your great mercy...). The chanting sounded so terribly woeful. It was only proper and fitting that Fr. Walz journeyed his "last earthly mile" from the Motherhouse that he so dearly loved. His earthly remains were carried in solemn procession from the chapel to the adjoining Community cemetery, to await Resurrection Day! It was fitting that his earthly journey should end where it all began for him, on ordination day.

Several weeks later found us riding our community's

open-air dump trucks to the voting polls in Casella, Ohio. Since we read no newspapers or magazines (those were forbidden), we knew nothing about local politics other than the reports by our Rector. Regardless, we had a "civic duty" to fulfill and fulfill it we did. Our rector explained our options very carefully, reminding us to use due diligence in casting our vote! At the polling place some students decided to reward a priest faculty member who was not very well liked. Using "write-in ballots" they placed the faculty member's name onto the ballot for Animal Control Officer. Later that evening the call came to the seminary from election headquarter announcing that the "write-in candidate" won. We could hardly contain ourselves. Wow, our priest faculty member had been elected the County Animal Control Officer. The rector was outraged. "Never before had a group of seminary students been so derelict in their duty," he said. Of course, the priest tendered his immediate resignation from the office to which he had been duly elected. We obedient and humble seminarians had some fun fulfilling our "civic duty!"

Classes were cancelled on November the 15th. Rabbit season opened. Enough shot guns to supply an army came into sight as they were removed from our lockers. With guns in hand, anxious seminarians headed for the surroundings. One of the seminarians was eager to get the squirrel he had so often seen from his room as it jumped around those black walnut trees. He sat on a tree stump and waited for the squirrel to appear. Jim felt movement in his private area not long after he sat on that stump. He stood up, looked at the stump and saw hundreds of termites squirming all over that stump. Those buggers had entered his trousers through a slit! Dropping his shotgun he ran lickety split towards the infirmary. There the Brother Infirmarian doused the invaded area with turpentine. It was indeed a very painful cleansing. There would be another hunting day for Jim but not on that day. The Infirmarian had refrained from laughing all the while, but he lost it as Jim was pulling up his trousers. He burst into uncontrollable laughter and Jim joined him. The rest of that day was spent joking about the incident with his fellow seminarians.

Meanwhile I joined a foursome for the rabbit hunt with a borrowed 4-10 shotgun. It was a cold, damp, misty November morning. But no mind as the adrenaline pumping through our bodies provided all the needed body comfort. The four of us got six rabbits. All told about eighty rabbits were brought in from the hunt. Amongst the group of hunters were "rabbit skinning experts." The next day a baked rabbit feast was enjoyed by all. Those German Nuns, who worked in the kitchens, flavored those rabbit morsels with just the right amount of herbs and spices. Brother Eugene's home made bread, a daily staple, added to the wholesomeness of the rabbit feast. Cherry pie baked by the talented nuns of the Precious Blood Order made for a grand meal finale. As always, each pie was cut into four parts giving each of us a full quarter of a regular 8" round pie! Yum! Yum!

The curriculum for us "First Philosophers" was: "Introduction to Philosophy" with Father Henry Lucks, former president of St. Joseph's College. Dr. Lucks was a respected and dedicated community priest member. In "Cosmology" we received our first all Latin textbook! Now we knew why it was so important for us to learn Latin during our minor seminary days. The footnotes in this Latin textbook were in Greek! Now we also knew why we were exposed to Greek for two years during our minor seminary days. "Introductory Psychology" was also taught by Dr. Lucks; "Rural Sociology" by Father Harold V. Diller; "Ancient History" by Father Edward F. Siegman; "Public Speaking" by Father Othmar F. Missler and "Constitution" (of the Precious Blood Community) by the Rector, The Very Reverend Lionel E. Pire. There were fifteen priest faculty members for the hundred and some of us seminarians. What a favorable ratio!

It was during Constitution class that I first observed "snuffing by nose." Our rector, Fr. Pire, taught the Constitution class from a raised platform set up in the tower of the seminary building. There we sat in awe as he lectured about the Constitution of the Precious Blood Community. He was an authoritative person who ruled not only the students but also the professors with a strong hand. As he lectured, out came his metal oval snuff container. With his right thumb he gathered those tobacco morsels and gently raised them to his nose. With his left thumb blocking the other nostril Fr. Pire placed the snuff covered thumb to his open nostril and inhaled. An aura of delight enraptured his face. Before repeating the process he took out his "**khaki**" colored handkerchief and relieved his nose of the spent snuff.

Our day began in silence with rising at 5:40. Recitation of the Angelus was at 6:00 in the chapel, followed by Morning prayers, meditation and Mass at 6:30 AM. At about 7:10, we proceeded in silence to the refectory where breakfast was taken in silence. The "*SILENTIUM ALTUM*" (High Silence which began with the 8:00 P.M. Study period the night before.) ended once we left the refectory. We then had until 7:50 to take care of our room and the assigned priest room. A half-hour study period followed. Classes began at 8:25 and lasted until 11:30 followed by a twenty minute Particular Examen of Conscience and meditation in the chapel. Each of the three morning classes lasted 55 minutes. We had 5 minutes to get from one classroom to the next. Most of us young bucks had no trouble with that.

During the noon meal, which also was taken in silence, as were all meals, inspirational readings, as explained earlier, were read by one of the seminarians. We each took turns at reading. There was a one-hour work period after the noon meal. We all reported to our assigned stations: to the farm gang, to the house gang, or to whatever our work assignment called for. Following the work period was an hour of recreation. The three afternoon classes began at 2:30 and ended at 5:55. It was not unusual to hear growling of stomachs as we headed towards the end of the last afternoon class.

A 6:00 PM supper was eaten in silence as we listened to inspirational or spiritual readings. Benediction and Evening prayers followed after which we were free for about forty minutes until summoned to chapel for the recitation of the Rosary. A study period and the "great silence" began immediately after the rosary. Silence occupied eleven and a half hours of each twenty-four hour period. Thank God that more than half of that silence period took place while we slept! Our day ended as it began - in silence with lights out at 10:00 PM. To sum it up, our school day consisted of about three hours of prayer, six hours of classroom study, three hours of study hall, three hours of recreation and one hour of manual labor. Putting study and work into a weekly perspective, we had thirty hours of classroom study and thirteen hours of work. There were no classes on Wednesday and Saturday afternoons. On those days our work period began at 12:30 and continued to 5:00 PM.

On Sundays we followed a more prayerful schedule.

5:40 Rising; 6:00 Angelus & Mediation; 6:30 Mass and Chaplet of the Precious Blood; 7:10 Breakfast, care of rooms, recreation; 8:30 High Mass, 10:00 Studies and Meetings; 11:40 Particular Examen and Spiritual Reading; 12:00 Dinner & recreation; 2:00 Vespers & Benediction; 2:50 Recreation; 5:30 Supper & recreation; 7:50 Evening Prayers, Rosary and Studies; 10:00 Retiring!

It was at an evening meal just before my first Christmas that our Rector announced that there would be a limit as to the number of Christmas Cards that could be sent, a regulation governing Christmas Cards! Each student would be limited to mailing forty cards. Coming from a large family and with many hometown benefactors, I already had 43 cards addressed. There was no way to send more cards since all of our mail passed through the Rector's office unsealed. Some seminarians snuck Christmas cards to Joe Link's store just a short mile distance from the seminary. Joe was happy to oblige knowing that all our mail passed through the rector's office. Fr. Pire censored (in his Germanic accent he said "senjured") all our incoming and outgoing mail. It seemed as though he enjoyed his responsibility of "senjuring." We had no need for letter openers.

The Christmas spirit was further dampened on that first Christmas at the seminary when the rector made the announcement that we were to be in bed within ten minutes after Midnight Mass! The fact that it was Christmas morning made no difference. The fact that we were all in our late teens and early twenties also made no difference. Discipline, discipline, discipline! Our rector had a flair for "training" in good habits! What he referred to as training, some seminarians referred to as a restraining confinement of liberties.

That first Christmas vacation away from our seminary studies found us at work for about seven hours each day. Our house gang scrubbed and waxed and buffed the entire length and width (about 500'x14') of the terrazzo floors on each of the three floors plus the basement. We scoured all the walls in all three of the third floor "jigs" (bathrooms). "Jet" Bolan, the house boss, saw to it that we were kept busy. He didn't like the song that we sang one Christmas vacation day while scrubbing those tiled shower stalls. Sung to the tune of "My Bonnie Lies Over the Ocean" it went something like this: "They promised us plenty of free days, they promised us plenty of fun, they promised us plenty of good things, but we didn't get nary a one. No free days, no free days, no free days, not even a one."

The community spirit prevailed in most everything we did. We worked creatively together. We prayed and played together creating a bond as nothing else could. We helped each other to form priestly qualities, qualities that would serve us well as missionaries of the Most Precious Blood.

Nicknames abounded throughout the classes. Jet was John Bolan, Dutch was Jim Zimmerman; then there was Jumps Wohlwend, Flit Reed, March Boehle, Spooks Gelhaus, Zeke Zogran, Bow Schiml, Whispers Woytych and "Bishop" Froelich. Others were nicknamed Pops, Ubi, Gloves, More, Spike, Heiney, Bulldog and Phones. My nickname was "Unhitch." And, last but not least, the name for Joe Herber, the one who coined most of the nicknames, was "Crisco Kid" meaning "Lard-In-The-Can." It was a perfect name for Joe since he had a protruding posterior.

The first semester of major seminary studies provided a full 18 credit hours of arduous classroom pursuits. It was in a Psychology class taught by Fr. Lucks that we were given a very interesting assignment. Our term paper for that semester was to grade each of our classmates on 195 characteristics as they related to the following: Spiritual, Physical, Social, Intellectual and Personal qualities. The grading was to be done on a 1 to 7 basis, one being the lowest and seven the highest. A "1" in a good quality was the worst possible grade while a "7" was the highest. A "1" in a bad quality was the best grade while a "7" was the worst. Some of the "Spiritual" quality characteristics were: Charity in speech; Love of prayer, Scrupulosity, Suggestive speech, Prudence, Fortitude, Proper decorum, Giving of good example, Forgiveness, Patience, Acceptance of trials, Egotism, Honesty, Obedience and Pride. Under the "Physical" quality some of the characteristics were: General cleanliness, Good posture, Personal Hygiene, Effeminacy, Gracefulness, Exterior cheerfulness, Neatness, Halitosis and Manliness, etc. Under the "Social" quality some of the components were: Promoter of schemes, Emotional Equilibrium, Opportunist, Punctuality, Introvert, Sportsmanship, Loyalty to friends, Rusticity, Loyalty to community, Amiability, Affability, Impartiality, Cooperation, etc. Under the "Intellectual" quality some of the characteristic components were: Application to duty, Native talent, Ability to correlate, Plagiarism, Perspicacity, Works for grades more than for knowledge, Argumentative, Asks intelligent questions in lecture, Crams for tests, Slovenly enunciation, Stickler on small points, Power of apt expression, Balanced judgement and a host of others.

We were then asked to name any special talents of the subject under consideration, any outstanding good characteristics and any outstanding character defects. The final question was: "Do you consider the subject a fit candidate for the priesthood in the Society?" All eighteen of my classmates said yes. It was comforting and reassuring to know that every one of my classmates confirmed my vocation. There were 9 entries under the heading of "special talents" and I received 14 entries under "outstanding good characteristics." Under "outstanding character defects" I received 5 entries. All in all this exercise gave us an excellent insight as to how our classmates, with whom we had lived for years, regarded every aspect of our Spiritual, Social and Intellectual behavior. It prompted us to examine ourselves as we had never before. It was the most positive and exhilarating "term paper" during all of my studies.

A slew of new words and concepts were brought to light during that year of study. Some of them were contractility, proprioceptivity, reciprocal, enervation, endocrine, autocides, hyperthyroidism, subalternated, and *a priori* and *a posteriori*, to name just a few. We became adept in the etymology of words. One such interesting word was "cadaver." It contained three syllables, each of which were prefixes for Latin words. Ca - *caro* (flesh), da - *data* (given), ver -*vermibus* (given to the worms). Therefore "cadaver" stands for "flesh given to the worms!"

Axioms such as "*Caveat Emptor*" (let the buyer beware), "*In Vino Verita*" (In wine there is truth), "*Nemo dat quod non habit*" (you cannot give what you do not have), and of course, the Peripatetic axiom "*Nihil est in intellectu quod non prius fuerit in sensibus* (Nothing is in the intellect that was not first in the senses) are among some of the thought provoking truisms to which we were introduced early on. So it was with the study program during the first year at the major seminary. Our class had completed the first of six years of study at the major seminary. Of the original twenty-three students in our class, four had dropped out and nineteen remained to begin the second year of

Philosophy.

There were benefactors of the Society who contributed monetarily to help defray the costs of a seminarian's education. One such benefactor was a Rosalee Bauer from Kentucky, a parishioner of Father Bartholomew Besinger, C.PP.S. For whatever reason, Fr. Pire chose me to be the recipient of her generosity. The Community benefited from her generosity by an annual stipend. I benefited from her generosity with monetary gifts on holidays and special occasions. This helped to keep me in smokes, nickel candy bars and three-cent postage stamps for all those letters that needed to be written.

Ordination of 4th Theologians to the Priesthood

In May of that first year I witnessed the ordination to the priesthood for the first time. The Assumption chapel was filled with family and friends. Seminarian porters and acolytes assisted at this most solemn function. Those not so assigned were in the choir loft along with those of us who sang in the choir. The organ prelude announced the grand solemnity of the occasion.

Carrying the vestment of the priesthood and a lighted candle, those to be ordained processed into the sanctuary. The Bishop summoned each by name, each candidate answering "*Adsum*" (I am here). The vested candidates, holding a folded chasuble on their left arms and a candle in their right hand, went forward to kneel before the bishop. Addressing the congregation, the Bishop asked if anyone knew why any of these candidates should not be ordained. As the Bishop knelt before the altar the candidates lay themselves prostrate on the sanctuary floor. The Litany of All Saints, a powerful prayer of the Church, was chanted for them. Sung in Latin the Gregorian Chant was a powerful invocation for the aid of all the saints. It was as if the heavens themselves opened and all the saints joined in solemn prayer over those about to be ordained.

At the conclusion of the Litany the *ordinandi* (those to be ordained) rose and came forward to kneel individually before the Bishop. He lay his hands on the head of each candidate in silence. A very impressive move followed. All the priests who were present processed into the sanctuary laying hands on each ordinands in succession! As the head and hands of the candidates were being anointed with sacred oils, the Bishop intoned the "*Veni Creator*" and the choir responded.

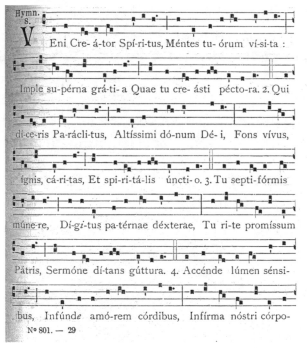

Crossing the stole over the breast of each, the Bishop vested each with the chasuble (the outer priestly vestment worn at Mass) saying "*tu est sacerdos in aeternum secundum ordinem Melchizedech.*" (Thou art a priest forever according to the order of Melchizedech.)

At the conclusion of the Offertory the Bishop sat himself before the middle of the altar and each of those ordained made a symbolic offering to him of a lighted candle. The Mass continued as the newly ordained priests concelebrated it with the Bishop.

Before Communion, the Bishop extended the kiss of peace to one of the newly ordained. He in turn extended the *"pax tecum"* (peace be with you) to another of his classmates. And so, the "Kiss of Peace" was extended from one to another and to all those in the sanctuary.

After Communion the newly ordained priests again approached the bishop and, standing before him, recited the Apostle's Creed. Laying his hands upon each, the bishop said: "Receive the Holy Ghost, whose sins you shall forgive they are forgiven them, and whose sins you shall retain, they are retained." The ordination was complete and the church erupted in solemn and glorious praise. *"Te Deum laudamus, te dominum confitemur, te aternum Patrem omnis terra veneratur, Tibi omnes Angeli, tibi coel, et universae Potestates. Tibi Cherubim et Seraphim incessabili voce proclamatur. Sanctus, Sanctus, Sanctus Dominus Deus Sabaoth...."*

The *Te Deum* continued as the congregation spilled out into the corridors of the seminary building. The long years of discipline and study had culminated in the glorious and solemn act of ORDINATION. The newly ordained priests mingled with the crowds imparting their "first priestly blessing."

In that crowd were those of us who studied and prayed with them. What a magnificent gesture as we knelt at the feet of the newly ordained and said "Father, may I have your blessing?" And Fathers Zupke, Kissner, Volk,

1950 Ordination class (the first witnessed by me) Fathers Zupke, Ruschau, Green, A. Herber, Rodak, Volk, W. Schenk, Kissner, Gerlach.

Schenk, Gerlach, Rodak, Ruschau, Green and Herber, each one individually, extended his first priestly blessing.

SUMMER SCHEDULE

Our school year had ended and with summer came the summer schedule. We awoke at 5:40 and were in chapel by 6:00 AM for morning prayers followed by a Community Mass. Breakfast, taken in silence, was served at 7:10. After breakfast we were free until 7:45. A study period was assigned from 7:45 to 8:45. It was during this summer morning study period that I learned how to type. My sister Mary sent me her high school typing book and an alarm clock. Typewriters were available in the typing room. Day after day for an hour at a time, all summer long, I sat at the typewriter. By summers end I was typing 45 words per minute. I had put that one hour morning study period to excellent use as my typing ability served me well during all my years.

Our morning work period began at 9:00 and lasted until 11:30. At 11:40 we presented ourselves for particular examen in the chapel. Dinner served at 12:00 noon was eaten in silence while we listened to a student reading from selected spiritual readings. The afternoon work period

lasted from 1:00 to 4:30. We were allowed to relax from 4:30 until supper, which was served at 6:00. Again supper was taken in silence while listening to spiritual readings. During the summer the Rector would often signal a *Tu Autem* which meant that there were no readings and we were allowed to talk during the meal. We were free after supper until 8:15, at which time the *Silentium*

Farm Boss Brother Oliver with seminarian workers Spitzig, Boehle, Kapitan.

Altum was in effect until after the following morning's breakfast. The community recited the Rosary in chapel at 8:15 PM, followed by Benediction of the Blessed Sacrament. The study period that followed lasted until 10:00 PM. So our summers were, true to monastic discipline of "*ora et labora*" (pray and work), were spent in work and prayer.

A reprieve from the summer schedule was affected by the allotted ten-day vacation. Early on the appointed morning, Sub-deacon Richard Cody, one of the seminarians in his last year of studies, drove me to the train station in Van Wert, Ohio. The Pennsylvania Clipper, traveling at sixty miles per hour, arrived in Gary later that morning. There I was reunited with family members. What a joy to be back home in Indiana. Since I was last home, my younger brothers and sister had grown noticeably. Ambrose, the 14-year-old, reminded me that in 15 months he would be able to drive the bakery truck and that his boss told him that he would then be able to drive out to Ohio to the seminary. Mary, my older sister, had become engaged to be married. Mom was her typical busy self, running off to the six o'clock Mass and then working at home all day long. Dad continued his struggle with his constant coughing; gasping for breath during his coughing spells. (Damn that mustard gas used in WW I!) I couldn't get enough of that delicious Slovak food, as only my mother knew how to prepare. Each day there was a table adorned with a special favorite of mine. Crammed into that ten-day period were movies, lots of pinochle games and plenty of lively Slovak conversation. The good times came to a quick end as I tearfully waved good-bye from the train ready to take me back to my seminary studies. The good days of so short a summer vacation at home had come to a quick end!

Second Year at the Major Seminary

The major subject of study during the second year of Philosophy was Metaphysics. It was a five credit hour course taken in both semesters. As such, it was the epitome of our philosophical studies as we attempted to understand the essence of composite beings. Father Ambrose Heiman, the Community's brilliant philosopher, explained the "highest metaphysical concept" thusly: "existence of a being is something which cannot be taught and when once grasped dominates the existence of him who grasped it." We struggled with that concept throughout that year of Metaphysics. Father Heiman also taught a 3 credit course in the History of Philosophy, using the brilliant text of Etienne Gilson, a masterful Thomistic Philosopher and Theologian.

Father George J. Lubeley, another community genius,

and a recent graduate of The University of Fribourg, was our Ethics professor. He also taught the course in Moral Philosophy.

Father Aloys Dirksen, a doctor of scriptures, taught the Scripture course. A large structured priest he had a head of wavy white hair. When he spoke, he rumbled. His voice was stentorian and as bass as bass could be. On occasion, as celebrant for one of the Community High Masses, he turned to the choir loft and, in his deep bass voice, shouted out, "Give me a lower note!"

Of all the scripture passages, those from the Book of Ecclesiastics were some of the most profound. The passage that most impressed me was: "Vanity of vanities! All things are vanity! What profit has a man from all the labor which he toils at under the sun? One generation passes and another comes, but the world forever stays. The sun rises and the sun goes down; then it presses on to the place where it rises.

Blowing now towards the south, then towards the north, the wind turns again and again, resuming its rounds. All rivers go to the sea, yet never does the sea become full. To the place where they go, the rivers keep on going. All speech is labored; there is nothing man can say. The eye is not satisfied with seeing nor is the ear filled with hearing.

What has been, that will be; what has been done, that will be done. Nothing is new under the sun. Even the thing of which we say, 'See, this is new!' has already existed in the ages that preceded us. There is no remembrance of the men of old; nor of those to come will there be any remembrance among those who come after them." Father Dirksen presented that passage as a penetrating assessment of reality and applicable to all seasons of our lives.

Other priest faculty members were Fathers Bierberg, Dorenkemper, Feldhaus, Gaulrapp, Goettemoeller, Knapke, Linenberger, Rohling, Ryan and Siebeneck. There was a lot for us to learn and these professors were willing, able and eminently qualified to sit in the "master's chair." Since this province was established by C.PP.S. Members who came from Germany in the mid eighteen hundreds, it is no wonder that the vast majority of its members were of German extraction. It was not surprising then that there was such a demand for excellence and perfection. Those were qualities inborn in members of the Germanic race.

It was during the second year of Philosophy that temporary professions were to be made to the Precious Blood Community. To prepare for that, Father Othmar F. Missler, our spiritual director, asked that we each make a general confession of our entire life. "I do not want you to confess that you committed this sin or that so many times a month." "I want you to multiply it out. You are 21 years old and, at age 7 you reached the age of reason, which is over 5000 days ago. I want you to say I committed this sin 2375 times or that sin 3650 times, etc. etc." Whew, none of us were prepared for that!

Father Missler heard our confessions in his private room. He scheduled each of us about a half-hour apart. At the appointed time, I knocked on his door. With great trepidation I entered as he said, "enter Rudolph." There he sat at his desk, rosary in hand, his purple confessional stole draped over his missionary cross. His face expressed a seriousness I had never seen before. I knelt down on the wooden floor in front of him and began my confession. I concluded by saying that these are, to the best of my ability and knowledge, the sins of my entire life. I received absolution and exited his room in great relief. "Whew," I said as I left the spiritual director's room, "I hope I never have to do that again!"

The next day, in our Metaphysics class, we were discussing the essence of separated substances and especially the essence of intelligences. As interesting as it was, I found it difficult to concentrate. My mind drifted off. Thoughts of married life, of a wife and of children whirled around. They were pleasant thoughts. Should I make my temporary profession to the Community? Was I really called to be a priest? Could I really lead a celibate life? I was devastated. Why should these thoughts enter my mind just before profession?

Profession – our class

The day of profession neared and my doubts increased. I made an appointment to speak with my spiritual director. Fr. Missler and I sat in conversation for what seemed like hours. He dispelled my uncertantity with these simple yet profound words, "The will of God is made known through your superiors. Remember, you have not chosen me, I have chosen you."

The central theme of the eight-day "pre-profession" retreat was the "construction of our spiritual edifice." We were to consider such questions as: "Why am I here?" "How am I to build?" "What have I built thus far?" "How shall I continue to build?" Under the guidance of our retreat master, Fr. A. Traeser, we meditated, prayed and sang. We chanted the little hours of *Prime*, *Tierce* and *Sext* (first, third and sixth morning hours as sung by cloistered monks at one, three and six AM.). On a daily basis, in order to get all the "nonsense" off our chests, we were allowed to talk after our noon meal. Fr. Traeser, was a stern man who voiced many inspiring words. At mid retreat, the sixteen of our class (we had lost seven classmates since we entered the major seminary) were asked to sign profession papers. And so it was that we entered into the written part of our three-year contract with the Community during the retreat.

Profession day came. It was December 3, the feast day of St. Francis Xavier (my Confirmation patron Saint). This day was not only "temporary profession day" for our class but also the "final profession day" for the third theologians. We processed into the chapel taking our places in the sanctuary. Even though the choir was short handed (many of us choir members were to be professed) the Gregorian chant of ancient days was masterfully rendered under the direction of Richard Wise, a second theologian.

At the Gospel of the Solemn High Mass, Fr. Seraphin W. Oberhauser, our Provincial, dressed in ornate gold vestments, took the seat of Community authority in the center of the sanctuary. He admonished us to be imbued with the spirit of poverty and to have a holy and blind obedience to our superiors. Henceforth we were to love the community, live for it and be prepared to die for it! We who were about to be professed, proceeded towards our Provincial. The choir began singing *"Veni Creator Spiritus, mentes tuorum visita...."* With one hand on the gospel I made my promise of fidelity, my three year temporary profession: *"Ego Rudolph Kapitan coram Omnipotente Deo, Beata Virgine Maria, Auxillio Christianorum, Sancto Francisco Xaverio, Protectore nostro, ac Beato Patre Gaspare, mea sponte promitto fidelitatem Congregationi Missionis a Pretioso Sanguine, ad tempus trium annorum. Sic me Deus adjuvet et sua sancta Evangelia."* (I Rudolph Kapitan, in the presence of Almighty God, of the Blessed Virgin Mary, Help of Christians, of St. Francis Xavier, our protector, and of Blessed Gaspar, our Father, of my own free will, promise fidelity to the Congregation of the Mission of the Precious Blood, for the period of three years. So help me God and these His Holy Gospels.) I was then invested with the cincture, a symbol of chastity. From henceforth, C.PP.S. (*Congregatio Pretiossium Sanguinis*—Congregation of the Most Precious Blood) would be a part of my name. On the first Sunday in December of 1950 I became Rudolph F. Kapitan, C.PP.S. an official son of Blessed Gaspar. My joy knew no bounds as congratulatory praises were heaped upon me by my brothers in the "Blood of the Lamb!"

The second year of life at the major seminary continued to be a blessing as I concluded my college courses by receiving a Bachelor of Arts degree from Dayton University. Our seminary administration had the foresight to have our Philosophy Department established as an upper level division of the college of Liberal Arts of the University of Dayton. We were listed in the University Bulletin as the Carthagena Division.

During the ensuing summer an "Oat Bug" infestation invaded our fields and buildings. The screens could not keep those pests out. These minute bugs got in everywhere. I captured a couple of them under a piece of scotch tape and present them here. Having been entrapped by scotch tape for  over fifty years, they remain perfect specimens. Those oat bugs were short lived and it was not uncommon for us to sweep shovels full of them off the portico as they struggled to enter the building through the main entrance.

One day in late summer Ray Gatza and I were assigned to work with Brother Walter, the "lil ole wine maker." There was a wine cellar in one of the old buildings near the chapel. To enter the cellar there were four steps down into an anteroom. From the anteroom you entered the wine cellar through a lock fitted door. This room contained a number of fifty and hundred gallon barrels of wine in various stages of fermentation. Our assignment was to fill 350-ml. bottles with wine from premarked barrels. As we began, Brother Walter told us that he had to go into town and said "remember boys, I have not counted the bottles." Ray and I, having had a few swigs of that heavenly nectar decided to put a bottle away for later consumption. So, long before Brother Walter returned, we each took a bottle and hid it in a dark corner of the anteroom. The anteroom always remained unlocked.

Later that evening, after Rosary, I walked over towards the wine cellar to retrieve my prize. I entered the anteroom, placed the bottle of wine in my deep cassock pocket and exited the room. Once outside I looked about very nervously to see if anyone saw me. The windows of the three-story seminary building looked onto the courtyard. Confident that no one had seen me, I hurriedly walked the two hundred and some feet through the rear courtyard towards the back stairs of the seminary building. I took those stairs, two steps at a time as I rushed to my third floor room. Gasping a huge sigh of relief, I placed the bottle of wine into my upright portable closet and covered it with some dirty laundry.

No sooner had I sat down than the unmistakable footsteps of our portly rector could be heard pouncing down the hallway. Clump, clump, clump and the footsteps stopped at my door! My heart began beating rapidly. There was a knock and I tripped over my chair as I went to answer the door. A very serious Fr. Pire said, "Rudolph, I want to see you immediately in my office." "Yes, Father," I responded nervously. Had Father seen me through the second floor hallway windows as I hurried through the rear courtyard with wine bottle in cassock? Thoughts like "But he couldn't have!" "Well, maybe, he did!" raced through my mind repeatedly. I concluded that he must have. I was devastated and prepared myself for the worst, immediate expulsion!

It took just moments for me to come down from my third floor room to the Rector's second floor room. My hands were clammy and I was totally unnerved. Envisioning many forms of punishment including my immediate expulsion, I tapped a very light knock on the Rector's door. "Enter, Rudolph," came the stern voice from within. My knees shook as I entered with trepidation. "Have a seat," he said. As I sat down he took a sheet of paper and gave it to me. I began to perspire thinking that these were my "walking papers." "I want you to translate this Slovak letter for me!" he said. I was emotionally drained as I stammered, "Sure, Father, sure!" "Yes, Okay, I will be haaappy to do that for you Reverend Father!" He looked at me quizzically and asked if everything was alright. "Just a little tired from working," I said as I left the room.

Since all our outgoing mail was censored, Father Pire knew that I wrote letters to my parents in Slovak. He saw all the letters that I wrote and knew that I understood Slovak. So that was why he wanted to see me, I said to myself, as I sighed a deep breath of relief! He didn't have the slightest idea that I had taken that bottle of wine! I returned to my room (cubicle) and, totally exhausted, plopped myself down on my bed. I was unable to do any studying for the rest of that evening.

Later I shared that bottle of wine with a few of my classmates. Filling a cough medicine bottle I went to the "jigs" for an after hour, "lights-out," forbidden smoke. During one of those illegal smoke sessions I convinced several of my classmates to take a swig from that cough medicine bottle. We had a pajama party as the contents of that bottle disappeared rather quickly. There was enough wine for several of those illegal smoke sessions. Had any of us been caught smoking after lights out, we would have lost our room privilege and been returned to the dorm and study hall.

During the summer we enjoyed various summer sporting activities. A favorite of many was croquet. The lawn gang cared for the croquet court meticulously. It was not uncommon for one of us to make a mad dash to save the court after a community activity. At times a game remained unfinished and was concluded the next free period or even the next day. When approached from a philosophic perspective, the more we made demands of the game and the court, the more we enjoyed the game. Some students were so hooked that they even played it on a snow-covered court.

A game of croquet <u>in the snow!</u>

Winter activities were carried on indoors in the basement of the seminary building. A two-line bowling alley was available. Teams were formed and tournaments were held. It was not uncommon for a student to challenge one of his professors to a line or two of bowling. A small basketball court provided the space to expend further energies. The boundaries were the walls. There were no refs. The idea was to make the rules as you played and to get all the points you could! Many times games were delayed to wipe the blood off the floor. It was a "bloody" basketball court.

Then there was Turner Hall (the old original seminary building) where exercise equipment had been set up. On entering that large second floor room (the first floor contained the laundry sorting room), the rumble of a punching bag could often be heard. Much pent up energy was expended in this exercise room, pumping iron or jabbing that punching bag with rapid lefts and rights. So as not to bruise our knuckles, each of us had our own pair of leather gloves with cut out fingers.

A bit more civilized recreation was carried on in the

Rec room scene

recreation rooms. Bridge was a favorite card game as was pinochle. Other games of cards were played. The two pool tables were in constant use. In the far corner of the main recreation room was a candy bar counter. If you had a spare nickel, it was easy to satisfy any sweet tooth cravings. The choices were many

in this well stocked
candy counter. Don
Vogel saw to that.

Our country was
engaged in a war in
Korea. Since we had
no newspapers or
magazines we knew
very little about it.
Young men our age

Rec room scene: Shea, Lang, Fullenkamp, Spitzig, Thieman, Wellman, Volmer, L. Barga, W. Eilerman, Bolan

were shedding their blood, giving their lives. The question arose, "How might we help?" It was suggested that as many as possible give blood as often as possible to help in the war effort. It was the least we could do. So it was that every six to eight weeks, truckload after truckload of seminarians arrived in open-air trucks at the local Red Cross facility to donate blood. Thanks to the seminarians at St. Charles, hundreds of gallons of that precious, life saving fluid were given during the Korean War years.

Third year at Major Seminary

Our Philosophy studies were completed. The next four years of Study would be in Theology. The courses to be pursued were as published in the Bulletin of the School of Sacred Theology, the Catholic University of America, with which St. Charles Seminary was affiliated. First year of theological studies encompassed thirty-seven credit hours over the two semesters. There were ten credit hours of Fundamental Dogma, six hours of Moral Theology, seven hours of Scripture, four hours of Church History and six hours of Canon Law. Two hours of classroom work were spent on each of the two auxiliary subjects of Homiletics and Asceticism.

Our professors were Fr. Mark Dorenkemper (a recent

doctoral graduate of the University of Fribourg) -Dogma; Fr. Edmund J. Ryan -Moral Theology; Fr. Aloys Dirksen - Scripture; Fr. Paul J. Knapke -Church History and Fr. Herbert J. Linenberger -Canon Law. We had an excellent line up of professors. Each of them had earned doctors degrees in their respective fields. There was very little time for levity as demands were made on us for scholastic excellence. There was so very much subject matter to cover and so little time in which to do it. Many an hour was spent under my bedcovers in my darkened room with a flashlight, studying after the ten o'clock "lights out" deadline.

One day while discussing laws governing baptismal certificates, our Canon Law professor, Fr. Linenberger, told us about an interesting case that happened right here in our seminary. Prior to the profession of a class of students, we were told that the seminary rector would call for the delivery of Baptismal Certificates from the parishes of all to be professed. As Fr. Linenenberger said this he looked at me and said, "We received a baptismal certificate of a student who was about to be professed and found that it had been altered!" Immediately my thoughts sped back to another time, a time when I, as a 15 year old lad, altered my baptismal certificate (to make it look like I was 16). I did this so that Inland Steel Company would employ me. Never for a moment did I think that my altered baptismal certificate would be returned to my parish priest and come back to haunt me. Needless to say Fr. Linenberger mentioned no names. Despite the fact that my classmates were unaware of the fact that he was talking about my baptismal certificate, I was totally embarrassed. As I left class that day, Fr. Linenberger smiled and winked at me. What a relief to know that he did not hold that indiscretion against me.

As in our Philosophy studies so also in our Theology studies, all our courses were modeled after the teachings and writings of that brilliant Doctor of the Church, St. Thomas Aquinas. Presented to us were concepts regarding the existence, nature, matter and form and efficacy of the sacraments. Discussions were held regarding basic human acts and the obstacles to them; moral and meritorious acts; the natural law and the positive divine law, ecclesiastical law, conscience and the moral system. We used the Latin language as though it were our primary language. We "feasted" on the written word of St. Thomas, the "Angelic Doctor."

Distractions continued to plague me during these classes. I wrote about some of them to my parents. In his letters regarding these distractions Dad would always remind me that "the devil howls the loudest around seminary buildings." "The devil never sleeps and is most voracious as he seeks to destroy those who would be faithful priests of Christ." Dad wrote about his brother Father Ambrose who overcame many distractions and went on to be an exemplary priest, loved by all of his parishioners. Fr. Ambrose attributed his priestly success to the power of prayer, especially prayer to our Blessed Mother Mary. Despite my prayers there was no resolution to the problem regarding my distractions

During that annual ten-day summer vacation, time was spent on the Whiting beaches of Lake Michigan with my brothers and sisters. Parading up and down the beach in front of me were young ladies clad in two piece bathing suits. I lay on the blanket and looked heavenward. I said to myself, Kapitan you have never dated a girl; you have never kissed a girl. Sure you danced with some of your high school class mates but you were never alone with a girl, to as much as, to hold her hand. You had better experience this before you make a life long commitment to lead a celibate life. Songs heard during that summer vacation like "Come-On-A-My House" by Rosemary Clooney intrigued me. Other songs kept popping into my mind, such as: "Walking My Baby Back Home," "My Heart Cries For You" and "I Get Ideas," were some of them. Songs like that, although on the hit parade, did not belong in the repertoire of a major seminarian. I was humming them and I liked what I was humming.

Fourth year at Major Seminary

I returned to the seminary that summer of 1952 and began my second year of Theology in September. It became most difficult to concentrate on my studies. The distractions were so upsetting that I thought I was going to lose my mind. I was now counseling more frequently with Fr. Missler, my spiritual director. My world was in turmoil and I couldn't seem to help myself. After long and serious deliberation, we both agreed that it would be in my best interest to discontinue my studies for the priesthood. So, it was on a **Friday, the thirteenth** of November, that I received a written, formal dispensation from the Community's Moderator General in Rome. It absolved me of the unexpired term of my temporary promises of fidelity to the Precious Blood Community. In return, I signed a "hold harmless" agreement in which I agreed never to hold the Community liable for any acts of commission or omission that I might have experienced while a member of the Community. Was my leaving on Friday the thirteenth an unlucky omen? A dark cloud enshrouded my entire existence. I was in a state of nervous anxiety as negative thoughts threatened my stability.

I was leaving. Friendships formed over many years

were coming to an abrupt end. There were some tearful farewells as I parted with classmates and friends. I said farewells to each of my priest professors. I remember well the words of my Dogmatic Theology professor Father Mark Dorenkemper. "Rudolph, it must have been very difficult and painful for you to decide to leave. It would have been much easier for you to stay. You are just a little more than two years from the priesthood. I do not fault you. I give you credit for making such a difficult decision." And difficult it was!

An Ex-Seminarian

As Father Lubeley drove me off, I glanced back tearfully toward the seminary building. With mixed emotions I recalled happy times when life, although very demanding, was both rewarding and fulfilling. I had spent all those years of training for what? I was now an ex-seminarian. Communication with fellow classmates and seminary friends was henceforth strictly prohibited. I automatically became a "*persona non grata.*"(An unwelcome individual) Even a letter to and from my friends and classmates would not be allowed! At the train station in Van Wert, Ohio, I said a sad farewell to Father Lubeley, the Community representative. I was headed for Fort Meade, Maryland to spend some time with my older brother John. I didn't want to face distraught parents. I didn't want to face the pointed finger of the neighbors back home. Even though I planned on returning to a seminary after I resolved my uncertainties, I was at the moment an ex-seminarian! I was a discredit to my family and to my parish. My life was in a state of turmoil. My God, what was I going to do? How was I going to make a living? Where would I live? How was I going to adjust to a world from which I had been totally removed for six long years? Question after question caused uncertainty after uncertainty. For the moment I felt that I wasn't prepared to make any of those decisions. I came to a keen realization that prayer, and a lots of it, would be needed.

After spending a few anxious weeks in Maryland, I returned to my parent's home in Whiting. It was indeed a sad homecoming. I was overwhelmed at the sight of my tearful parents. What made it even more difficult for them was the fact that I was the second of their sons to have left the seminary. Mom always prayed that one of her sons become a priest. Perhaps I would return to the seminary and perhaps not. The transition was difficult for all of us.

Being the "ex-seminarian" that I was, I felt like a fish out of water. I was not in sync with the outside world. After all I had spent years at the seminary living, thinking and breathing philosophy and theology. These concepts continued to be at the forefront of my everyday thinking. How could I ever erase, from my daily thinking, the importance of the "Principal of Individuation" for material composites, or the concepts of "prime matter and substantial form," or the psychology of the "average norm"? What about the "Metaphysical Essence of God" and His Divine Attributes and the "Hypostatic Union," etc. etc. The nature and properties of justification and proper disposition remained matters of importance. The natural law and the positive divine law as applied to moral systems, etc. etc., were thoughts that occupied some of my every day thinking. The world around me was altogether oblivious and uninterested in these or other philosophical or theological concepts.

Chapter XII - Life Outside the Seminary

Father Lefko, mentor of my seminary days, continued to be concerned about my welfare. One morning after Mass he called me over to the St. John rectory. We chatted about my future over a cup of coffee. "How would you like to work in a bank?" he asked. Since I had nothing better in mind at the moment, my answer was in the affirmative. The next day I went for an interview with Mr. Joseph Grenchik Sr., President of the American Trust & Savings Bank. And so on that day I began my thirty two year banking career as a teller and concluded that career as a Vice President and Comptroller of the American Trust & Savings Bank.

The CYA - Father Lefko further acquainted me with the CYA, Catholic Young Adults. It was an organization whose members were over 18 years of age and unmarried. There were about sixty of us representing all six Whiting-Robertsdale parishes. I joined reasoning that this was to be the instrument through which I would resolve the questions I had regarding dating; questions which plagued me during the last years at the seminary. I became very involved and the group chose me to be their president.

First Car - To facilitate my comings and goings, I purchased a used 1953 Mercury from Pop Hart at Jim Moran "The Courtesy-man" dealership in Chicago and, at age 23, I learned how to drive. Now I had the liberty of asking young ladies if I might take them home after our Thursday functions. I began dating in earnest, and even, on occasion, came home late at night. When that happened, Dad stayed up late waiting for me. Although I was twenty-three years old, he chastised me when I came home at a late hour.   In his mind I remained the son who was going to become a priest.

Standard Oil Co. Explosion   It was early one Saturday morning following a very late Friday CYA outing that I was rudely awakened. I had been thrown from my bed onto the bedroom floor. "What happened," I asked myself as I sat on the floor in a semi daze. "Had an atomic bomb exploded?" The clock on the bedroom wall read 6:15. I cleared the cobwebs from my eyes and raced to the bedroom window to take a look at what could have happened.   I had never experienced an explosion so powerful that it knocked me right out of my bed. The sky to the south was thick with flames as smoke bellowed high into the air above the Standard Oil Company refinery. There had been an explosion, flames were flashing up hundreds of feet into the air. My family was huddled around the kitchen table listening to the radio. It seemed to us that the end of the world had come. The radio commentator announced that a huge 26-story cat cracker unit, making high-octane gas, had exploded, spewing wreckage for miles around. Several sixty million-barrel storage tanks had gone up in flames. The blast shattered windows for miles around. We were among more than a thousand homes to be evacuated as policemen using bullhorns announced imminent danger. Up and down the streets of Whiting drove the police in their squad cars making emergency announcements. Route 12 & 20, the main highway into Whiting, was closed. You could not get in but you could leave.

Gasoline from the explosion had found its way into Whiting's sewer system, creating an extremely hazardous condition. With precious little clothing and bedding, we left for my married sister's house in East Chicago. We remained at the Germeks for several days until the all-clear was signaled. It was remarkable that only two were killed during all those explosions. There were many injuries. Ten per cent of the world's largest oil refinery had been destroyed. As a result of this fire and explosion Whiting lost acres of its residential area. All of "Stiglitz Park" and "Goose Island" were permanently vacated. Streets named Ann, Alice, Grace, May, 130th and 131st, along with Barry Ave. and Louise Ave. all disappeared from the map of Whiting. The Gypsy population living in that area exited Whiting, never to return. The Oil Company purchased all the homes and businesses in that part of town. A much larger disaster was avoided thanks to the immediate response of the Company's Fire Department and the Whiting Fire Departments. Their expertise and dedication won praise from the many fire departments that came to help from near and far. Even the Chicago Fire Department helped in the fire fighting team effort.

Mary Kasper - Our CYA meetings and functions continued unhampered by the largest fire in Whiting's history. As president of the group it was my responsibility to appoint group leaders. One such person was Mary Kasper. Her responsibility was to direct Social and Sporting programs for the organization. What a job she did! She organized trips to Chicago area functions. There were beach parties and square dances and sporting competitions. I liked how Mary took charge and followed through in arranging successful, fun filled social activities. It was at these gatherings that I gradually shed myself of the philosophically and theologically way of seminary thinking. No longer was I prone to discuss the "Principal of Individuation" or the "Average Norm," or quantitative and qualitative theological and philosophical theories. God was leading me in another direction. I began to realize that the priesthood was not to be my vocation. As time went on Mary Kasper directed more than our programs. She began directing my heart.

A song we loved to sing as we traveled to and from the functions was "Sweet Violets." It went:

"Sweet violets, sweeter than the roses,

covered all over from head to toe,

covered all over with sweet violets.

(Verse 1) There once was a farmer who took a young miss

in the back of the barn were he gave her a

.....lecture on horses and chickens and eggs

and told her that she had such beautiful

......manners that suited a girl of her charms,

a girl that he wanted to take in his

.....washing and ironing, and then, if she did,

they could get married and raise lots of.....

(repeat chorus). (Verse 2) The girl told the farmer that he'd better stop,

and she called her father and he called a

.....taxi and got there before long,

'cause it's always been my belief marriage will bring a man nothing but

......(repeat chorus). (Verse 3) The farmer decided he'd wed anyway,

and started in planning for his wedding

.....suit which he purchased for only one buck

but then he found out he was just out of

......money and so he got left in the lurch

standing and waiting in front of the

......end of this story which just goes to show

all a girl wants from a man is this......(repeat chorus).

In 1956 I traded my 1953 "Merc" for a brand new Pontiac "Chieftan." It was fully loaded except for a "padded dash" which cost $28.00 more. Since it was not that easy to get a new car, I didn't want to add the cost of that additional luxury. I was fortunate enough that, with my trade-in, some additional "saved-up cash," and a bank loan, I was able to get a sparkling brand new car right off the show room floor.

The Auto Accident - On a Sunday afternoon in November of that year, while returning from visiting a friend at a Dyer hospital, Mary Kasper and I were involved in a serious automobile accident. Route 30 was covered

After the Accident - What was my brand new 1956 Pontiac

with ice. Mary, my soon to be fiancée, and I were on our way home, traveling eastbound. From the west came an orange streak skidding and sliding across all three lanes as it smashed against the left front of my car. Continuing to skid, it then bounced off hitting the front and then the right side as it rolled over into the ditch and off the road.

Thank God that both Mary & I suffered only minor injuries— some broken bones, black eyes, contusions and cuts. The occupants of that "orange streak" didn't fare as well. The injuries sustained by that Chicago dentist couple were more severe. Settling with their insurance company, all that Mary and I wanted was what we had before the accident, if that were possible. An attorney friend suggested that, since we did not want to initiate a lawsuit, a fair monetary award would be three times the cost of injuries and all other expenses, plus, of course, a car to replace my automobile. That is exactly what we settled for, except that the car I received was a "Star Chief," a top of the line Pontiac, four door hard top model.

Several weeks later I received notification from the attorney for the dentist couple that they were suing me for the "negligent" operation of my automobile. How could that be? They came across three lanes hitting me and ending up in the ditch. My car remained on the roadway where it was hit. Their insurance company had admitted liability and settled with me! The offending couple was the one who came skidding across three lanes striking my auto, causing injury and trauma to Mary and to myself. They demolished my newly purchased automobile with only 6000 miles on it, my pride and joy.

Contacting their insurance agent, the one who settled with us, I was told not to worry. The agent speculated that since we did not initiate a lawsuit their "ambulance chaser attorney" presumed we felt liable. They were unsuccessful. Their lawsuit didn't get past first base. Afterwards our attorney friend cautioned that we "left them off the hook" too easy and that prompted their lawsuit. We were content that we had conducted ourselves as Christians. "Do unto others as you would have others do unto you!" That policy had served us very well. When we least expected it, blessings came our way.

Chapter XIII - Getting Married

On May 18, 1957 Mary Kasper and Rudy Kapitan "**graduated**" from the CYA as we exchanged marriage vows at the Immaculate Conception church. Custom had it that couples were to be married in the bride's church. Ours was a large wedding reception with over five hundred in attendance. We both came from large families. Mary was the youngest of six and I was the third oldest of seven. Our parents were happy with us, happy with our "marital union." After all, we possessed the three important ingredients for a successful marriage. My bride and I were, first of all, both Catholics. Secondly we were both first generation Slovak Americans and, thirdly, we were both of the same social caliber. On our return from a Florida honeymoon we registered as Mr. & Mrs. Rudolph F. Kapitan at St. John's Parish. Custom had it that once married the new couple was to enroll as parishioners in the groom's parish, and so we did.

Our first Christmas as a married couple proved to be the saddest of my life. At age 69 my Father finally succumbed to his life-long battle with severely damaged lungs. He had been gassed during World War I with that horrendous mustard gas that the German army used in France. Dad struggled during his entire life as he coughed up greenish-yellow phlegm. At night he put water in a *sherblik* (spittoon) and put it on the floor next to his bed. In the morning that *sherblik* was loaded with his spittal and phlegm. Day or night there was no reprieve from his coughing which often caused a choking spell as he gasped for breath. He gasped his last breath on Dec. 20, 1957. Before he died, he came to know that his daughter-in-law was pregnant and he was elated about that. What he didn't know was that my wife was pregnant with the first Kapitan boy and that his grandson would be named Rudolph after his grandfather and father.

Dad was buried on December the 24th, the day before Christmas. As the twenty one-gun salute sounded at Dad's graveside, I remembered what one of my grade school Sisters at St. John's said about that salute. "The sum of the numbers in 1776 totals 21," Sister said. Then it came to mind that just as the soldiers of 1776 served their country in the Revolutionary war, so did my Dad in WW I. So, the honor of a 21 gun salute was his as he was about to be placed to rest to await resurrection day

We were not going to put up a tree that year. My wife Mary convinced me that Dad would want us to celebrate Christmas with the traditional tree. So, we bundled up and went out into the cold and snowy afternoon to look for a tree. It was the day before Christmas and we knew that finding a decent tree would be difficult. Time had run out and the Christmas trees had surely been picked over. Driving from Christmas tree lot to Christmas tree lot we finally found a tree that was to our liking. We asked how much. "A dollar sixty five for this one" said the lot owner. "Will you take a dollar fifty?" I asked. Why not bargain; after all, I had learned bargaining from my Dad during all those trips to "Jew Town." I knew that Dad would be proud of me. The Christmas tree lot owner said, "You last day shoppers are all alike. You come on the last day expecting a bargain!" "We are not last minute bargain shoppers," I said. "My Dad just died and we buried him this afternoon." "We wouldn't want your tree for free," Mary and I said simultaneously. As we were leaving, the owner came after us telling us that we could have the tree for the dollar and fifty cents we had offered. "Keep it," we said. "We wouldn't want it for nothing!" My young bride and I came away with a valuable lesson about being judgmental. Perhaps that negative encounter served a purpose after all, we mused. The tree that we bought at the next lot, although not as perfect, was in memory of my dear father. It made our first Christmas together a bit more meaningful.

A few months after we were married, Mary and I were playing tennis at the Whiting park tennis courts. It was a bright sunlit Saturday morning, perfect for strenuous exercise. I twisted my ankle by stepping on a rock. An X-ray proved that I had fractured the 5th metatarsal in my left foot. Dr. Stecy, our family doctor, put a cast on that leg all the way up to the knee. He gave me a set of crutches with the admonition to stay off the injured leg. When I arrived at work on Monday no one believed that this happened to me while I was playing tennis with my wife. "Yeah, sure," they chided "tell us another one." "We know both you and Mary, she probably gave it to you." I did not live that incident down.

Several months later I came to work with a patch over my left eye. "A ha, now what did you do to deserve that from Mary?" my fellow workers chided. I explained that while helping my brother-in-law drive a well, the old fashioned way, a bit of rusty metal flew off the driving iron weight and flew right into my eye. At the clinic my eye was frozen and the piece of metal was removed. A patch was placed over the eye. "yeah, sure," chided my fellow workers, "what's the next story going to be like, in the episode of this newly married couple?"

Our First House - There was a "For Sale" sign in front of a house at 1627 LaPorte Ave. The asking price was $12,500.00 for this frame two-story, six-room house with a full basement. There was a detached two-car garage, which was located in the back yard just on the alley line. The lot size was a huge 40'x125'. Mrs. Kasper, my mother-in-law, said, "Offer them 10,000.00." Mary and I both said, "Ma, they will never settle for that." I said, "Besides that Ma, I would be too embarrassed to offer them such a low figure." "Just do it," she insisted. We took her advice and to our amazement the sellers took our offer. We bought our first house for $10,000.00 in February of 1958.

With the help of my father-in-law, Joe Kasper, we rebuilt the whole thing. As a Whiting fireman Pa Kasper had time to learn many of the skills and trades of his countrymen. He was a "jack of all trades." We removed the front and back first floor walls of that structure, shoring up the second floor walls and added twenty-four feet to the gutted first floor. At his recommendation we converted the second floor to a rental apartment. "Having rents is how you will get ahead," Pa suggested. "That's how I got ahead," he said.

We began the complete reconstruction in April and moved into our newly reconstructed house in September. Besides my father-in-law, I received help from my brothers and also from newly ordained Father Ron Schiml, C.PP.S. He was a seminary classmate of mine and had just been assigned parish work at St. John's. From seminary days I knew that he swung a mean hammer. Pa Kasper often teased us by calling us "shoemakers." Even if I have to say so myself, the carpenter work the "shoemakers" did was quality work.[1]

An "Apartment for Rent" sign was placed in our front-room window. We planned on renting the apartment for seventy-five dollars a month. The very next day we answered a ringing doorbell. There stood the town drunk with a rugged looking stranger. "What's the rent for your

---

[1] Some forty-five years later the house is still standing.

135

apartment?" they asked. Surely, we didn't want these bums as renters. I hesitated for a moment and said, "One Hundred Fifty Dollars a month." My wife added "and one hundred fifty dollars for a deposit." The rugged looking stranger said, "I'll take it." He reached in his pocket, pulled out a wad of money and counted out one hundred and fifty dollars. "I'll be back tomorrow for the key and I'll bring the one hundred fifty dollar deposit," he said. Ernie Orr turned out to be the best renter we ever had. Another valuable lesson in life was learned: "Don't judge a book by its' cover!" We considered ourselves blessed with the rental arrangement. Our house mortgage payment was $68.00 per month and we paid that from my pay. The $150.00 we received as rent income was banked. We had established a savings account for our children.

Starting a family—RUDY Our First Child - On Saturday, May 3, 1958 our firstborn, Rudolph Joseph Kapitan left the comfort of his mother's womb at 4:36 PM at St. Catherine's Hospital in East Chicago. I was ecstatic. Our parents were overjoyed at hearing the good news of the birth of the first Kapitan grandson. My father-in-law was skeptical when I

Mary has just announced that she is pregnant with our first child!

called him. We always joked around. He said "stop kidding, Mary probably had a girl."

Rudy was baptized at St. John's church. Father Ronald Schiml, a seminary classmate of mine, performed the ceremony. He also performed the "Churching" ceremony for Mary. It was a custom for the new mother to receive a blessing given by the Church after the recovery from childbirth. During the blessing the new mother prayed that she would obtain, by means of the priestly blessing, the graces necessary to bring up her child in a Christian manner. Up to this time Mary never ventured out until the baby was christened and she was "churched." This "Churching" ceremony was symbolic of the Mother of Christ carrying her Child to the Temple to offer him to the Eternal Father and to receive the special blessings prayed for at the presentation.

MICHAEL Our Second Child - Fourteen months later on July 25, 1959 our second son, Michael Kasper Kapitan was born. Father Ron also baptized him and Mary presented herself again for the Churching ceremony.

SUSAN Our Third Child - Blessings kept on coming and, again, fourteen months later, on September 19, 1960,

Our children in 1961 - Rudy, Sue, Mike.

our first daughter Susan Marie was born. Father Ron also baptized her and Mary was "Churched." Each of these precious charges, bundles of joy and gifts from heaven, came home from the hospital to a newly rebuilt home provided by Mary and I.

The year before Susan's birth was a traumatic one for me. One morning while shaving I was startled by the fact that the left side of my face was numb. The left side of my tongue was also numb. Peering intently into the mirror I noticed that my face was disfigured. I called to Mary. My speech was slurred as I began telling her of the paralysis of the entire left side of my face. I couldn't believe that at age

30, a malady as serious as this afflicted me. After all, I was responsible for the support of my wife and two small children. The doctor saw me that very same day. The diagnosis was Bells Palsy. "What's Bells Palsy?" I exclaimed in trepidation! "It is a facial palsy which, for some, remains permanent," the doctor said, "and for others, it remains partial." "For the more fortunate it disappears altogether." He continued saying, "We will need to wait and let nature take its' course." He said that the medication he was giving me would hasten the recovery, and so it did. Over the next several months the paralysis began to disappear. Then, as if a miracle happened, the palsy disappeared altogether. Our prayers were answered. I was among the more fortunate.

In early 1962 Mary was in charge of planning her parents' 50th wedding anniversary. The golden anniversary of Joseph and Anna Kasper would be in November. Plans for a well deserved party were well underway when Ma got sick. She never recovered from her illness and Anna Wagner Kasper died on April 17, 1962, at the age of 68. The well-deserved party to celebrate the Golden Wedding Anniversary of Joseph Gullak Kasper and Anna Wagner Kasper was cancelled.

Fighting the Sales Tax - It was in 1963 that legislation was passed to establish a Sales Tax in Indiana. I wrote a letter in opposition to the Hammond *Times* "Voice of the People." As a result of that letter an organization called the "Hoosiers For Good Government" was formed.

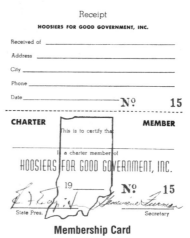

Membership Card

The ten initial members of the Board of Directors came from all walks of life. I served as the first president. A membership drive followed. Because of the urgency of the matter we held semi weekly meetings in each other's homes.

Judge John L. Niblack, a Marion Circuit Court judge, ruled in our favor. He ruled twice that the tax bill was unconstitutional. Proponents of the sales tax bill, our Governor being among them, had appealed to the State Supreme Court. The Judge encouraged our organization

Hoosiers For Good Government: Meeting Agenda & Petition.

June 15, 1963

TO THE PUBLIC RELATIONS OFFICER OF YOUR ORGANIZATION

A LAKE COUNTY CITIZENS COMMITTEE REPORTS:

On May 24, 1963 a group of Lake County Citizens, opposed to the 2% Sales Tax, met to briefly outline a procedure to organize our County in a fight against this new tax. We felt it to be our civic duty to arouse our people and ourselves from the lethargy which has given some of our politicians a free rein over tax matters. Ever aware of increasing expenditures by the State Government and of increasing budgetary needs, we were, nevertheless, convinced that a Sales Tax under the guise of a Gross Retail Tax was absolutely unnecessary.

We are deeply concerned that our great Hoosier State treads along a route directed towards an almost calculated goal which would make each of us more depended on the State for our existence.

Gentlemen, our great Country was founded in order that this should not be. Our tax methods and structures as they exist today, in many instances flout the liberties of man, sapping from him ounces of freedom with the passage of each new tax law.

We of Lake County have organized and fought. Our efforts were not in vain. In just fourteen short days, 135,000 Lake County taxpayers signed our petition asking for a repeal of the State Sales Tax. Armed with these petitions we traveled to our State Capitol in time for the June 10th Constitutionality hearing of the Sales Tax law before Judge Niblack of the Marion County Circuit Court. The judge took the case under advisement and should rule shortly.

We conferred with Governor Welsh who appeared unimpressed with our efforts. Gentlemen, our goal now is to have 65% of Indiana's taxpayers sign this petition. Attorney Nelson Grills of Indianapolis will file a law suit for us, the people of Indiana. A meeting is scheduled with Attorney Grills in Indianapolis on Tuesday, June 18th.

We now look to you for financial support and to your leadership and organization in furthering our mutual cause. We enclose a copy of our petition which, I am sure, you could stencil and reproduce. For uniformities sake, we have asked our people over radio and in newsprint, to sign petitions at the local stores which display our "FIGHT" sign."

If you would carry this through, the approach of the entire state would be identical. Our sign is 11" high by 14" wide; black lettering on an orange backgroun. It reads:

FIGHT (letters 4 3/4")
The 2% Sales Tax (letters 1")
Sign Here (letters 2")

Your efforts in promoting this petition campaign will be appreciated for generations yet unborn.

Yours for a greater Hoosierland

The Lake County Committee

by: Rudy F. Kapitan
1627 La Porte Ave.
Whiting, Indiana

A PETITION

We, the undersigned taxpayers, through the signing of this petition, wish to express our vigorous opposition to the Indiana Gross Retail Tax enacted by the 93rd Session of the Indiana General Assembly. It was enacted without any reasonable opportunity for taxpayers to express their opinions. We view it as an unfair and unreasonable impost upon those least able to bear additional taxation. We feel it is likely to operate to the disadvantage of retail business in Indiana. We are concerned about the unfair and uncompensated burden placed upon retail business in the collection and remittance of the tax, particularly the very small businesses unequipped to handle the record-keeping involved.

NAME	ADDRESS	CITY, STATE

Return to RUDY KAPITAN, 1627 La Porte Ave., Whiting, Indiana
(Before June 8, 1963)

to proceed using these words: "We must continue our battle if we are to prevent the passage of a sales tax bill." Our organization proceeded to continue the battle in opposition to the proposed sales tax.

A plan of action to defeat the Sales Tax bill was formulated. 18"x12" "FIGHT" signs were made

YOU ARE INVITED

TO ATTEND A PUBLIC MEETING TO PROTEST THE 2% SALES TAX

PLACE: HAMMOND CIVIC CENTER

TIME: THURSDAY, JULY 11, 1963 AT 8:00 P.M.

SPONSOR: HOOSIERS FOR GOOD GOVERNMENT

SPEAKERS: SENATOR JOHN F. SHAWLEY, Michigan City

SENATOR EARL LANDGREBE, Valparaiso

SENATOR WILLIAM CHRISTY, Hammond

SENATOR WALTER BARAN, East Chicago

REP. PAUL HRIC, Hammond

REP. BEN LESNIAK, Jr.

REP. JAMES HUNTER, East Chicago

REP. WM. BABINCSAK, Munster

SEC. OF SENATE, DAVE COLOSIMO

MR. JOHN ALEXANDER, SAVE THE DUNES COUNCIL

Despite the tremendous efforts of Mr. Clinton Green of the Indiana Port Commission and Governor Welsh, to pass legislation appropriating money for a port at Burns Ditch, no such funds were appropriated.

However, a 2% Sales Tax passed the legislature in the closing days of the session. This law has since been declared unconstitutional. However, Governor Welsh and the state administration plan to contest that decision in the courts.

If the 2% Sales Tax is declared legal, it will produce about a 70 million dollar surplus two years hence when the state legislature convenes.

Governor Welsh and Mr. Green have by no means relinquished their plans for their pet project--a port at Burns Ditch. We can be certain that at the next session of the legislature, with that 70 million dollar surplus, they are bound to get their port.

Every Indiana citizen should vigorously protest this misuse of public funds. Join the thousands of Hoosiers who have voiced their objections to the sales tax.

140

up on hard cardboard. The signs were made of orange stock with the word **FIGHT** printed in large black letters. These signs appeared in most all business storefront windows throughout Lake and Porter Counties. A week after the signs appeared, petitions in opposition to the sales tax began to circulate. Within two weeks we had over one hundred thousand signatures. We announced that an open forum would be held at the Hammond Civic Center to discuss the pros and cons of a State Sales Tax. All local and state legislators were invited including Governor Matthew Welsh.

About four hundred attended the meeting. Tax experts and local politicians presented the pros and cons of a sales tax. It was clear that the majority of those in attendance were opposed to the tax. Most agreed to join in the fight against the sales tax. Petitions began coming in from Newton and Jasper counties. We were on a roll. It wasn't long after that we had over two hundred thousand

signatures petitioning to void the sales tax legislation. Armed with those thousands of signatures, we traveled to Indianapolis, asking for a repeal of Indiana's new 2% sales tax

Warren Krill, Mrs. Krill and me with over 250,000 signatures, petitions against the proposed new Sales Tax.

legislation. Indianapolis television covered our story. Despite support from about ninety per cent of our Lake County State representatives, our efforts failed and the bill became law. All attempts to change the Governor's thinking on the tax bill failed. Governor Welsh continued to oppose our undertaking and resisted all attempts to change his course. The 2% sales tax went into effect despite statewide opposition. Our mission, however, was not a total loss. The Hoosiers For Good Government saw to it that Matthew J. Welsh was not reelected as governor.

A Continuation of (Chapter 13) - Married life

Not long after the sales tax battle, Joe Lampa, a local real estate agent, approached me. "Hey Rudy," he said, "there is an income producing property on Atchison Ave. which I will be offering for sale. The rents from the property will really help your income picture." (Having worked at a savings and loan he knew that banks paid very poorly). "You and Mary should look at it," he said. We did and we bought it. The eighteen hundred dollars that we had saved from the rental of the upstairs apartment served as the down payment for this three-income unit. The mortgage payment was $115.00 per month and the rents were $260.00. We banked the difference.

Within the year we purchased a beautiful fawn colored Chevrolet impala nine-passenger station wagon for cash. "Didn't I tell you that with rent income you would get ahead," Pa exclaimed as we showed him the new station wagon. "Yes, but we had to sacrifice some good times," we said. Often our friends called for us to go out for pizza or bowling and we couldn't because we were too busy removing wall paper or painting; working to prepare one of our apartments for rental after a renter had moved out. We gleaned another fact of life: "Sacrifice does produce results and does not go unrewarded."

My Mother Stricken with Cancer - Not long after I was cured of my palsy, mother was diagnosed with terminal cancer. It wasn't fair to Mom, we all said. Her life had not been an easy one.   Of ten pregnancies she carried seven of us to full term, lost triplets during her fifth month of that pregnancy and suffered two miscarriages. Caring for a sick husband for most of her married life and raising the seven of us had not been easy. Now when she was ready to enjoy the rewards of her fruits and efforts, she was diagnosed with terminal cancer. "Lord," we prayed "let this pass from our dear mother; allow her some good years to enjoy the fullness of life."

A body scan proved that the cancer had spread throughout her spinal column. She began losing control of her extremities. Her doctor recommended that she have her adrenaline gland removed. It would not prolong her life but would ease the pain during the last three to six months of her life. To the proposed surgery mom's response was: "*Nie viac rezania, ja sa dam do Božich ruk,*" (no more surgery, I will place myself in God's hands). All of her life Mom believed in prayer, and so she began praying for a cure, and so did we.

As if from heaven above, we heard of cancer treatments available to residents of Illinois. The Djurovic brothers from France had established a cancer clinic in Chicago where they administered Krebiozen. An important member of that Krebiozen foundation was Dr. Ivy who had represented the AMA at the post WW II Nuremberg trials. We contacted Dr. Ivy who referred us to a Dr. Phillips. Since time was of the essence we drove to Dr. Phillips' Chicago office without an appointment. Ambrose and I assisted our mother from the car into the Doctor's office, as she was barely ambulatory. Upon being called into Doctor's office we identified ourselves and explained the urgency that prompted us to come to his office without an appointment. We acknowledged that our "Indiana plated" car was parked in front of his office. With that, using a few choice words, he became totally unnerved and asked us to leave immediately; he wanted nothing to do with an "Indiana resident." He explained how the FDA invaded his office several days before. They closed his office, told a room full of patients to leave and seized all his records. He was now under investigation and was allowed to treat Illinois residents only. No interstate patients were to be treated in his office!

As we left Dr. Phillips' office we vowed to return with Mom as an Illinois resident. We applied ourselves diligently to the serious task ahead. With the help of my sister Mary and a few of her Illinois friends we established an Illinois residence for our mother. And, just in case that was not enough for those Illinois doctors, we even got Mom an Illinois voter's registration card. This was accomplished with the help of some local politicians and also with the help of an Illinois Senator.

Within a week we had an appointment for Mom to see Dr. Phillips. He welcomed us as we showed him Mom's Illinois voter's registration card, proof positive that she was an Illinois resident. Mom's condition had worsened, as she remained just barely ambulatory. It was in February that the doctor began immediate Krebiozen treatments. By the end of May, Mom's condition had improved significantly to the point that she wanted to go to a Krebiozen foundation testimonial being held at the Drake Hotel in Chicago.

We met the famous Dr. Ivy at that testimonial. The AMA was now referring to him as an incompetent old man because he supported Krebiozen and the Djurovic brothers. Yet, it was Dr. Ivy whom the American Medical Association held in high esteem as they chose him to represent their elite medical association at the Nuremberg trials. We listened as many gave testimony of the cure they had experienced through Krebiozen. Several months later, thanks to those weekly Krebiozen treatments, Mom experienced a total remission of her "terminal" cancer. Her earnest prayers and our prayers were answered. Mom lived for another twenty years enjoying good health throughout all those years.

It was long about this time that we realized that the nine-passenger Chevrolet Impala station wagon with facing rear seats, purchased several months earlier, would really come in handy. Mary was expecting our fourth child.

CAROL Our Fourth Child - It was on November 29th, just before the Christmas of 1964, that our second daughter was born. She was christened Carol Jean. What an apropos name for this baby daughter of ours, born just before Christmas.

Teaching CCD - During the next several years I became engrossed in the CCD program at St. John's. Father G. Richard Danielak, a new assistant at St. John the Baptist parish, had a need for a CCD teacher for his high school junior class. I felt honored that he asked. How could I refuse such a call to expound on the teachings of our Catholic faith! My seminary training had prepared me well for the task and Father Dan knew that. Many interesting and thought provoking sessions were held with my students on those special Monday evenings.

Yearly Vacations - During the Christmas holidays it was customary for us to plan a summer vacation. The children were of an age where it didn't make much difference as to where we went. The following summer vacation, taken with our family of four small children, was to Michigan. We piled into our Impala Wagon and headed for a Michigan resort where the children played on the beach, fished, swam and picked fruit at an orchard. On that Michigan vacation we responded to a "puppy for sale" ad. Our five-year-old son Mike was rather fearful of dogs, so we decided to help him overcome his fear. There were six puppies in that litter of cocker spaniels. We picked a feisty black one and named her Blackie. By the time we returned to our cottage, Blackie had snuggled up to Mike. Whatever fears Mike had for dogs were being dispelled by that lovable puppy.

A year and a half later Blackie had her own litter. Our children marveled as they watched the birth of seven little puppies. What intrigued them even more was how much they looked like their mother and how they all nursed, each finding a nipple.

One evening as Mary was nursing our daughter Carol, six year old Mike sat down on the floor in front of his nursing mother and asked: "Mom do you have only two of those?" "Whyyy yes," Mom answered. "Whyyy do you ask?" "Because," Mike said, "Blackie has seven of them!" What an astute observation by a five year-old who watched Blackie nursing her seven puppies. Can you imagine women having more than two!

With the four of our children, the three-bedroom, LaPorte Avenue house was now becoming a bit tight. We wanted more room for the six of us. From the beginning, a dream of ours had always been to own "a bit of country." One day I spoke to a Joe Kuchar, a customer of the bank, asking if he would sell me a few acres of his land. Joe had purchased a fifty acre parcel out towards Crown Point. He said to "come on out on some Sunday."

The following Sunday we packed the four children into the station wagon and headed for the country. The two acres, which Joe said he would sell, had no "top" soil. The land which Joe owned had been farmed by a tree nursery and stripped of its top soil. We didn't want that kind of land. Joe's wife Helen told us of a house and acreage that was for sale "just down the road." We took a ride and parked at the entrance of the driveway leading to the house. The impressive brick and cedar tri-level house sat back about 150 feet from the lime stoned capped brick walls at the driveway entrance. Mary and I just shook our heads saying, "We could never afford this."

At Helen Kuchar's insistence we drove forward to meet the owners. We entered into a huge kitchen. The 22' x 20' kitchen had just been featured in "Better Homes & Gardens," they explained. They pointed out that the Muschler cabinetry was "top-of-the-line" and that the center island was equipped with a Thermador cook top. There were Thermador ovens which fronted on a built-in brick and stone barbecue pit. The cathedral ceiling had an exposed center beam. One wall had double glass sliding doors. The opposite wall had a single set of glass sliding doors. The walls were brick and 3/4" tongue and groove, varnished ash planking. Inlaid copper tubing heated the ceramic tiled floor.

Six-foot wide steps of solid oak, accented by a black wrought iron railing, lead from the kitchen into a huge living room. Again, an exposed wooden beam centered the living room's cathedral ceiling. The walls were 3/4" pickled ash, random width, planking. The floors were true pleated red oak random width and length. The massive fireplace was faced with Italian marble and Indiana lime stone. The wall opposite the fireplace was a 20' window wall. The back yard came into view as we looked out the living room windows. There in plain view was schoolyard quality playground equipment, a brightly painted merry-go-round and swings. A brick and frame "doll" playhouse sat to the side of the playground equipment.

Sitting on a five and one third acre parcel of fertile loam, this house with four bedrooms (one with a fireplace) and two baths, would certainly be the ideal home in which to raise our growing family. But how could we ever afford this five-year-old custom-built beauty?

For the next week or so Mary and I figured and refigured and thought and thought. Since my father-in-law's labor in reconstructing our house was gratis, that free labor added a lot to the equity we had in the rebuilt old house. Also we could sell the rental property we had acquired through real estate agent Joe Lampa several years ago. We sharpened and resharpened our pencils and we burnt some midnight oil. If we had half of the purchase price for a down payment, our mortgage payments would be $120.00 per month plus taxes and insurance, representing about 20% of my net pay. My gross pay for a half-month (we were paid on the 15th & 30th of each month) was $369.79. Subtracted from that was $34.79 for Federal Income Taxes, $7.25 for Social Security Taxes and $4.22 for Indiana State Income Taxes). So, my take home pay for half a month was $323.53. We could afford 20% of my net pay for a mortgage payment. Now we needed the down payment. If we sold our house and the Atchison Avenue rental property and all of our "E" bonds, we could do it. Both houses went on the market and both houses sold. We had the down payment. I was about to become a gentleman farmer.

Chapter XIV - COUNTRY LIVING

On December 15, 1965 we took occupancy of that country estate in Merrillville, Indiana. Our children were Rudy age 7, Mike age 6, Sue age 5, Carol age 1 and Blackie, our cocker spaniel. Our work was cut out for us and we were all eager to get started. Our neighbors were surprised that such a young couple bought the property. Mary & I thought "young?" why we are both already in our thirties!

To mow the acre of lawn with a riding Toro lawn mower, which came with the house, was a joy. Now I needed a tractor to farm the rear acreage. Early the following spring I saw an ad in the paper. There was a 1948 Ford 8N tractor for sale. All the implements for a three-point hitch were included. There was a two-bottom plow, an 8' disc, a harrow (4 sections), a two-row cultivator, a corn planter, a snow blade, a boom and a 3' x 6' metal wagon. I figured that I couldn't afford all that and so I hesitated to ask the price. What a relief when the gentleman said, "You can have everything for five hundred bucks, and I'll deliver it." I stood there in total disbelief. He noticed my consternation and explained that everyone in his neighborhood borrowed his tractor, and when he needed it, someone was always using it. As a matter of fact the tractor was at his neighbors' when I came to look at it. "I'm too good natured to say no to my neighbors," he said. "So, I decided to sell the whole kit and caboodle." I bought the tractor and the whole "kit and caboodle" for five hundred bucks! What a deal!

Farming – Growing Sweet Corn - That spring I learned how to use the implements. I plowed the field, disked it and ran the four-section harrow over it. I filled the corn planter with seed and the fertilizer buckets with fertilizer and began the planting. Four different maturing corn seeds were used to get corn maturing from early August to mid September. What a joy to behold as tiny corn plants began sprouting out of the ground, row upon row spaced just to perfection. It was with great care that I straddled those rows of young corn shoots as I began the delicate process of cultivating. I was becoming a "gentleman farmer."

From time to time Mary and the kids looked out into the field in eager anticipation of harvesting our very own sweet corn. It was in late July that the sixty-four day corn began to mature. At long last it was time to harvest the eight to ten inch long, lush green ears. With potato sacks in hand the boys and I went from stalk to stalk picking those fully ripened ears.

Inside the house, Mary was in the process of preparing several pots of boiling water. Rows of golden kernels appeared on each ear as it was husked. Mary dunked the freshly picked corn into the boiling water while the children sat at the table in eager anticipation of the soon to be feast. Never before had we feasted on freshly picked corn which came right from the field and into the pot in less than twenty minutes. The children oowed and ahhed as the platter of steaming ears of corn was brought to the table. What a delight to watch the children as they bit into those juicy, milk-filled kernels. Our first picking of corn was a "sweet" success.

We picked our home grown sweet corn all summer long. Each picking produced larger and larger ears of corn. The last rows of corn to ripen were the eighty-eight day corn. It was long about Labor Day that we began picking our final harvest. These were no small ears that hung from stalks that were seven-to eight feet high. They were fifteen to eighteen inches long and loaded with twenty-two to twenty four rows of golden kernels. Each ear was a meal in itself.

The following year I decided to try my luck by planting not only sweet corn, but also a full-fledged garden. Seed catalogues proclaimed the availability of a number of unusual vegetable colorations. Along with red tomatoes, we planted yellow and white tomatoes. We also had success with yellow and white watermelon. Potatoes and peanuts were planted as were peas, carrots, beets, parsley, pickles, dill and a host of other vegetables and herbs. At harvest time it was not only a thrill but also a treat for our children. It was especially rewarding to see the excitement in their faces as they pulled peanut plants from the rich fertile loam. The acres planted in sweet corn produced an even more successful growing year than the first. We harvested corn all summer long. Car after car pulled into our driveway in response to our ad "Pick your own corn - three dozens for a dollar." As the growing season progressed, Rudy, Mike and Sue went door to door selling corn in the Merrillville area. At forty cents a dozen each of the children contributed to their very own Christmas Club.

Then, on Fridays, we loaded the station wagon with sacks full of freshly picked sweet corn, about a hundred dozen ears. It was a special day for Rudy and Mike as they traveled to Whiting with me. Our first stop was Grandma Kapitan's house, home base for corn sales. There we unloaded sack after sack of homegrown sweet corn. The boys kept their delivery wagon in Grandma's garage. How quickly they filled that red wagon with fresh sweet corn and, off they went door to door. The corn sales were excellent, not only because the corn was farm fresh, but also because it was Friday. For us Catholics, Friday was a meatless day. At forty cents a dozen, they sold out before noontime.

Just after lunch Rudy and Mike hurried to the bank with pockets full of money. Their well-earned wads of dollars were converted to big bills, twenties and an occasional fifty-dollar bill. One Friday, while returning from Whiting, the boys wanted to stop at Griffin's Marine and Bicycle store to look at some new bikes. It didn't take much persuasion on their part for me to agree to the purchase of two Schwinn bicycles, a gold one for Rudy and a blue one for Mike. I was one proud Father as I watched each of them count out fifty-four of their own hard earned dollars. I knew that my sons were developing an excellent work ethic. Apart from the financial success, they were building character traits, which would serve them well in later life. They were learning a life long lesson.

I enjoyed another delightful experience after the boys purchased their Schwinn bicycles. Turkey Creek was about a half mile north of our house. I passed over the Turkey Creek Bridge each day as I traveled to and from work. Once the boys had those shiny new bikes they pedaled to the bridge to wait for me as I returned home after work. Heading southward on Hendricks St. and approaching the Turkey Creek Bridge I would often spot Rudy and Mike on their bicycles waiting for me to come home. As I approached the bridge, I slowed down and rolled down the car windows. With Rudy pedaling on one side and Mike on the other side we raced for home. "How fast are we going, Dad?" they would shout out. "I yelled back, "We're going twenty miles an hour; then thirty miles an hour." They always beat me to our driveway where they jumped off their bikes as I exited the car and gave me great big hugs. What a beautiful home coming greeting I often received from my two sons! Those gestures really made my day!

Towards the end of that second summer's growing season Mary and I decided to have a "corn-boil." We invited about twenty couples who had belonged to the CYA (Catholic Young Adults) organization with us during our single days back in Whiting. They came with children in tow to our "little bit of country." The majority of those couples married mates whom they also met during their CYA days. The children watched as I hooked up a farm wagon to the tractor. "Jump in," I said, and, in no time at all, we were out in the field picking lush green ears of sweet corn.

It was an excited group of children who helped their parents unload the precious cargo from the wagon. Inside, in the kitchen, Mary had four large pots of boiling water ready to accommodate what would soon become a feast without equal. Husking began in earnest as each couple chose enough ears for their family. Jumping with delight the children masqueraded with moustaches of corn silk. Our kids ran inside and brought out some big red wax lips. What happy musketeers parading around picnic tables set with pounds of butter along side crystal salt shakers. The feast was ready to begin. We all bowed our heads in prayer, giving thanks not only for the bountiful feast but also for the friendships that had been formed many years ago. Platter after platter of steaming sweet corn disappeared from the picnic tables. Expressions of satisfaction soon appeared on the faces of our guests. Most of our friends had never before eaten sweet corn just minutes after harvest.

LAURA Our Fifth Child - Earlier that summer I was pleasantly surprised when my wife broke some happy news to me. "I'm pregnant with our fifth child," Mary said. It was at 1:23 A.M on four-five-six seven that cries of a newborn filled the hospital's delivery room. Shortly after the birth I exited the waiting room to be with my wife and our newborn baby daughter. The next day I hung a life sized cardboard stork at the front of our house. The inscription said: "It's a GIRL —Laura Ann arrived on 4-5-67."

Within six months Laura was back at the hospital with pneumonia and respiratory problems. Mary and I were in shock as we stood at her crib. We couldn't physically comfort her or even hold her hand. An oxygen tent covered the entire crib. We prayed as we watched her labored breathing. Her tiny chest heaved upwards and downwards as she struggled for survival. Towards nightfall her breathing became more labored. It appeared that we were going to lose her. A kindly old Sister came into the room and prayed with us. She observed our concern and asked that we come with her to a room just across the hall. She wanted to show us some new baby furniture. We hesitated; we didn't want to leave Laura's crib. "It will just take a minute," she said.

We crossed over the hallway and into the room supposedly filled with new baby furniture. There, instead of the furniture, lay a child with an encephalitic head, caused by an inflamed brain. "This is Nancy," said the Sister. "She was born six months ago, on the same day as your Laura. She has not left the hospital since she was born." Not only did she have a head twice the size of normal, she also had an open hole at the base of her spine. The nun spoke in a soft and gentle voice as she continued. "Although Nancy has a brother and sister at home, her mother finds time to come to her daughter's hospital bedside to feed her twice a day. Nancy's father has taken

154

on a third job to help pay for all the medical bills." "This little girl," she continued, "will never go home. Her brother and sister keep asking their mommy, 'When will Nancy come home?' We left that room teary-eyed and whispered a thank you for such a tactful and considerate Sister.

Mary and I returned to Laura's bedside resolved not to be so despondent with our present situation. Although our hearts continued to be heavy with anguish, our lives could not be as sorrowful and weary as that of Nancy's parents. Laura's chance for survival was a hundredfold better than that of Nancy. That kindly old nun eased our sorrow by proving that there were others with more serious problems. Laura improved and the day came that we brought her home. Meanwhile, Nancy remained at the hospital. She never did come home. We learned a valuable lesson that there are always others with problems more serious than ours.

Sadly, on May 20, 1969, Mary's father died at age 74. Joseph G. Kasper was buried next to his wife Anna at Calumet Park Cemetery. Now, our children were without a Grandpa.

The Beginnings of a Tree Farm -

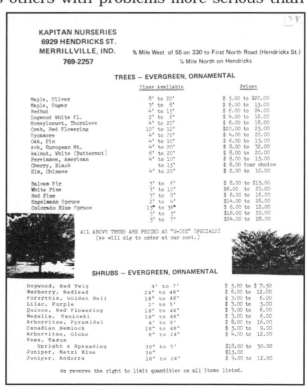

KAPITAN NURSERIES
6929 HENDRICKS ST.
MERRILLVILLE, IND.
769-2257

¾ Mile West of 55 on 330 to First North Road (Hendricks St.)
¼ Mile North on Hendricks

TREES — EVERGREEN, ORNAMENTAL

	Sizes Available	Prices
Maple, Silver	8' to 20'	$ 5.00 to $20.00
Maple, Sugar	3' to 8'	$ 6.00 to 15.00
Redbud	4' to 15'	$ 6.00 to 24.00
Dogwood White Fl.	2' to 6'	$ 4.00 to 12.00
Honeylocust, Thornless	4' to 20'	$ 6.00 to 18.00
Crab, Red Flowering	10' to 12'	$20.00 to 25.00
Sycamore	4' to 20'	$ 4.00 to 20.00
Oak, Pin	4' to 10'	$ 6.00 to 15.00
Ash, European Mt.	4' to 20'	$ 8.00 to 32.00
Walnut, White (Butternut)	6' to 20'	$ 8.00 to 20.00
Persimmon, American	4' to 10'	$ 8.00 to 15.00
Cherry, Black	to 15'	$ 8.00 Your choice
Elm, Chinese	4' to 20'	$ 2.00 to 10.00
Balsam Fir	3' to 6'	$ 8.00 to $15.00
White Pine	3' to 10'	$6.00 to 20.00
Red Pine	3' to 8'	$ 6.00 to 16.00
Engelmann Spruce	2' to 4'	$14.00 to 28.00
Colorado Blue Spruce	15" to 36"	$ 6.00 to 12.00
	3' to 5'	$16.00 to 20.00
	5' to 7'	$24.00 to 28.00

ALL ABOVE TREES ARE PRICED AS "U-DIG" SPECIALS!
(We will dig to order at our cost.)

SHRUBS — EVERGREEN, ORNAMENTAL

Dogwood, Red Twig	4' to 7'	$ 5.00 to $ 7.50
Barberry, Redleaf	24" to 48"	$ 6.00 to 12.00
Forsythia, Golden Bell	18" to 48"	$ 3.00 to 6.00
Lilac, Purple	2' to 5'	$ 3.00 to 5.00
Quince, Red Flowering	18" to 48"	$ 3.00 to 6.00
Wegelia, Vaniceki	18" to 48"	$ 3.00 to 6.00
Arborvitae, Pyramidal	4' to 8'	$ 8.00 to 16.00
Canadian Hemlock	18" to 48"	$ 5.00 to 9.00
Arborvitae, Globe	8" to 24"	$ 4.00 to 12.00
Yews, Taxus		
Upright & Spreading	30" to 5'	$18.00 to 30.00
Juniper, Hetzi Blue	36"	$15.00
Juniper, Andorra	18" to 24"	$ 9.00 to 12.00

We reserve the right to limit quantities on all items listed.

Early the following spring I prepared a section of land for a tree nursery. Seedlings of several tree varieties and shrubs were planted. Each year thereafter more varieties were set out in row after row. With twelve to eighteen inches of rich black topsoil it didn't take long for the seedlings to develop into nice sized specimens.

Back at the house our five children were growing by leaps and bounds enjoying the fresh country air. Each one was physically fit and pleasing to the eye. Mary was comfortable in her role as wife and mother; and I was diligent in my responsibilities as husband, father and provider. We concluded that another child would be a blessing and not a burden. In any event, from the very beginning of our married life, we always wanted a large family. Now with five beautiful children why not, if it were the will of God, add a sixth.

DOROTHY Our Sixth Child - And so, on income tax day, April 15th of 1970, Dorothy Ellen was born. Each of the eight chairs around our large round oak kitchen table would now have an occupant.

It was shortly after the birth of our last child that Mary and I came to appreciate, in depth, the words of Joseph Cardinal Mindszenty when he wrote:

*"The Most Important Person on earth is a **MOTHER**. She cannot claim the honor of having built Notre Dame Cathedral. She need not. She has built something more magnificent than any cathedral—a dwelling for an immortal soul, the tiny perfection of her baby's body. The angels have not been blessed with such a grace. They cannot share in God's creative miracle to bring new saints to Heaven. Only a human mother can. Mothers are closer to God the Creator than any other creature. God joins forces with mothers in performing this act of creation. What on God's good earth is more glorious than this: **To be a MOTHER**?"*

Before the end of that 1970 summer, Dorothy joined her brothers and sisters in the backyard pool. How careful they were as they pushed her around in an infant bassinet made especially for water flotation. Often Mary and I would join the frolicking group as they played and swam to their hearts' delight. A favorite of the girls was the "little old tug boat" flotation toy. As they sat on the inflated toy, I pushed them around singing: "Little old tugboat works on the river, little old tugboat works on the bay, here she comes chug chug chug, down the river, down the bay." Around and around we went during those fun filled summer days.

In order to stretch my bank paycheck of eight hundred dollars per month, it was necessary for Mary to be frugal in her budgeting for our family of eight. Jacob Reder, a neighboring farmer, raised beef cattle. Mary arranged to purchase beef in bulk, forty pounds of freshly ground pure beef hamburger meat at sixty cents a pound and forty pounds of fresh cuts of steaks at ninety cents a pound. It was fresh, corn feed, quality beef at bargain bottom prices. Mrs. Marich, a church friend, raised laying hens and sold eggs. She belonged to Our Lady of Consolation church as did we. She often waited for us after church as Mary and I, with our six children in tow, exited the church building. "I've got some cracked eggs for you this morning," she often said as she smiled approvingly at our brood. At twenty cents a dozen, the cracked eggs were a "fresh-from the-hen-house" bargain. Laying hens, whose productive days had ended, were available for chicken soup. At twenty-five cents a pound, they made many excellent chicken soup dinners and chicken salad sandwiches. Bakery products were purchased from area outlet stores. At the supermarket she purchased dry food products and cereal in bulk. The reduced section in the supermarket was always a favorite stop for Mary. If the reduced section did not have what she was looking for, her purse full of coupons helped purchase the necessities at reduced prices. We never were in want of fresh, wholesome food.

Our children's friends marveled that sit down dinners were daily occurrences at the Kapitans. They would often stay over for a meal. Mary said it's not a problem to feed a few more faces. And so it was at many a meal. A favorite lunchtime meal was bologna, cheese and pickle "mini sandwich squares." A slice of bologna and a slice of cheese were placed between two slices of bread. Three sandwiches were made at a time. Each sandwich came out of the toaster oven portioned into four tasty squares. A container of chip dip was placed on the revolving Lazy Susan table center. Batches of those delicious bologna-cheese squares were washed down with glasses full of ice cold Kool-Aid mix. The money we saved by not splurging on fast foods was put away for our annual summer vacation, and that made those tasty hot sandwich snacks even more appetizing.

Not only did Mary excel in getting the best for the least amount of her food money; she also excelled in getting the best for the least amount of money that was set aside for clothing. With a keen eye for sales and coupons, the children's closets and dressers were never empty. They always had a nice selection of comfortable dress wear. The clothing outlet stores were also a source of great savings. Again, money saved by using coupons was put aside for our annual summer vacation. We vacationed somewhere every year and never borrowed a dime for our vacations. Mary and I were of the same frame of mind when it came to our family's annual vacation. We agreed that vacation memories would last our children's life time.

Chapter XV - A Colorado Vacation

That winter as the snow flew around the countryside, we planned for our summer vacation. Lying in front of the crackling fireplace with an atlas on the rug laid out in front of us, we began dreaming of a vacation full of warm summer days. The children leafed through the atlas page after page. They kept coming back to the map of Colorado. Two of the children were studying about the mountain ranges in the United States. Our boys wanted to visit the "Estes Rocket Factory" in Colorado They wanted to visit the factory that produced the toy rockets and parts which they frequently purchased by mail. The map of the Rocky Mountains' terrain looked extremely inviting. The more we examined the map of that unique state, the more it became evident that Colorado was going to be this summer's vacation destiny. "Let's go to the Rocky Mountains," we all said. We closed the atlas, knelt down to say our evening prayers, and it was off to dreamland for the children.

The end of school came before we knew it. We had planned an early June vacation and arrangements had been made to rent a fold down travel trailer to sleep eight. Our nine-passenger station wagon was fitted with a hitch. Mary made curtains for the rear side windows. We planned our route westward with the aid of the Chicago Motor Club. Since the weather in the mountains would be near freezing, we packed the travel trailer with both summer and winter clothes. Every nook and cranny of that travel trailer was packed with all the necessities for a fun vacation. Mary purchased a large package of those new disposable diapers to take along. The cloth diapers would be used when we were at campsites and the disposable diapers would be used as we traveled. What an ingenious and liberating invention those disposable diapers proved to be for a mother who didn't have that luxury with Dorothy's two brothers and three sisters.

Back at work, I discussed our family's vacation plans with fellow workers. Several of my bank colleagues suggested that I have my head examined. "You are going to travel over a thousand miles, pulling a travel trailer and with a station wagon full of children! Why, you must be insane!" they said. "And when you get home, you'll need another vacation," they continued.

We arose early on the day of departure. The three older children sat in the second seat. The third seat was laid flat and a bed was made for the three younger children who were taken from their beds dressed in their pajamas. It was just before five in the morning that our dog Sabu, a spayed female cross between a collie and shepherd, knowingly let out a melancholy howl as we departed the driveway. Grandma and Uncle Tony Kapitan would take care of Sabu during our absence.

The curtains that covered the rear windows of the children's sleeping area filtered the brightness of the rising sun. By the time the children awoke, we were on the banks of the Mississippi River where we enjoyed our first breakfast in our travel trailer. An early morning departure always guaranteed us a head start as we traveled a hundred miles or more before a breakfast stop. It was an uneventful drive as we drove over 400 miles that first day through the flatlands of Illinois and Iowa. We were a weary eightsome as we arrived at our first campground in Council Bluffs, Iowa at the Big Timber KOA. The cost for the campsite was $3.00 for the night.

As I backed into our campsite I remembered the instructions of the trailer storeowner. "If you want the trailer to go to the left, turn your front car wheels to the right. If you want the trailer to go to the right, turn your front car wheels to the left." It was easier said than done. Mary was on one side of the campsite giving directions; Rudy and Mike were on the other side giving directions. One hollered go left and the other hollered go right. I saw the faces of smiling campers at adjoining campsites as I backed up, pulled up, went to the left, then to the right and backed up again! At long last the trailer was where it was supposed to be. How it got there was a surprise to me. The boys unhitched and leveled the trailer. I made myself a stiff Manhattan and sat down to wait for dinner. Meanwhile the girls prepared the outside picnic table and Mary heated stuffed green peppers that she had prepared at home. After supper Mary and I sat outside watching our children running around excitedly, making new friends. We were miles away from home and we were all enjoying our temporary surroundings at the Missouri River. The hooting of owls did not keep us awake on that first night.

Early the next morning we went into town. Mass at the local church was at 8:00 AM. We had located the church and a bakery the night before as we drove into Council Bluffs. To find a Catholic Church for Sunday Mass and a bakery for Sunday morning breakfast, was always a priority on every vacation we took.

On our return to the campsite we enjoyed our usual Sunday morning breakfast of donuts and Danish.   The boys hitched up the trailer, the girls did the few breakfast dishes, and we were off. We stopped for lunch in Mitchell, South Dakota at the Corn Palace, a remarkable structure faced with multi-colored ears of corn. "Visit Wall Drugs," announced roadway signs as we traveled through the "Bad Lands" of South Dakota. It was dusk as we passed the faces of the four presidents looming out of Mt. Rushmore in the Black Hills of South Dakota. The road down the mountain to the campground was perilous, especially so with the weight of the trailer behind the station wagon. I switched the transmission to engage it in second gear. The three hundred and sixty degree winding curves led to narrow bridges and more winding three hundred and sixty-degree curves as we descended the steep grade. "Yoj Millie" shouted our six year old Carol. Mary asked "What did you say Carol?" "Yoj Millie, Yoj Millie, that means I'm scared," Carol answered.[1]   Those of our children who were not petrified enjoyed the challenge of that steeply descending road winding its way to the campground entrance below. We were lucky that there were several unoccupied campsites; no matter the $4.25 fee for the overnight stay.

The kids (ages 13 to 1) Mike, Rudy, Dorothy, Sue, Laura, Carol & Me (age 42) at Mt. Rushmore.

A bright moon shown upon the darkened camp-ground as we drifted off to sleep. The thought of the difficult ascent that awaited us the next morning kept me awake. Breakfast eaten at the base of picturesque Mt. Rushmore was nourish-ment for both body and soul. I began the ascent in first gear. The quiet that prevailed in our vehi-cle was broken only by the sound of the laboring

transmission. There were no "yoj Millies." The children sat in silence; their little minds occupied with the rugged vast-

---

[1] Later in life Millie, coincidentally, would be the first name of Carol's mother-in-law, Millie Sanders.

ness of nature as it unfolded before them. It was onto Mt. Rushmore's observation point. The children looked on in awe experiencing what the older ones had only read about in school.

Ticket prices for the Passion play at Spearfish, S.D. were quite pricey. Thanks to spring tree sales at our home nursery, we were able to buy tickets for all eight of us. We could not have afforded this luxury from my monthly salary. Although I had just been promoted to Vice President, I cleared about a thousand dollars per month. The Passion Play presentation was awesome and well worth the ticket price. We, along with many other spectators, jumped at the thunderclap when Christ died on the cross.

The next morning while driving through Wyoming, en route to the Rocky Mountain National Park, we noticed antelope grazing in the green pastures along with deer. The children began singing a very appropriate song; "Home, home on the range, where the deer and the antelope play...." We pulled over to a diner just outside of Cheyenne for lunch. The older four children sat in one booth, Mary and I and the two younger children sat in an adjoining booth. The waitress was taken by surprise when she learned that we were all together. "These are all your children?" she asked looking at my wife. Mary responded by saying "Yes, and put it all on one bill." We all agreed that the waitress did an exceptional job while serving all eight of us.

Later that afternoon, four days after our Merrillville departure, we arrived at our Rocky Mountain destination. Estes Park Campground would be our home base for the next week or so. Our campground, equipped with a swimming pool, was at the entrance to the Rocky Mountain

National Park. The snow-capped mountains provided a spectacular view as we sat back, swam and relaxed. The campground office was equipped with a candy counter. There were Rocky Mountain candies that were not available back home. One of our children's favorites were "Sioux Chief" candy sticks.

Early the next day we packed a lunch, threw some winter jackets into the station wagon and up into the mountains we went. There, as promised, the children had a snowball fight. How exhilarating it was for the children to romp around in snow during the middle of June. It was a memory they would keep for the rest of their lives and a story to tell their friends back in Indiana.

Pouder Canyon - We read that one of the more spectacular tours was an automobile driving tour of Pouder Canyon. Several days later we set out for Pouder Canyon. As we drove into the north side of the canyon we decided to stop for something cold to drink. We pulled into the parking lot of a soda and ice cream shop. There were picnic tables set outside the store. We sat down to enjoy our ice cream and pop. Dorothy, our fourteen-month-old, began running towards the road. There was quite a drop off where the parking lot met the road. At that moment Mary looked up and saw Dorothy running. She put down her purse and ran to grab Dorothy, just in the nick of time. That was enough excitement for the moment so we all got back into the station wagon and headed into the canyon.

About an hour later, while driving out of the canyon on the south side, we heard a dreadful sound of plop, plop, plop. Yes, the right rear tire went flat. I pulled off the one lane highway onto a very narrow shoulder. We were on the side of a mountain with a precipitous drop off into the rapids below. Fortunately the jeep that was following us stopped. The two men from the jeep saw my predicament, a station wagon full of children and two "shook up" parents. They told me to relax while they changed the flat. "You're lucky mister," they said. "Last week a family of six was driving this road, developed a flat, lost control of their car and fell off into the rapids below. To this day all of the bodies have not been recovered." We "hurried" out of that canyon at an oxymoron "snail pace." I paid no attention to the honking cars behind me. We were all praying the rosary.

The canyon road brought us to the main highway. We passed a tire store. "Great," I said, "this tire store is not far from our campground. I'll get tires here tomorrow." I did not want to use any of the remaining traveler's checks or cash. Mary said that she had brought along a credit card and we could use that. She looked for her purse to confirm the fact that she had the credit card. "My purse,'" she exclaimed, "It's not here! I think I left it on the picnic bench at the soda and ice cream shop when I ran for Dorothy." All of her important papers were in that purse. Her traveler's checks, her cash, her credit card, driver's license, pictures of her deceased parents and on and on. We pulled over to a roadside telephone booth unable to think of the name of that shop where we had stopped earlier that day. "Please, dear Jesus," Mary said, "help us to remember the name of that shop." With that Mike said, "I think the name begins with "Bear."

A Miracle (?) Happens - We opened the telephone directory and found the telephone number for *Bear Rock Soda Shop.* Mary dialed the number and explained her situation. "Lady," the man responded "You were here this morning, left your purse on the table and want me to go outside to see if it's there! There were hundreds of people here today; but I'll go out and check for you." There was a pause that seemed like an eternity. He came back to the phone and said: "You're lucky lady, the purse was where you left it and I have it in front of me. I cannot guarantee that everything will be in it, but I have it." We prayed as we drove back into the canyon not knowing what, if anything, would be left in Mom's purse. We also knew that we were taking a chance by driving into the canyon without a spare tire. We got to the soda shop and Mary jumped out of the station wagon. Moments later she exited the store purse in hand and a big smile on her face. Everything was in the purse; nothing had been taken out during all those hours that it sat out in the open, on a table in the parking lot of that roadside store. Again we experienced another important lesson in life: "The good Lord above hears the prayers of the faithful."

The next day we had a set of new tires installed on our station wagon. Although the station wagon, bought new just two years before, had only twenty eight thousand miles on the odometer, we couldn't risk another flat tire. Our return trip would be over a thousand miles. It was a well-relaxed Kapitan eightsome that began the one thousand plus mile trip homeward. Mary and I decided to leave after sunset. We knew that it would be easier for us to drive through Nebraska while the six children slept.

Danger Lurks on the Nebraska Interstate - Arriving at the Colorado-Nebraska border long about midnight, we switched drivers. The children were fast asleep as we traveled homeward along U. S. #80, a four lane divided highway. Long about three AM we stopped for gas at an all nighter where we again switched drivers. Once we got back on the road we noticed a ratty old pick up truck following right behind us. It seemed that we were the only two vehicles on that dark and lonesome Nebraska road. When we slowed down, he slowed down. When we sped up, he sped up. This vehicle continued to follow us for the next hundred and some miles. Mary was driving and I kept my eye on the movements of that sinister looking pickup truck behind us. Thank God the six children were fast asleep and didn't hear our conversation. We had no means of self protection and we were scared.

It was getting along onto daybreak as we came upon a gas station. "Yea," Mary and I said in unison as we pulled into the station. The ratty old truck slowed down and pulled in after us. Thank God the gas station was open. As the station attendant came to our car the rusty old truck took off. The children began to stir. We stayed at that station for a while and purchased some donuts and milk. We talked to the station attendant about our experience. He offered to call the police. "No," we said, "we will stay here for a while and besides, the traffic out on the road is beginning to pick up." We enjoyed our early morning breakfast with the three older children who had awakened. Checking our campground directory we located the perfect campground for our next stop. It was just an hour away. Before the children could ask, Mary said, "Yes kids, it has a swimming pool!"

When we returned to the road there was a flow of early morning traffic. We never did see that rusty old pick up truck again. At the campground Mary and I went to sleep and instructed the three older children to look after their three younger sisters. There was food and drink in the fridge and we needed some sleep. From this point on the rest of the return trip was uneventful.

Chapter XVI - BACK HOME AGAIN IN INDIANA

Within a month our corn harvest was in full swing again. We were all busy earning money for the next summer's vacation. It wasn't all work and no play. Rudy and Mike spent many summer days experimenting with the rockets they purchased from Estes Industries, a rocket factory we visited while vacationing in Colorado. The boys occasionally let their sisters blast off the rockets when they helped prepare the rockets for launching. That summer vacation was indeed a "blast" for the children.

In the fall our children continued their schooling at SS Peter and Paul School. Both Rudy and Mike were on the grade school football team. What a hard working and dedicated group of boys as they went undefeated, giving their all to win the diocesan championship. Having accomplished this, they were to play St. Victors of Calumet City, the champions in their Illinois diocese. Our family decided to treat the championship football players by having a cook out and bon fire for the team, coaches and parents on our property. Early on the Friday afternoon before game day, eleven-year old Susan was helping prepare for the bon fire. In her eagerness to help she swung an ax to chop out a tree stump. The ax bounced off the wood stump and into the shin bone on her right leg. What a brave girl she was; not a peep came out while the doctor stitched the open wound in her leg. Later that evening she was comforted by some of her sixth grade friends, sisters of the football players. The pep rally concluded with the burning in effigy of a St. Victor football player.

On the following Sunday, a brisk fall afternoon, we

Diocesan Grade School Football Champs

headed out to Gilroy Stadium in Gary where the championship game was to be played. It was a close game but we won. A long awaited and well deserved victory came to our boys. Coach Joe Chester, surrounded by his cheering team of boys, raised the victory trophy high overhead. "It was a hard fought battle," he said, "but we won!" He went on to thank the Kapitan family for hosting the pep rally and for their hospitality. The coach and boys applied themselves by working diligently to achieve victory. We were proud to be a part of this memorable event in the annals of diocesan grade school football.

Two of the Champs (Rudy & Mike) with their father.

Our Own Ice Skating Rink - Winter came and with it came the fulfillment of an idea I had when we moved out to the country. The front lawn provided the perfect spot to build an ice skating rink. A framework of twenty-four-foot long, 2 x 4's were set out. The length of the rink was seventy-two feet and the width was forty-eight feet. I spread a commercial grade of 4-mil plastic onto the area and attached it to the 2x4's by nailing wood laths over all the plastic edges. The entire framework was secured to the ground by pounding eight inch long; "L" shaped metal rods into the ground every eight feet around the entire perimeter. Once the framework was ready I began the chilling task of filling the area with water. Holding the hose I sprayed the ice cold flowing water from side to side. It was a painstaking labor of love.

Although I was bundled up, it didn't take long for the chill to get to my bones. Every hour or so I came into the house and warmed up by sipping on a couple of shots of blackberry brandy. The best "ice making" time came at night when the temperature was generally much colder than during the day. The most effective way to make layers of ice was by spraying a fine mist of water onto the rink area. The colder the temperature the quicker was the freezing capacity of the water. The girls, watching from bedroom windows above, would rap on the glass to get my attention. They would then wave to me and blow an occasional kiss. Their antics made my efforts more than worth while. Also, they helped to keep my mind off the bitter cold.

One Sunday morning after church, while refreshing the top layer of ice on the rink with a fine misty spray, a car pulled into the driveway. Out jumped a man. "My friends and I would like to talk to you," he said. "What about," I replied, as I continued to hold the hose, spraying water from side to side. "We are Jehovah Witnesses. May we talk to you inside the house?" "Talk to me out here," I said. "Not out here" the man replied, "it's too cold." It was a bone chilling two degrees above zero that morning. Needless to say the Jehovah Witness got back into the warmth of his car and drove off. They were not about to freeze their butts off talking to me!

Crack the whip was a favorite game the kids played with their friends while skating on the ice. Hockey was a favorite of the boys. Two goal posts were fabricated by twelve year-old Mike. Teams were chosen from among school friends and neighborhood kids. Games of hockey were played into the early evening under spotlights shining from the house. When the skaters tired they skated over to benches which the boys helped make from 2'x12' planking. After the first basement window was broken, Rudy suggested that we place sections of plywood in front of the basement windows during play. Not a single window was broken after that.

Another winter treat that the kids enjoyed was being pulled on sleds with the farm tractor. Two and sometimes three, sleds were attached to our "Ford 8" as we slid and zigzagged over acres of snow packed terrain. As we went along I looked back at the children every once in a while. It was exhilarating to hear the children's laughter. They sang as they wiped the wind blown snow from their faces. Mother stepped out and called for us to take a break. She had prepared refreshments of hot chocolate and home made chocolate chip cookies. As we walked around in our stocking feet, the heated ceramic tiled kitchen floor was especially soothing to our cold feet. Many a snowy winter day was spent by the children in childhood abandon as they skated and sledded in our part of God's country.

Chapter XVII - Spring In The Country

Living out in the country, each spring gave more meaning to the saying, "Five Acres and Freedom." The last gasps of winter were being stilled by the new life of spring. Along the roadside and in the fields the yellow-green of each branch of the Weeping Willow was the first sign that new life was beginning. Winter bulbs planted in the fall pushed their delicate blossoms upward as they crowned the earth in a rainbow of royal colors. The celebration of new life was not unique just to nature around us. The Catholic Church and the Christian Community joined in the celebration of new life at this beautiful time of the year. Although Vatican II changed some of the methods and manners of the Easter celebration, the more things changed the more they stayed the same. The practice of visiting five churches on Holy Thursday evening and reciting 5 Our Fathers, 5 Hail Marys and 5 Glory Bes for the intention of the Holy Father is a blessed practice which we keep to this very day. The blessing of Easter baskets continues to be another reminder of the glories of Easter. On the more mundane side, Easter Monday remains as "sprinkling day," a day when the boys sprinkle the girls. Custom has it that Roman soldiers were ordered to sprinkle the women who gathered in groups to talk about the resurrected Christ, in order to disperse them.

Our Christmas Tree Farm

Meanwhile, during the spring before Rudy's grade school graduation, I decided to begin a Christmas Tree Farm. Several thousands of evergreen seedlings and transplants were ordered from Nurseries in Pennsylvania and Michigan. The shortest needle Christmas tree, the spruce, was ordered from Pennsylvania, as was the fir, an intermediate needled Christmas tree. Pine seedlings and Pine transplants, the longest needled Christmas trees, were purchased from Michigan Nurseries.

Since the Michigan nurseries were nearby I decided to drive to those nurseries to pick up my orders. So, on a sunny Saturday morning in early April, my two sons Rudy and Mike and I made the first of many trips to Michigan to pick up our Christmas tree nursery stock. A delightful scent filled our station wagon, jam-packed with evergreen seedlings. The scent was reminiscent of the many fragrances of Christmas. As we drove homeward we felt like the Three Kings in the Christmas story. We envisioned Christmas tree shoppers with their children romping through our acreage ornamented with full-grown Christmas trees. Christmas songs came easily. "We Three Kings of Orient Are" was sung as: "We three Kapitans of Merrillville are, bringing trees from Michigan afar, over interstates we traveled afar, following yonder star. Oh oh fields of wonder, fields of trees, what a wonder you will be, as you grow to be full grown Christmas trees."

Within seven years some of those seedlings were ready for harvest. Signs out on the road proclaimed "*Christmas Trees -Choose & Cut your own.*" There was a second sign, which the sign painter painted in jest. It said "*Christmas Trees - You May Cut yourself.*" What I had envisioned years before while driving from

Scene of Christmas tree farm

Michigan with a station wagon full of Christmas trees seedlings had come to fruition. Happy families romped through "Grandpa Rudy's Christmas Tree Farm" looking for the perfect Yuletide tree. Mothers aimed their cameras to capture the rapture of fathers and children as they cut down the tree of their choice. Many a tailgate celebration followed with Christmas cookies and hot chocolate, as car radios filled the air with Christmas music.

One Saturday morning in mid December, a young couple, husband, wife and two girls, ages six and eight, came to choose and cut their tree. They seemed to be no different from other couples who came that day. The wife got out of the car, as did the girls. The husband opened his window and waved as his family headed for the field of Christmas trees. "Is it O.K. for me to stay in the car?" the young man asked haltingly. "Go with them," I said. "I can't," the man replied. "I've got M.S. and I cannot get around very well."

It was customary for me to haul the customer's cut trees from the field in a six-foot wagon. The wagon was attached to my John Deer 345, a small but powerful tractor. Since the wagon was empty. I encouraged the young man to get into the wagon and I would take him out to the field. I helped him out of his vehicle and into the wagon. In no time at all we caught up with his family. The girls shouted, "Goodie, goodie, here comes Daddy." The wife broke out into a great big smile as she heard him say excitedly, "I'm going to be able to help pick out our Christmas tree." The girls took pictures of their tearful parents next to the Christmas tree of their choice. The mother took pictures of the smiling girls and their joyful Dad as they rode merrily out of the field with the husband holding the tree lying in the wagon. The young man couldn't thank me enough. Tears streamed from the eyes of that young mother as she gave me a great big Christmas hug. "Merry Christmas" we said to each other as they drove off. That whole Christmas season of selling Christmas trees was worth that one thought provoking experience.

Our First Grade School Graduation - It was in the spring of 1972 that Rudy, our eldest, was preparing to graduate from the eighth grade at SS. Peter & Paul school. One day in early May he brought home an envelope. The letter was from the pastor Monsignor Senderak. In it he called our attention to the fact that we had been paying the "parishioners tuition rate" for our four children. That being the case, as non-parishioners, we owed SS. Peter & Paul some fifteen hundred dollars for that school year. The letter stated that payment was to be made before our son Rudy's graduation.

We asked for an appointment to speak with Monsignor Senderak. An appointment was granted and we went to the rectory. Mary began by stating that Father Wozniak, our pastor at Our Lady of Consolation Church, had made those tuition payment arrangements with approval of Father Beckman. The Monsignor would not hear of that. "You have the tuition bill and I expect payment in full." Mary reminded the monsignor that she volunteered many hours of her time as room mother, Volleyball coach, worker at many of the school's fund raisers, etc, etc., all *gratis*. Her comments were falling on deaf ears. We mentioned that it would be impossible for us to pay the one thousand-five hundred-dollar tuition bill as demanded. There were several reasons; lack of income was one and the fact that we were raising six children on one salary was another. I suggested that I would sign notes with interest to pay for our children's Catholic education. We were not a family to ask for dole outs, nor would we accept them. We always were, and would continue to be, a responsible family paying our way. Monsignor asked, "Where do you work?" I said "at a bank." "When do you get home?" he continued. "At about six," I replied. "Well then, why don't you stop by the school after work and perhaps you can work off your children's tuition by doing some janitorial work like cleaning the latrines and scrubbing floors."

I was in total disbelief of what Monsignor had asked me to do. I said, "When I get home after a long days work, my

Posing for a First day at school photo: Mike & Rudy, Dorothy, Sue, Carol and Laura.

children need me and we spend quality time together." "Then, if you cannot afford the tuition" the Monsignor said, "take your children out of this school and put them into the public school. <u>They will get just as good of an education there as they get here</u>." Mary and I couldn't believe what we heard. His statements shocked us. I reminded the Monsignor that our parents were obligated to send us to a Catholic school <u>under the pain of mortal sin</u>!

We told him that we felt a moral obligation to have our children educated in the only Catholic School in Merrillville. Whatever Mary and I said made no difference to him. We were exasperated as we concluded our visit. I told the good Monsignor that he should clean his own toilets instead of going golfing! With that we left in a state of shock as to what had transpired at the rectory that night!!

As we drove homeward Mary and I agreed that we would not allow the Monsignor's attitude and his lack of charity and understanding to dampen our resolve to remain steadfast in our faith. Despite the hurt inflicted by so uncharitable a priest, the faith of our fathers would remain firmly planted in our hearts. After all, he was a man who put his pants on the same way I did. We would not allow him to impact negatively on our faith. Rather than losing our faith, it became firmer. We learned how to respond positively as another of life's valuable lessons was presented to us. We took what could have been a spiritual tragedy and transformed it into a triumph. The depth of our Catholic faith came to mean much more to us than the words and actions of that impudent priest. We were being tested and, thank God, we passed the test.

Rudy graduated without further incident. In the year that followed, we paid the full-parishioner tuition rate for two of our children who were left by us to continue their education at Sts Peter and Paul School. Michael was to graduate from the eighth grade and Carol was to make her First Holy Communion that year with her second grade classmates. We did not want to disrupt what was to be so important for Mike and Carol.

Catholic Grade School Education Continues - In the years to follow our girls attended St. Michael's Byzantine School. Here is how that happened. One "fish fry Friday," Mary spoke to Father Michael Evanick, pastor of St. Michaels, about our predicament. She stressed our resolve to see that our children receive a Catholic grade school education. What a blessing when he informed her that the tuition at St. Michael's School would be One Hundred Dollars per child per year. Father Evanick was a godsend in our time of trial. Because of his generosity we were able to fulfill what we considered to be our grave moral obligation to have our children educated in a Catholic grade school. Mary continued to be untiring in her efforts as she volunteered her time in promoting the causes of St. Michael's Byzantine School. Her donation of time and talent at school functions and at their Friday pirohy dinners, did not go unnoticed and unappreciated by Father Evanick.

It was at St. Michael's that a classroom discussion was held on the feast of St. Nicholas. Sister Mildred, the second grade teacher, asked the children to talk about St. Nicholas. When it was our youngest child's turn, Dorothy told the class that she and her two brothers and three sisters all put a pair of shoes by the fireplace on the night before the feast of Saint Nicholas. The next morning the shoes were filled with all kinds of goodies. There was candy, nuts, gum, cookies and a box of each child's favorite breakfast cereal. Dorothy continued that this year was extra special for her because she found a fifty-dollar bill in one of her shoes.

Dorothy's teacher, Sister Mildred, called our house after school that day to tell us that Dorothy had made up a story about a fifty-dollar bill that St. Nicholas brought her. "She told the truth," Mary said, "all the children get money from St. Nicholas to buy Christmas presents for each other. The younger children get more because they are too young to earn any." As Sister hung up she apologized for doubting Dorothy's story about St. Nicholas.

Chapter XVIII - Our Celebration
Of Christmas

Christmas was just around the corner. Our children were anxious to get started on the house decorations. A large manger scene was set out on the front lawn. Carol noticed that "Gloria" was missing and she asked about her. "What do you mean Gloria?" I asked. "The angel above the manger scene is missing," she said. "Isn't her name Gloria?" Carol thought that the "Gloria Banner" above the angel's head indicated the name of that angel! To this day Carol gets chided about "Gloria."

To complete the outdoor Nativity set we placed a steel-plated star, studded with lights, high up in an elm tree just above the nativity set. Laura loved to climb that tree and was quick to ask if she could take the star to the top of the tree. That star was visible for several miles around. The exterior of the house was bedecked with hundreds of Christmas lights. Inside Mary and the girls were baking ethnic Christmas delicacies. We all helped decorate the tree that ascended to the very top of the living room's ten-foot tall cathedral ceiling. The ornaments were hung with great care including several from Mary's childhood. Those favorites were positioned on the tree so that they were immediately visible.

On Christmas Eve, just before we left for a *Vilia* dinner (Christmas Eve Dinner) at Grandma Kapitan's house, the youngest girls set a plate of cookies and a glass of milk by the fireplace for Santa. We all piled into the station wagon for the trip to Grandma's house. Invariably I had to return to the house having forgotten something. The children and Mary remained in the car while I came in to check on Santa's cookies. It didn't take but a few minutes to make all the necessary arrangements to complete Santa's visit. I returned to the car and off we drove to Grandma's house.

Chapter XIX - Children's Antics In And Out of School

Children's Educational Aids - As the children returned to school after the Christmas holidays, Mary's knack at forming educational aids helped the kids remember certain facts. Many an educational aid was discussed during those holidays. For instance, an easy way to remember the names and positions of the planets was: M-VEM-J-SUN-P (Mercury Venus, Earth, Mars, Jupiter, Saturn, Uranus Neptune and Pluto). Another memory aid, remembered from her own grade school days, was a way to remember the names of the Great Lakes It was HOMES, an acronym for the names of the Great Lakes: Huron, Ontario, Michigan, Erie and Superior. The names of musical notes on lines and spaces were: All-Cows-Eat-Grass (A,C,E,G) and Every Good Boy Does Fine (E,G,B,D,F).

The Funny Things Children Will Say And Do - It was not uncommon for our children to come up with some real gems. One day after school Rudy, a first grader at the time, was excited about a new word Sister had taught them that day. The word was "tavern-apple." Mary asked him to repeat the word thinking she didn't hear him correctly. Again, he said "tavern-apple." She asked him to use the word in a sentence. He said, "Jesus lives in the tavern-apple." "Rudy," his mom said with a smile on her face, "it's tabernacle, not tavern-apple."

While living in Whiting our neighbors on Laporte Avenue were the Smiths. Susan, at age three, always referred to Mrs. Smith as "Sissy Miss."

One Sunday morning on exiting the church, our Pastor, Father Wozniak, an avid Chicago Bear fan, greeted us with the words "Pray for the Bears, pray for the Bears." Our five year old daughter Carol said, "I'm going to pray for the other animals in the zoo."

Our ten-year-old son Mike came home from school one day with the "golden rule" as interpreted by one of his schoolmates. It went like this: "<u>Do one to others before they do one to you</u>."

In church one Sunday morning "clap your hands and shout with joy" was a phrase repeated several times. At the third repetition of "Clap your hands," our attentive four-year-old Carol did exactly that. She clapped her hands! It was five year old Carol who often talked about her "imaginary" friend Mary Johnson. Once while returning from kindergarten with Carol, Mary stopped the car as she pulled up in front of a strange house. "Mary Johnson lives here'" she said to Carol. "Would you like to go and visit with her?" Carol whimpered saying that she does not live in this house. Mary insisted that Carol visit her friend Mary Johnson. When Mary noticed that Carol was quite overcome she stopped her kidding and they drove home. Carol never mentioned the name Mary Johnson again. Susan remembered certain Slovak phrases by Anglicizing them. For instance she said *dobru noc* (the Slovak for "good night") as "double nuts." Another phrase with which she had fun was *na zdravia* (a Slovak toast to "good health") was said by her as "nice driveway!"

One day while Laura and Dorothy were playing a "hiding" game, Laura was having a difficult time finding the object hidden by Dorothy. She asked Dorothy for a hint. Dorothy responded by saying that the hidden object could be found by the "V trees." Laura asked, "Where are the V trees?" "Right next to the 'U' trees," was Dorothy's response. In our tree nursery there was a row of Yews.

Our four-year-old Dorothy knew her alphabet very well and assumed correctly that V comes after U! So, in her four-year-old mind the row of trees next to the yews had to be, what else, but a row of "V" trees.

Music Lessons - As our children grew; each was involved with learning how to play a musical instrument. Rudy was first as he learned how to play the trumpet. My Mother's eyes glistened as we listened to a Christmas musical presented by the gradeschool CYO band. The trumpets had a special arrangement along with the drums during "Drummer Boy." Grandma Kapitan paid special attention to her grandson Rudy as he played his little heart out! A favorite of ours, from that Christmas musical, was "Hey Jude." Many a day Rudy could be heard whistling "Hey Jude." Rudy loved to whistle.

Michael who took organ lessons played many a festive arrangement on our Hammond organ. He loved to play, especially during the Christmas season. Susan took clarinet lessons and also performed in the children's CYO band. Her grandmother Kapitan couldn't praise her enough for her excellent performances. She called her "*moja krasna dalka*" (my beautiful doll).

Carol, Laura and Dorothy took guitar lessons. On Mondays and Wednesday, as soon as I got home from work, I drove the three of them to the Sherwood School of music. The lessons lasted a half-hour for each daughter. Generally I spent the hour and a half of wait time reading that day's newspaper. We were a hungry foursome as we sat down to a late homemade supper which Mary kept hot for us even though it was some two hours later than usual.

Children's Pets - There was ample opportunity for our children to have their very own pets since we lived out in the country. Rudy and Mike had ducks and Doberman dogs. Susan had a pony called "Thunder." Carol had

Siamese cats named "Kiki" & "Maitai." Laura had rabbits and Dorothy had fish. Each took on the responsibility of caring for their pets. Along with that responsibility came an opportunity for some to make money. Carol's Siamese cats, for example, produced some valuable litters. With the kitten sale proceeds Carol not only paid for all the cat food and cat litter, but she also had spending money for vacations. Our children learned about the responsibility of caring, albeit it for an animal, at a very early age. They too were learning that life's pleasures can be had by diligent application and effort.

Fire Flies - The kids also had fun earning money by catching fire flies. One summer a fire fly promotion was aired on the radio announcing that a Chicago firm would make payment for fire flies at a penny apiece. As daylight ebbed away and darkness fell, the flashing lights of thousands of fireflies lit the entire countryside. It looked as though a sea of thousands of miniature stars had fallen to earth. Mary and I sat in lawn chairs marveling at the children's firefly romp. It warmed our hearts to watch their agility as they jumped and chased around grabbing those luminous wonders of the night. Each child had a pint sized glass jar with a "full of holes" lid cover. When the glass jars were filled, they were emptied into plastic zippered bags two hundred to a bag. Since the instructions were to freeze those little buggers, the bags of fireflies were placed in the freezer. At redemption time the kids collected over sixty-five dollars for the six thousand and some fireflies collected to promote a scientific experiment. Apart from the financial rewards that they received, they were happy to be part of a scientific experiment.

Other Flying Insects - While on the subject of flying

insects an interesting incident happened. Luther Kilbourne, a bank customer of mine, spoke of his sadness at being asked to "get rid of" his two hives of honeybees. He lived within the city limits of Hammond where the keeping of beehives was prohibited. Knowing that I had some acreage out in the country and that I had planted fruit trees, he explained the benefits of bees and asked if I wanted them. He offered to teach me the ropes about the honeybees. Luther brought the two hives and set them out in the tree nursery near my south property line. He explained that two hives might very well develop into a miniature apiary. Before long there would be more than enough honey for family and friends. Also, the bees would be of tremendous benefit, as they would pollinate the nursery trees and especially the fruit trees. I was excited about the prospects of an apiary

One day while at work, Mary called to say that hundreds of bees were flying all over the back yard. "The children," she said, "left their merry-go-ground and swings and came running into the house. What am I to do" Mary asked, "with all those bees buzzing around?" Hurriedly I called Luther Kilbourne, the bee expert. In a few minutes I was back on the phone with Mary giving her instructions. Luther said to take pots and pans and go outside and beat the heck out of them with big spoons, make as much noise as you can. The noise will cause the bees to settle down. The swarm did settle down on the lower branch of a nearby Birch tree. Luther came and gently shook off the swarming bees onto a white sheet that he had spread on the ground, under the tree. Finding the queen bee he placed her into the spare beehive he had brought with him. The swarming bees followed the queen into the beehive. This all happened without incident to the cheers of the watching children.

Another interesting bug story is one that involves the birch bore. Several White Birch trees became infected with the birch bore. I cut them down and cut the trunks into fireplace size logs. There was about a cord of these elegant looking logs set outside the garage. There they sat all summer long as they cured to make the perfect fireplace log. One cold morning before going to work I brought in several arms full of those interesting white logs and set them in the holder next to the living room fireplace. It was a picture perfect fireplace scene.

Later that morning as Mary prepared to place several of those logs into the blazing fireplace she noticed bugs crawling around the pile of logs. On closer inspection she noticed that they were crawling all over the twenty feet of living room window wall. She was quite beside herself and didn't know what kind of bugs they were nor did she know how to get rid of them. I received a less than calm telephone call from my wife. My secretary interrupted a telephone conversation I was having with a client saying that my wife needs to talk to me immediately. Once she explained that the bugs were crawling all over the living room windows, it became apparent to me as to what kind of bugs they were. They were birch bores whose dormancy had been interrupted by the warmth of the house and they were looking to get outside. So, they were all over the windows. I suggested that she immediately take all those white birch logs outside. She did and then she killed and vacuumed the bugs and washed the windows. Those fashionable logs were placed on the outside burn pile and destroyed.

Of Interest - An interesting name assignment came when Mary and the three younger girls joined the "Indian

Maidens." They were asked to pick a word from nature and develop it into names for themselves. "Water" was the word chosen by our girls. Mother became "Sparkling Water," Carol became "Laughing Water," Laura was "Still Water" and Dorothy was "Bubbling Water." Today, some twenty five years later, two of our daughters belong to the Indian Maidens with their daughters. In fact, Carol Kapitan Sanders is the Nation Chief of 14 tribes! Dressed in regal Indian head gear, with colorful feathers from head to toe, she is the perfect picture of a Chief of many nations. This sure is evidence that we gravitate towards those good and fun things of our childhood and tend to repeat them with our own children.

Our children were an active bunch. Besides the Indian Maidens they participated in all kinds of school sports. There was the Little League and Cub Scouts, Brownies, Girl Scouts and Pom Poms and the CYO band and all those music lessons. Church activities and school plays and choral groups all helped to develop personality traits that would serve them well in their adulthood.

Dorothy, Laura & Carol as Indian Maidens and Sue as a Merrillville H.S. Pom-Pom Girl.

Chapter XX - Mary's Inheritance

Our Travel Trailer - It was in 1973 that Mary received her portion of the inheritance from her Dad's estate. Pa died in 1969 and it took over three long years for the estate to settle. Meanwhile the income producing assets continued to produce an income all of which became part of the estate assets subject to attorney fees. The more income generated by the estate assets, the higher would be the attorney fees. Had the estate been settled in six months to a year, as it very well could have, the attorney fees would have been about a third of what they ended up being. One of those blood-sucking attorneys is still alive today, more than likely doing now what he did back then and probably doing it better. The attorney's estate distribution cover letter dated just before Christmas made it sound as though it were his assets that he was distributing as though he were Santa Claus. In retrospect I recall that he was the same attorney who refused to pay a solitary dime for his cup of coffee at a morning "coffee counter" meeting we had regarding the estate. Rather than making a scene, I paid for it.

Disney Land Vacation - With a portion of Mary's inheritance we purchased a 22 foot, eight sleeper, 1973

Wilderness Travel Trailer. We so enjoyed the camper which we had rented for our Colorado vacation a year earlier that we decided to buy one. The first use of our Wilderness was that

Rudy and Laura getting travel trailer ready for (1975) Disney World Vacation. '

188

very same year as we traveled to New York and points east. The following year our annual vacation found us in Disney Land in Florida. Camp Wilderness was our campground located right on the premises of Disney Land. Travel from the campground to the attractions was by monorail or streetcar, or by walking if you wished. Rudy, Mike and Sue went their way seeking more mature attractions while Mary and I took Carol, Laura and Dorothy to kiddy attractions.

The cost of theme park food was prohibitive. Mary made sandwiches, put them in a cooler on the kiddy stroller and took along an empty plastic bottle and packets of "Kool Aid" mix. When we got

Our Family at Disney World Campground - Fort Wilderness.

thirsty the Kool Aid powder was poured into the plastic bottle which we then filled with cool water from a drinking fountain. Presto, we had glasses of delicious fruit flavored drink. When we got hungry, we sat down to a feast of delicious homemade sandwiches that Mary made earlier to each child's specific order. For what it would have cost to feed just one child, we "fed 'em all and we fed 'em to their heart's content." What a delight to see such enjoyment on the children's faces as we strolled through the theme park for three breathtaking days. We enjoyed as many attractions as time permitted. The kids marveled at the animations, which were beyond description. "It's a small world after all, it's a small world after all, it's a small, small world. It's a world of fun, it's a world of ...." was a song which the children sang with all the childish gusto they could muster up. That was the song the kids sang often as we were returning from our Disney vacation.

Southern Indiana - A Geode Haven - On our last stop homeward we camped at a campsite in southern Indiana. There, next to us was a Florida plated travel trailer and car. That campsite was occupied by a mother and son who had traveled from Florida to southern Indiana for a vacation. We told them we had done just the opposite. We couldn't understand how there could be anything so interesting in Indiana. The mother explained that her son was a Geology major and that southern Indiana was loaded with caves full of age old stalagmites and stalactites. It also was a paradise for geode exploration, she explained. How interesting it was to learn about our state from Floridians. We vowed to come to southern Indiana on our second summer vacation in August of that year.

Later that summer, thanks to the "Floridians" whom we had met earlier, we returned to southern Indiana to do some rock hunting and cave explorations. We experienced breath taking scenes as we explored two nationally prominent caves right here in our very own state. The formations in Wyandot cave and Marengo Cave were sensational. The deeper we got into the caves the more splendorous they became. We stood there in awe gazing at the magnificence of God's creation! How could we, living in this state for all these years, not have heard of these wonders!

We stopped at a geode shop to ask for directions as to where geodes might be found. The shop owner gave us directions, all right! Why should a seller of geodes want us to know where to find the kind of rocks he was selling? We went south for a mile to a dirt road. There, according to his directions, we turned left. The dirt road wound around for over a mile until it ended in a wooded area with no exit. We should have known better. We had been led up a blind alley

Returning to the black top road, we drove past the geode shop and I believe the children thumbed their noses at the shop owner who sat in a rocking chair in front of his dilapidated shop. Just up the road was a gas station where we inquired about geode locations. The attendant directed us to a dried up riverbed, which was nearby. "Eureka," I exclaimed, as I lifted a cauliflower look-a-like geode from the hardened clay of that dried up riverbed. It didn't take long for us to fill several bushels of those fascinating rocks that had been formed eons ago.

We returned to our campground with our treasure, anxious to get home and anxious to share the exciting news with family and friends. When we returned home, I immediately called my mother. I told her how excited we were about bringing home five hundred pounds of rocks from southern Indiana. *"Čo, či si rozum stratil muoj syn,"* (What, did you lose your mind, my son) she said. *"Prečo ste urobili taku sprostu vec?"* (Why did you do such a stupid thing?) She continued. I assured her that she would change her mind once she saw the formations inside one of those rocks. She did change her mind and even complimented us on our find of those "geodsky" as she affectionately called them.

Chapter XXI - Some Milestones

Kids **Learn To Drive** - The following year was an exciting year for the Kapitan children. Rudy, the eldest, got his beginner's permit for driving a car. Freedom time was just around the corner for the Kapitan kids. In rapid succession Mike would be next and the following year it would be Sue's turn, and so on and on and on. Rudy was a quick learner, and it wasn't long after that he graduated from the "Alvarez Driver's Training School." He wanted to learn how to drive a "stick-shift," something not available at the driver's training school. So, his Mother, an excellent stick-shift driver, helped him. She took him to a nearby cemetery where she explained the intricacies of "stick-shifting." It was at the cemetery where traffic was almost nonexistent that Rudy and Mike and Sue and Carol and Laura and Dorothy all learned how to "stick-shift" from their mother.

High School Graduation - Then came our family's first high school graduation. There were over five hundred in the 1976 Merrillville High School graduation class. Mary and I sat teary-eyed as the graduates came marching into the auditorium to the tune of "Pomp and Circumstance." We were one set of very proud parents as we watched a smiling Rudy march past us, all grown up and dressed up in his purple cap and gown. This was the first of many milestones for the parents of six talented and beautiful children.

A Big Hurt For Laura - The following year was especially trying for our daughter Laura. In April of 1977, she broke her femur and was in a body cast for three months. While Mary and I were attending a Calumet College of St. Joseph's fundraiser at the Martinique in

Chicago, we received a long distance telephone call to hurry home; one of our children had been hurt and taken to the hospital. As I sped homeward on the expressway, Mary and I prayed for something for which we had never prayed before. We prayed that we be stopped by a policeman, but that didn't happen. On our arrival we learned that Laura fell off her bike as it entered a rut alongside our driveway. Rudy picked her up, brought her indoors and laid her on the living room couch. Unable to reach us, they called my brother Ambrose, a police captain in Whiting. In a matter of minutes he was at Laura's side with my brother Tony. Laura's femur bone was broken completely and it was plain to see that the broken bone was overlapping.

The paramedics were called. One look and they knew that it would be necessary to adjust the broken femur. So that Laura would not bite off her tongue, the paramedics placed a one-inch thick piece of wood into her mouth and told her to bite down on it. Uncle Ambrose held one of Laura's hands and Uncle Tony held the other. Laura screamed as the broken bone was adjusted. She was then whisked away to the hospital. Ambrose jumped into the ambulance and went with her. She needed an adult's permission to be admitted to the hospital, and in our absence, Ambrose would sign her in. Tony stayed behind to comfort the rest of the kids.

Meanwhile, as if all this excitement was not enough, our seventeen-year-old daughter Sue had an automobile accident. She was returning from Pom Pom practice and was run off the road by an unknown driver. Thank God she was not seriously injured even though the car was totaled.

The following morning, Dr. Bicahlo, a bone surgeon,

Laura in full body-cast posing with friend and sister Dorothy

used a hand drill to drill a hole just below Laura's knee. A metal pin was inserted. Weights and pulleys were attached to complete the traction apparatus. X rays were taken daily and additional weights were added to pull down on the broken bone. Laura lay in her hospital bed in traction for one month. While at the hospital her sister Carol brought Laura her homework from St. Michael's School. Despite her absence from school during the last months of that school year, Laura finished at the very top of her class. When the break was back in place, Laura was placed in a full body cast and was released from the hospital.

At long last we brought Laura home. Being in a full body cast we procured a hospital bed for her. We placed the bed in the living room next to the twenty-foot window wall of that room. Laura wanted to be up in the living room so that she could watch her brothers and sisters at play in the back yard. From that vantage point she also had an excellent view of her brothers and sisters swimming in the pool down below her.

There was a spiritual highlight for Laura during her disability. It was a special visit from Father Louis Gelhaus, C.PP.S., a friend of mine from seminary days. On one of his visits we all sat around her hospital bed laughing and playing games. Having spent time as a hospital chaplain, Father Lou knew how to ease the sufferings of the bed ridden, especially children. He asked Laura if she would like to go to Confession and then receive Holy Communion. Laura was overjoyed and arrangements were made for a very spiritual visit. Laura went to confession and received Holy Communion on the very next day, which was the "First Friday" of that month. Thanks to Fr. Gelhaus that was a special day not only for Laura but also for all of us. We concluded that very special day with Father Lou's favorite dinner, Mary's famous "filled steak." It was a special dinner prepared by Mary for many of my priest friends from seminary days.[1]

[1] The recipe can be found in the Addendum on page 309

Chapter XXII - Kapitan Motors - Our Corporation

In the year that followed, Mary who had given birth to our six children, gave life to yet another entity. She drove to Indianapolis, our State Capitol, bringing with her all the legal papers necessary to form a corporation. On October 15, 1978, Kapitan Motors, Inc., came into existence. Our eldest son, Rudy had an affinity for automobiles and wanted to be involved in the sale of cars. We purchased an abandoned Phillip's gas station in the Ranburn Woods section of unincorporated Calumet Township, and opened shop. Mary became the President, Rudy the Vice President and I was the Chairman of the Board.

As with any new venture, it takes time to become recognized as a business worth patronizing. To minimize our expenses, Rudy and Mary took no salaries during the entire first year. Rudy continued his day job at Inland Steel Company. A sign at 4085 Cleveland St. read: "If you see what you like, call 769-2257." That was our home phone number. When called upon, Mary would leave her household tasks and make the ten-minute drive to our lot. She became quite adept at selling cars and preparing all the necessary paper work.

Before the end of the second year in business, Rudy wrote this letter to his supervisor at Inland Steel Company announcing his retirement from the mill: The car business was showing profits sufficient to justify a payroll. So, Rudy came aboard full time. The business increased by leaps and bounds. We began financing car purchases for customers who were unable to get conventional financing. In fulfilling this need, Kapitan Motors, Inc., gained recognizable prominence in the community. We were not only pro-

INLAND STEEL COMPANY
INDIANA HARBOR WORKS

DAILY MECHANICAL REPORT   28" Mill   DEPARTMENT
Crane Repair.   Feb. 17, 1980

To Herb Kruzan,

I wish to retire from this mill in good keeping & standing on my records. Therefore I am giving you fair notice, so you can get someone to replace me. My last working day will be Wednesday Feb. 27, 80.

Todays date: Feb. 17

Termination date: Feb. 27

Rudy J. Kapitan
#7159

MECHANICAL SPARES USED

QUANTITY	DESCRIPTION	BLUE PRINT	WHERE USED	STORAGE LOCATION

Foreman

NOTE—Reports should cover all Mechanical Delays, complete information regarding Pinions, Boxes, Spindles, Bearings, Metallic Packings, Materials Being Tested, and all information of special interest.

A written notice of retirement by a conscientious 22 year old.

viding transportation for the underprivileged but we were helping them to reestablish their credit.

The City of Gary was promoting a "hire a disadvantaged youth program." Kapitan Motors, Inc., decided to become a part of that program. After all, we were a responsible member of the Ranburn Woods-Glenn Park business community. The City sent a young man to apply for an auto mechanics job. His interview was successful and he was hired. Rudy checked his toolbox and found it to be presentable. Shortly thereafter Rudy sold a seven year-old Buick to a friend of his. The car was sold as is and shown. "The check engine light came on by the time I got home" explained the frustrated customer. "I know that I bought the car as is and shown," he continued. Rudy said to bring it back and we would correct it. After all we ran a respectable shop and our policy was to do whatever it takes to satisfy the customer. After all, our motto was, "We'll steer you right!"

The newly hired mechanic corrected it all right. He corrected the problem by pasting black electricians tape across the "check engine" light on the dash. The newly hired "disadvantaged youth" was fired. He applied for unemployment compensation and got it despite our protest. As a result the unemployment rate was increased for our entire payroll. That experience, needless to say, prompted us to exit that program. Our business was succeeding because of satisfied customers and we wanted to keep it that way. We didn't need incompetent workers to play havoc with our efforts to succeed.

On our fifth anniversary in business, Rudy and I set a five year sales goal for our business. The goal was to sell one million dollars worth of cars in a year. At that time the average sales price of a car was about $2500.00 to $3,000.00, and our sales for that fifth year were $330,000.00. Was our goal attainable? Were we dreamers to think that we could triple our sales in five short years? Would we ever achieve that lofty goal? "Well," we both said, "time will tell." And Rudy added his favorite saying, "Being the good Lord willing!"

As we increased our sales, each year was more successful than the preceding one. During one of those years Rudy convinced me that we should purchase a

Rudy & his Porsche

Mary and her "Vette"

Porsche. "It would add prestige to our operation," he said. In retrospect I was happy that I agreed to the purchase of that toy. It became his pride and joy. Rudy was shooting for the stars. His next dream was for his Mom and Dad to own a Rolls Royce. In the meantime, to make do, he purchased a sporty Corvette for his Mother. We were coming to the top of the mountain. It would all be down hill from this point on!

Chapter XXIII - Family Vacation Participation Diminishes

As the children grew into their teen years they no longer wanted to go on family vacations. They wanted to do their own things, and we encouraged their independence by not trying to convince them otherwise. One thing for sure, was the "life instructions" they received at this time especially from their Mother: "Boys keep your zippers zipped and girls keep your blouses buttoned." We further made them aware that whatever they did as individuals would reflect on the family. The kids were receptive and our admonitions were well taken. Again, we were blessed.

On our 1981 summer vacation we had more than enough room in our Wilderness travel trailer as we traveled to California with just the three younger children. It was to be a more relaxed vacation in comparison to earlier ones with six children aboard, well almost. Going westward we traveled a southern route through Oklahoma, Texas, New Mexico and Arizona. On our return we planned a northern route which would take us through Utah on our way to Yellowstone and Grand Teton National Parks in Wyoming.

A Miracle? - On our return from that California vacation, our first stop in Utah was the Bryce Canyon National Park. We were in awe as we drove along the canyon roads paying little attention to the gas tank gauge. The drive along the scenic canyon route brought us out to a two-lane highway, just as we had planned. Once on that highway we headed north towards Salt Lake City. We were miles away from any major highway when I noticed that the gas gauge registered just above empty. Mary checked the map for the next city and estimated its' distance at about twenty miles. We had at least two gallons of gas left and at twelve miles to a gallon would just make it to that city. As we approached the exit for that city, we found that it was closed and our gas gauge read empty! We were on a desolate Utah highway, in no-mans-land!

We pulled off onto the shoulder, turned off the engine to conserve fuel, and waited for traffic to come. We waited for some thirty minutes to no avail. There was no traffic on that godforsaken road. We were in the wilds of Utah and the sun would be setting in about three hours. We knew not what kind of human evil might lurk out there or what kinds of wild beasts roamed there at night. We huddled mustering up all the brainpower that we could. Should we unhitch the trailer and try to make it to the next town? We would get farther without the trailer. How safe would an unoccupied trailer be out there? Perhaps I could stay in the unhitched trailer and Mary and the girls could drive on to get help. We rechecked the map. There should have been a town where we were and there was none. The map showed the next town to be about twenty miles away. Would there be a town there?

We decided to stay together, leave the trailer hitched to the car and go for the next town powered by prayer. In order to conserve on whatever fuel was left, we turned off the air conditioning and opened the car windows. It was hot and stuffy on that parched and desolate road. We pulled out a rosary and began to pray. We decided to say the Glorious Mysteries of the rosary. By the end of the first decade our lips were dry and our voices began to quiver. Towards the end of the fifth decade, "The Coronation of the Blessed Virgin Mary as Queen of Heaven," our voices were barely audible. We finished the rosary and then there was complete silence in the station wagon. Not a sound, not even the sound of another automobile! Our hearts were racing when all of a sudden a church steeple appeared on the distant horizon. As we chugged along, the church steeple came closer and closer and the gas gauge registered empty, empty, empty!

A road sign ahead said exit open. "Our prayers were answered," shouted the girls. As we arrived at the exit we proceeded very cautiously not knowing what awaited us. There right next to the church was a gasoline station. The girls burst into tears as Mary and I let out a sigh of relief. Our prayers had been answered. We filled our **twenty-one gallon** capacity gas tank with **twenty-two gallons** of gasoline! We were unanimous in our thanksgiving to the Blessed Mother for the "free gas" that she gave us. It was a miracle! How else could we have driven over twenty miles, and pulling a trailer on top of that, without any gas? The station attendant directed us to a nearby campground where we arrived in total exhaustion.

The rest of that vacation went as planned other than for the minor inconvenience of a punctured gas tank! Our left rear tire was losing air and we asked a gas station mechanic to repair it. He placed the jack under the rear quarter panel of the station wagon rather than under the bumper. In so doing he punctured the gas tank as he raised the vehicle in order to remove the tire. That happened over the Fourth of July weekend when all the automotive parts stores were closed. We waited two days at the Laramie, Wyoming campground for the replacement part. The new gas tank had to be trucked in from Cheyenne.

Chapter XXIV - Open Heart Surgery

Later that summer I noticed that the heart medication which had been prescribed two years earlier was beginning to lose its effect. After a battery of tests my cardiologist, Doctor Nazzal Obaid decided that an angiogram would prove what he had suspected. Yes, there was serious blockage in several of my heart arteries. An open-heart operation needed to be performed to bypass the blocked arteries. On the eve of my surgery my family was assembled for a procedural explanation. My wife and our children ages 23, 22, 21, 16, 14 and 11 were intent as they listened to Doctor Obaid's explanation. Later that night, in the quiet of my room at St. Anthony's Hospital in Crown Point, I received the sacrament of Extreme Unction from the hospital chaplain. I was at peace.

Early the next morning on September 8, 1981, I said my good-byes, gave and got hugs and kisses from my wife and children as I was whisked away to the operating room. I was afraid! My wife reminded me that it was the feast of the Blessed Virgin Mary's birthday, and that she would pray to her. The surgery was a success not only because of the knowledgeable and proficient Thai surgeons, Doctors Porapaiboon, Thupuong & Suwan, but also because of all the prayers that were offered up in my behalf. I remained in intensive care for several days and in the hospital's cardiac unit for a week.

On the day of my discharge I had just removed my Holter Monitor when, to my utter surprise, a length of a two by six came crashing through from above, right through the suspended ceiling. The large piece of lumber just missed my head by inches. My heart began racing as I rang for the nurse. The nurse called for the construction supervisor. But what could he do? His apology was meaningless. For a while I thought, "Is God telling me something? Does He want me to stay in the hospital?" The falling debris was caused by the construction of floors above my floor. The cardiac floor at St. Anthony's Hospital in Crown Point was the top floor before the construction. I was one happy camper when I set foot into our house all safe and sound.

A poem was written to commemorate this very critical time in my life. My younger sister Tillie (Kapitan) Bryan wrote it. Tillie is the poet laureate of our family. Here is a photo of that poem card:

On October the 8th, exactly a month after my surgery, my mother Johanna Kapitan died. She was 80 1/2 years old and had been seriously ill for several months. As she lay on her deathbed she told me that she had offered her sufferings for my successful surgery. It was her prayers, the prayers of my wife and six children and my brothers and sisters and friends that helped pull me through this major heart surgery. The power of prayer did indeed prove to be efficacious.

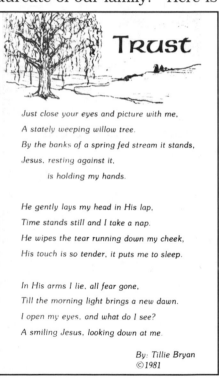

Trust

Just close your eyes and picture with me,
A stately weeping willow tree.
By the banks of a spring fed stream it stands,
Jesus, resting against it,
    is holding my hands.

He gently lays my head in His lap,
Time stands still and I take a nap.
He wipes the tear running down my cheek,
His touch is so tender, it puts me to sleep.

In His arms I lie, all fear gone,
Till the morning light brings a new dawn.
I open my eyes, and what do I see?
A smiling Jesus, looking down at me.

                    By: Tillie Bryan
                    ©1981

A poem written on the occasion of my open heart surgery.

Chapter XXV - Independence - Children Work and Buy Cars

As our children received their driver's license, they sought employment other than on our tree farm. The object was to earn enough money to purchase a car of their very own car. They knew their eldest brother Rudy would see to it that they would get the best car for the least amount of money. "Hey bee dee a bee dee a bee dee a" hollered the auctioneer as Rudy bid on a "cream puff" for his sister Carol who had just received her driver's license. Carol drove the car home joyfully knowing that it was just the right car and the right color, and of course, a good wholesale price. When we moved out to the country, little did I imagine that there would ever be six cars parked in our driveway, Rudy's, Mike's, Sue's, Carol's and our two.

An Honesty Test - Now it was Laura's turn to save money to buy a car. Waitressing at a local restaurant she saved every dollar she received as a tip. One day she saw a small white envelope lying on the floor of the restaurant. She picked it up and to her utter amazement there were six, crisp one hundred bills in it with a note that said "good luck." There were no names in or on the envelope to serve as identification. "Man," Laura said to herself, "the six hundred bucks will sure help me get a car pretty quickly." She dispelled that thought and, instead, went to the restaurant manager with the six-one-hundred-dollars in the envelope. The police were called and the envelope and its contents were properly noted. Laura was told that if the money were not claimed within thirty days, it would be hers. Her fellow employees were surprised that Laura turned the money in. Some of them told her that she was "nuts" and that they sure would not have turned it in.

"Who would know about it?" her friend said. Laura's response was, "It could have been someone's wedding present or maybe it belonged to someone who needed it more than I did. Besides, I would have known that I kept something that did not belong to me!" Laura's honesty was repaid. The waiting period elapsed and she received a telephone call from the police to tell her that no one claimed the money and the six hundred dollars were hers. We were proud parents knowing that Laura had put into practice what we had preached. She passed the honesty test.

Children's Sporting Ventures - Rudy and Mike had been racing in motocross events for a few years now. They traded their smaller Honda and Yamaha bikes for larger Suzuki and Husquavarna dirt bikes. The more they rode the more they improved. At a typical race, twenty bikes would be lurching at the starting line revved up and ready to go. The flag at the starting line dropped, announcing the start of the race. The entire area became engulfed in a cloud of dust as the bikes made their way towards the first turn. As the dust settled, many a bikester lay separated from his bike. How many times we prayed that our sons come out of that

Rudy & Mike just before the race

cloud of dust unscathed. Both Rudy and Mike came home with trophy after trophy one larger than the other. It was in this year that Mike placed 3rd in a State qualifying event.

The boys also participated in several of Leon Wolek's Triathlons held in Hobart each year. The grueling event encompassed swimming, biking and running. They swam for a mile, rode their bicycles for twenty miles and ran for seven miles. In their first ever Triathlon, of over 290 entrants, Mike finished 8th and Rudy finished 61st.

Rudy & Mike finish their first Triathlon.

Within a few years Laura joined her brothers in competing in the annual Triathlon. True to the old Slovak saying, "*Aka Matka taka Katka*'" (like mother like daughter) Laura displayed the athletic prowess of her mother in one sporting event after another. Laura also emulated her brothers Rudy and Mike who displayed their mother's athletic abilities.

Rudy's athletic prowess found him excelling in skiing.

He especially enjoyed the challenges of the Canadian Rockies in Banff, Canada. Snowmobiling in Wisconsin and Michigan was an exhilarating winter sport, which he truly enjoyed. During the summer, on his days off from the car business, Rudy could be found at his cousin Janet and Ted Pietrzak's lakefront home in Edwardsburg, Michigan jet skiing on the refreshing waters of those inviting twin lakes.

The entire Kapitan clan enjoyed outdoor sports. As a matter of fact enthusiasm for Volleyball was so captivating for our children that they invited friends over each Tuesday to play. During spring, summer and fall every Tuesday night was "Volleyball" night at the Kapitans. Scores of friends came to play at a court set up by Rudy and Mike on our country sized front lawn. The games began right after supper. As darkness befell the playing area, spotlights positioned high in adjoining trees bathed the entire playing area in a sea of light. Many a game continued well past midnight as team after team challenged each other to "one more game."

Miss Teen Pageant - Laura had just turned sixteen and entered a "Miss Teen" pageant. We traveled to Indianapolis with her where she represented our town of Merrillville. The finals of that pageant were held at the Adam's Mark hotel during the Easter break from school. It was on Good Friday, the first full day of that pageant that we experienced a very unique dining experience. The entrée for that Good Friday meal was <u>steak</u>. As Catholics, meat was strictly prohibited on so solemn a day on which we commemorated the crucifixion of Jesus Christ. We called for the maitre d' telling him that we could not and would not eat meat on Good Friday. He assured us that he would order a fish substitute for us. In a very short time a plate of fish was brought to us. The presentation was unique as only could happen in so exquisite a hotel. Each fish was wrapped in BACON! We were appalled that they did not understand the term meatless. Our table companions were amused as we unwrapped the fish from their bacon wrapping.

The Last Family Vacation - Our youngest Dorothy, aged thirteen, was the only one of our children to travel with us on our 1983 family vacation. The other five were all in their teens and twenties. What a difference traveling without a car full of kids. So that it would be more interesting Dorothy invited her cousin JoAnn Kapitan, my brother Ambrose & his wife Pat's daughter & also my godchild, to come with us. Each of the girls had an entire window of that huge station wagon to themselves as we traveled over four thousand miles. Our plans were to visit the Eastern Provinces of Canada and then return via our eastern states. There were conversions to be made on our first refueling stop in the Canadian province of Quebec. The gas pump readings were in liters! The dollar amount for those liters was priced in Canadian Dollars! The outdoor thermometer showed the temperature in Celsius and the roadway speed signs announced speed limits in kilometers! At first it was confusing as we traveled in that "foreign" country of English speaking people. As we continued, my hand-held calculator proved to be an informative asset in making the conversions necessary to understand those expressions of foreign measurements.

From Quebec we traveled eastward into New Brunswick and then onto Nova Scotia. As we traveled through Ottawa, teen-agers Dorothy and JoAnn were treated to a most exciting and memorable event. Prince Charles and Princess Diana were visiting the Province and made themselves available to cheering throngs lining a parade route. We were among those who lined the streets on that glorious sun lit day. The girls did all but swoon as the smiling and waving Prince Charles and Princess Diana passed within feet of us.

One of the most impressive sights of that entire vacation was at the Bay of Funde where the tides go out for miles. It was unbelievable as we watched miles of shoreline disappear and reappear as the forces of nature worked their daily wonder. This became one of our last "family" vacations. In a way it was sad as we reflected on all the vacations taken with a car full of children. And yet, from another point of view, we were thankful that our children had memories of fun times, vacation memories that could never be taken from them. Our family had reached another milestone.

While recalling the awesome powers of the Bay of Funde, I was reminded of a prayer which I, as a member of the parish council, was asked to prepare for a St. Stephen Martyr council meeting. Truly, the powers of God the Holy Spirit are manifest in all of creation. I wish to share that prayer, in abbreviated form, with you:

"Let us place ourselves in the presence of the Holy Spirit. ...At the dawn of creation the Spirit of God, source of life and energy, moved over the waters. In Numbers (XXIV 2) we read 'When the Spirit had rested upon the seventy elders, they prophesied.' Samuel (Kings 23-2) assured Saul, the first Israelite King that 'the Spirit of the Lord will come upon you and you shall prophesy.' David (Isias 48-16) declares in his last words that 'The Spirit of the Lord has spoken by me and His word by my tongue.' In John (14:15-17) Jesus, before His Ascension tells His apostles 'If you love me and obey the commandments I have given you, I will ask the Father and He will give you another Paraclete – to be with you always, the Spirit of Truth.' In the Acts of the Apostles (2:1) we read: 'When the day of Pentecost came it found them gathered in one place. Suddenly from up in the sky there came a noise like a strong driving wind which was heard all through the house where they were seated. Tongues as of fire appeared, which parted and came over them.'

O Holy Spirit, you were the breath of life at the world's creation; you spoke to us in every time and in every age through the prophets, the Evangelists and the Apostles, all of whose writings you inspired. We believe you are the Lord, the giver of life who proceeds from the Father and the Son, who together with the Father and the Son are worshiped and glorified.

We have been baptized in you. When we were confirmed, we received you as the giver of life. Renew us so that we may renew the face of our St. Stephen's parish community.... We humbly pray for your seven gifts: Wisdom—to relish the truth; Understanding—to enlighten us; Counsel—to guide us; Fortitude—to strengthen us; Knowledge—to distinguish good from evil; Piety—to enjoy true peace and the Gift of Fear—to avoid all danger of offending you.... Enable us to be fruitful in the works we undertake this evening...."

Our Last High School Graduation - Dorothy, our youngest, was bringing to conclusion the high school years of the Kapitan children. She was a graduate of the Merrillville High School class of 1988. The invitation for her graduation party read:

"As we have in the past....
So shall we for our last....
Give a party for our lass....
Who ranks high in her class...

For the efforts put forth...
We now reward our Dorth....
With a well deserved repast...
Given by the rest of the cast...
of 6929 Hendricks St., Merrillville....
Please come to the repast...
On June 12th from one till it lasts."

As usual, Kapitan parties were memorable.

Chapter XXVI - Other Family Milestones

The next milestones for our family were graduations from college. We became the proud parents of graduates from Purdue University and Ball State University. When Carol graduated from High School she wanted to go into business for herself. We purchased a business trailer and set it up on the large commercial lot at Kapitan Motors. There Carol opened her very own "Nut House," and we named it RUM-SCLAD NUT HOUSE. What a treat it was to sample fresh roasted nuts and to munch on healthy snack mixes. Imperial Mixed fruit was one of our favorite snacks followed by California Mix and the unbeatable "Inflation Fighter." Clever advertising promotions kept her business in operation for several years.

RUMSCLAD NUT HOUSE
4095 Cleveland
Gary, Indiana 46408   Rt. #55 & 41st

Phone (219) 769-2257
Hours
Mon-Sat 9 to 5:30 p.m.

Grand Opening Price List

	Price Per Pound
ALMONDS:	
* Whole Natural R/S	$3.25
Smokehouse	3.50
* Slivered & Blanched	4.75
* **BRAZILS R/S**	3.75
CASHEWS:	
Fancy Whole Roasted — NO SALT	4.95
Fancy Whole R/S	4.95
Cashew Pieces R/S	2.95
* **FILBERTS R/S**	3.75
MACADAMIAS R/S	9.50
MIXED NUTS: (No Peanuts) R/S	4.95
PEANUTS - REDSKIN R/S	1.95
PECANS:	
* Choice Mammoth Halves R/S	4.95
* Topper Halves - Choice Raw	4.25
Large Standard Halves R/S	3.25
PISTACHIOS:	
* Colossal Natural or Red In Shell R/S	5.95
Jumbo In Shell R/S	4.50
Shelled Pistachios R/S	6.95
YOGURT ITEMS:	
Yogurt Peanuts	2.95
Yogurt Raisins	2.95
* Yogurt Walnuts	3.75
* Yogurt Pineapple	3.25

HEALTH SNACK MIXES:

CALIFORNIA MIX: (No Salt) Raisins, Sunflower Meats, Pineapples, Banana Chips, Coconut, Brazils, Apricots, Walnuts, Almonds, Filberts, Pepitas, Cashews & Pecans ... 3.25

HOT'N SPICY MIX: Romy Kernels, Hot Nacho Peanuts, Blanched Peanuts R/S, Cashew Pieces R/S, Chinese Pumpkin Seeds R/S, Chili Bits ... 2.95

INFLATION FIGHTER: Sesame Sticks, Redskin Peanuts R/S, Sunflower Seeds R/S, Carob Bits ... 1.95

IMPERIAL MIXED FRUIT: Prunes, Turkish Apricots, Pineapples, Dates, White Greek Figs, Sulfured Pears, Peaches & Apples ... 3.95

MISC:	
FROSTED PRETZELS	3.75
GUMMY BEARS	3.75
GOURMET JELLY BEANS, ASSORTED FLAVORS	2.95
SESAME STICKS	1.95
SHELLED SUNFLOWER SEEDS R/S	1.95

* Items Available for the Holidays   R/S Roasted & Salted

11-83

business in operation for several years.

The years flew by swiftly as one season followed another. It seemed as though our six seedlings turned into mature flowers overnight. Mary and I were at once both tearful and joyful. A full circle was beginning to pass for our family. Our little boys became bridegrooms and our little girls became beautiful brides. There would be no more wet oatmeal kisses, no more tooth fairies, and no more dandelion bouquets. There would be no more admonitions of, "Why don't you grow up?." The silence of the house would say, "I did."

As our children departed to marry, the silence of our house opened the door to all the beautiful sounds that were about to permeate the households of our newly married children. Where we were one household there now would be six; what a blessing from Almighty God. There were wedding toasts that I proposed to each of our newly married couples. To our eldest son Rudy my toast was: "Today Rudy and Tammy you stand on the threshold of your life together as man and wife. Your parents' prayer for you is that you remain faithful to one another in the lifelong commitment, which you have made. May what you envision for yourselves, for your home and future family, come true a hundredfold. May your days together be full of unselfish love for one another and for your children. May that love serve to overcome the trials that will come into your lives and may those trials serve only to strengthen your marriage. May you, when you are where your parents are today, be as justifiably proud of your children as we are of you today. May you live to a healthy ripe old age together and may you through this marriage, blessed by Christ, come to receive for yourselves the eternal reward which is promised to those who remain faithful to his precepts."

Each of the six toasts, although similar in meaning, were a bit different in their wording. So as not to be repetitious, just one of the five other toasts is presented. It is: "Today you begin a glorious new adventure as husband

and wife.   In God's presence you have promised an unreserved love for and of one another until the end of your lives and then into eternity.   You have planted the seed of matrimony in your heart and in your soul.   As Father, it is my prerogative to echo parental blessings upon you my children.

May you nurture that seed with many tears of joy and may you learn how to nurture it with tears of sorrow, which may come into your lives.   May you look to Christ the author of love for solutions to any shortcomings.

May your marriage then be refreshed and invigorated by each watering as though it was a spring rain.   May the sun, which breaks through after the storm, provide you with a rainbow of matrimonial bliss, as your lives together blossom into a beautiful marriage, blessed with very special rewards - CHILDREN.

May you find comfort in each other's presence, that special kind of comfort that knows how to shut out all the sounds except the sounds of two hearts in love. May the fruits of your efforts be as blessed as are the fruits of your parents...."

Rudy & Tammy (Bowen)

Mike & Mary (Killam)

Sue & Richard Scuderi

Carol & Joe Sanders

Laura & Dan Small

Dorothy & Tommy Metcalf

Chapter XXVII - THE BANK

The following is a brief narrative of the memoirs of Rudolph F. Kapitan as an employee of the American Trust from 1952 to 1984.

It was in December of 1952 that I hired in at the American Trust and Savings Bank as a teller apprentice. At the end of that year the bank reported that its Capital, Surplus and Undivided Profits totaled $300,000.00 and that customer's deposits totaled $6,000,000.00. It didn't take long for me to learn the fundamentals and responsibilities of a bank teller. Within a week I had my very own cage as both a receiving and paying teller. As a receiving teller I accepted savings and checking account deposits and Christmas club payments. Savings deposits were receipted for by machine. The customer's savings passbook and the individual customer savings account ledger were posted simultaneously by machine. Checking account deposits were receipted for by hand posting to the customers deposit book. A commercial deposit clerk posted the customer's individual ledger with the bank from deposit tickets prepared by either the customer or the teller. Christmas club payments were hand posted to customer and bank Christmas club payment cards.

As a receiving teller I accepted loan payments on both installment and mortgage loans. The installment loan payment was receipted for using the customer's coupon book. The mortgage loan payment was receipted for by posting the customer's mortgage payment book simultaneously with the customer's mortgage loan ledger.

As a paying teller I cashed checks presented to me for payment. The bank's obligation was to cash checks drawn only on our bank. It was customary, however, to cash checks drawn on other banks especially other local banks. Generally we knew most of our customers on a first name basis. The cashed checks were spindled. Periodically, in between customers, the cashed checks would be removed from the spindle, then totaled and bundled. A "cash out" ticket was then prepared. The original of the "cash-out" ticket was included with the bundled checks and sent to the proof operator. An adding machine tape prepared by the teller was always included with the bundle of checks.

Installment loan payment stubs and mortgage loan credit tickets, which had been spindled throughout the day, were also totaled. A "cash-in" ticket was prepared to match the total on the adding machine tape and sent to the proof. At the end of the working day the teller was left with his cash, change in the till and all of the "cash-in" and "cash-out" tickets which had been generated throughout the day. Each teller prepared a daily "balance sheet" at the end of the day. The credit side contained the beginning cash total. To this total was added the total of all the "cash-in" tickets. The right side of the balance sheet carried the cages ending cash total plus a total of all of the "cash-out" tickets issued by the teller during the business day. If the left side total matched the right side total, the teller was in luck and the cage was balanced. If the totals did not match, the teller recounted the cash, checked for transpositions, checked with the proof for any errors and even rummaged through the waste paper basket. At times, this process consumed several hours of exasperating work. It was not uncommon for another teller to assist the teller having difficulty in balancing. Every effort was made to balance the cage "to the penny."

Banking hours were from 9:00 AM to 2:00 PM. Once the doors were locked each teller began balancing their cage. Many and varied were the assignments after the cages were balanced. For instance the next interest payment on the customer's individual mortgage loan ledger was individually calculated and penciled in on each mortgage loan ledger card after each posting. Savings account ledgers were divided into books, about five hundred ledgers per book. Each book was totaled and the total of all books had to be balanced to the bank's General Savings Ledger. There were many other "balancing acts" performed by the tellers until the 4:30 PM quitting time.

Interest was paid on all savings accounts as of the 1st of January and the 1st of July. Interest calculations were made during the last week prior to the payment of the interest earned on each of several thousand savings account. These amounts were penciled in on each individual savings account ledger. The interest earned on each savings account was then machine posted to the individual ledgers on the last day of June and the last day of December. Many unpaid hours of overtime were spent during those two "savings account interest calculation" weeks, calculating the interest and balancing all the savings accounts prior to and after the interest posting. As a result, the first week of July and the first week of January were exceptionally busy weeks as anxious customers flocked to the bank to have their savings passbooks "posted." Line after line formed at each of the cages as the customers presented their savings passbooks for interest posting.

The vault teller balanced his cage by including all the vault cash, bags of coins in the vault and all the loose rolls of coins in the "silver buggy." The silver buggy contained loose rolls of coins and was rolled out of the vault each morning and placed right behind the center cage. As tellers needed additional change, they bought rolls of coins from the silver buggy, paying for them by putting dollars into a cigar box located on the silver change buggy. As tellers needed cash, they issued debit tickets listing the denomination and amounts needed. The vault teller would then "sell" the cash according to the amounts shown on the tellers debit cash ticket. Conversely, when a cage accumulated excess cash, it would be sold to the vault teller. The vault teller was in an especially strenuous position as he balanced not only the vault cage's daily customer activity but also the bank's total vault cash position.

A special cage, under the auspices of the floor supervisor, accepted insurance payments, city water bills, real estate tax payments, Calumet Park Cemetery "plot" payments; issued traveler's checks, Bank Money Orders and Cashiers Checks and performed other sundry bank tasks.

On Fridays the bank hours were from 9:00 AM to 7:00 PM. Friday was payday for most of the local industries. Every other Friday was Standard Oil Company payday, the largest cash day in the Whiting-Robertsdale area. Standard Oil Company paydays were imprinted on large wall mounted calendars issued by the local banks. Everyone wanted a Standard Oil Company calendar. These one and a half foot wide and two foot long wall calendars appeared on virtually every kitchen wall throughout Whiting and Robertsdale.

On each SOCO payday there were lines of workers waiting for us to open. These were the 12 to 8 AM shift workers, waiting to cash their paychecks. To prepare for the assault of these customers, the vault teller issued $36,000.00 of cash to each cage. Each cage was issued a bundle of 20's ($20,000.00), a bundle of 10's ($10,000.00), a bundle of 5's ($5,000.00) and a bundle of 1's ($1,000.00), enough cash to cash about two hundred paychecks. Most of that cash was gone by noontime. There were lines of customers at each teller's window all morning long. Just before the next shift of cash hungry workers made their appearances at the teller's lines, there was a lull. During this lull each cage took turns to close and balance. Cash supplies were replenished once the cage balanced and reopened for "the next day's work." Again each cage "bought" another bundle of twenties, tens, fives and singles as they prepared for the onslaught of the second shift of check cashing. It was not uncommon for a cage to "go through" seventy to a hundred thousand dollars on a SOCO payday.

Next the 8 to 4 shift workers made their appearance, forming lines at each window until the closing at 7:00 PM. It was not unusual for a customer to present his paycheck and ask that so many dollars be deposited to his savings and checking accounts. The teller would prepare the deposit tickets and post the checking account deposit to the customer's passbook by hand. The savings deposit was posted to the customer's passbook by machine. Invariably the customers would also make mortgage loan or installment loan payments. It was not uncommon for a bank customer to have four or five transactions when presenting his paycheck. And then, after he received the balance in cash, he would return cash for deposit payments to his Christmas club: $5.00 on his club card, and a dollar or two on each of his four or five children's club cards, each entry being hand posted. With a little bit of luck the next customer just wanted his paycheck cashcd. It took about fifteen seconds to count out the $172.42 of the next customer's paycheck. Grabbing a handful of twenties I counted 20, 40, 60, 80, 100. Throwing whatever 20's were left back into the $20 bin of my cash drawer, I grabbed a handful of tens counting to one hundred sixty and quickly drew out two 5's and two 1's Zip, zip. zip, in a couple of seconds I doubled checked the cash, hit the 42 cent change button, checked the endorsement on the check, stamped the check with my cage "cash" stamp and spindled the check. The check cashing process took about ten to fifteen seconds. For some tellers like Tom Grenchik it took less time then that. Customers marveled at his speed and accuracy and even made complimentary remarks.

Tellers received instructions to get rid of the Silver Dollars, which the Federal Reserve Bank would ship out periodically. Many a customer would roll that Silver Dollar right back asking for a greenback. Very few, if any, wanted those "Cartwheels." Then there were the customers who asked for and received $2.00 bills. We always thought of the two dollar bill as "race-track money." At 7:00 P.M. the bank doors closed only to be reopened to the knocks of late-comers. "She's a good customer, let her in," came the words from the exhausted lips of one of the bank workers.

During the next five years I advanced from one cage to another. With increased responsibilities came increased wages. Then in 1957, being promoted to Assistant Cashier, I left the teller line up for a front desk. Hurray, as an officer, I no longer needed to punch a time clock, an official fringe benefit. At this time I began taking "Banking Classes" at the American Institute of Banking in Chicago. Several of us traveled to the "loop" each Tuesday and Thursday by way of the South Shore. We left immediately after work, grabbed a bite to eat and were ready for the first class which began at 7:00 P.M. Classes ended at 9:00 P.M. So the Tuesdays and Thursdays of the next several years were quite busy. On those days I didn't get home till about eleven o'clock at night. My study habits had been keenly honed during my seminary days having received a bachelor's degree in Philosophy from Dayton University. It was not uncommon for me to be at the top of my banking class where I received honors and even a cash award.

In 1965 bank president Stephen J. Kovacik asked that I become involved in the business politics of the Indiana Banker's Association. I had just been promoted to Assistant Vice President, a more fitting title for the bank's liaison to the Indiana Bankers Association. It was in that year that a meeting was held in the Indiana State Senate chambers. Proposed banking legislation detrimental to small state banks was being discussed. I received a standing ovation for my remarks and was instrumental in defeating the proposed legislation, legislation which would have negatively impacted small state banks throughout Indiana.

The following year the Indiana Banker's Association held their annual convention in French Lick, Indiana. That prestigious group honored me by electing me to membership on the Executive Committee of Region Two. My efforts in behalf of small, family owned banks, such as the family owned Grenchik bank (not my family), were especially rewarding as I was chosen by my statewide banking peers to represent them.

Indiana Bankers Association 55th Annual Meeting

Meanwhile back at the shop, I became involved in most every aspect of the bank's services. I served as first floor supervisor and as such was the officer in charge of new accounts, advertising and promotional officer, customer stock and bond sales rep., bank rep for Tuzex and other foreign remittances, safe deposit box officer and bank statements reconciler. As internal accounting officer I prepared the bank's Call reports as directed by the FDIC, also all the banks financial and interim reports and prepared the banks semi annual Statement of Condition for publication.

Subsequently I was promoted to Trust Officer and Loan officer. As Trust Officer I represented the bank in all fiduciary matters relating to the Trust Department, including court appearances. As Loan Officer I served in the personal loan department, commercial loans department and mortgage loan department. Not long after I assumed responsibilities in the mortgage loan department, I became the bank's appraiser for real estate home loans. Serving on the banks Investment Committee, I was the officer in charge of the banks entire Municipal and Government bond portfolio, responsible for the record keeping and executing of all the bank's buy and sell orders. With each passing year I became involved in most every aspect of banking. I thrived on the challenges that a small, family owned bank offered and I thoroughly enjoyed what I did as a banker. I was proud of my accomplishments as I watched the bank's footings grow by leaps and bounds.

I served on all the bank's committees: Trust, Investment, Loan, and Budget. The Retirement Committee is one that I was never invited to serve on. I didn't know why but I would come to know why when my retirement was at hand. That committee was more or less reserved for the OWNERS - THE GRENCHIK FAMILY.

So that employees would not know each other's salary, the method employed by the bank in paying its employees was not by individual paycheck but by cash in an envelope. One expense check was cut for the entire payroll. As accounting officer I was responsible for generating the credit and debit tickets to reflect the total payroll expense and the total of all the payroll withholdings and deductions. As the year went on I became aware of the fact that, generally, the FICA (Social Security) contributions began to decrease in May. It was not difficult to conclude that someone's wages had reached the maximum subject to FICA tax for that year. Norbert Grenchik, the bank's president didn't know that I knew what his salary was. To keep the peace, I kept all that information confidential, not revealing that his salary was equal to the combined salaries of several officers and to, perhaps all of the tellers or the bookkeepers and secretaries.

Who said you can't have your cake and eat it? The bank did; they formed a Bank Holding Company. The Holding Company, owned or controlled by the Grenchik family members, bought all the bank stock with proceeds of a loan from a Chicago correspondent bank. Although they received a cash payment for all of their bank stocks, they continued to maintain a majority ownership through the Bank Holding Company. That certainly was a shrewd maneuver, to say the least. The interest on the Holding Company's loan was paid for from, naturally, the bank's profits. It was in the first years of that arrangement that there were minimal, if any, salary increases. The interest expense of the Holding Company's loan claimed a substantial portion of the year's bank profits. There was very little left for increasing the salaries of all the dedicated workers who made that possible. "The rich got richer and the poor got poorer."

There were certain fringe benefits awarded bank employees. For instance we received discounted loan interest rates! To keep the record straight I need mention that we did receive preferential loan interest rates, like maybe 12%! How was that for preferential? The rewards for employee work ethic and disciplined honesty were given very sparingly; certainly not commensurate with some of the outstanding performances of so many dedicated bank employees.

Despite all the disparity I did not falter in my work ethic. It demanded a loyal and faithful dedication to service and duty. In so doing the bank's goals were enhanced and the bank's profitability and success were being promoted. My dedication to service and duty is exemplified by the fact that, on retirement, I had accumulated over 260 sick days. On one occasion, rather than take a day off work, I asked my wife Mary to drive herself to the Michigan City Hospital where she was to have surgery. I needed to be at the bank that day. I had a mortgage loan to close and several million dollars of investments to make. I was also working on a "Call Report" as demanded by the FDIC. I convinced her that some day when we needed the bank, it would be there for us. How sorely I was mistaken as will be explained later.

In 1979 the bank lost a valuable employee, Richard C. Hajduch. At the very young age of 59, Rich died of an aneurysm of the aorta. That condition was no doubt accelerated for him by the stresses to which he was subject on a daily basis. Many were the times that Rich complained to me of the unfair treatment he was receiving at the hands of Norbert Grenchik. He was Norbert's "whipping boy." His heart ached so many times because of the unfairness to him and especially because of a certain letter of reprimand issued to him by Norbert. That letter was similar to one I later received from Norbert, as he sought to MASTER over the life and death of those unfortunate enough to be the recipients of his ignominy.

It wasn't long after Rich passed away that I became Norbert's "whipping boy." It was in that same year that I began experiencing chest pains. It was much too late to seek employment elsewhere. Two years of treatment with heart medication proved futile, and my condition worsened. Then in 1981 I underwent open-heart surgery to bypass blocked heart arteries. Since, over the past twenty-nine years I had accumulated more than three hundred sick days, I received full compensation during the four months of my recovery. Because of my work ethic and diligence in reporting to work, sick though I may have been, there still remained about two hundred and fifty sick days in my "sick day bank" account. It was consoling to know that I had built up all that security. I was further consoled by the thought that, someday when I needed it, the bank would compensate me for those sick days. Well, as I said before and I will explain later, the bank did not compensate me.

Upon returning to full-time employment, after my heart surgery, I experienced less stress. Norbert's evil mindedness and unjust treatment towards me subsided. That calming atmosphere, however, did not last very long. At a review of the loans made during the year 1983 I was chastised for poor performance. I took it upon myself to review the bank's "loan charge off" records for that year. To my utter astonishment, some of those charged off loans were loans which were originally rejected by me; and, after my rejection were subsequently approved by Norbert, our Jekyll and Hyde bank President. It sure made me look like a jackass, especially when it was my responsibility to write "dun" letters to delinquent loan customers, customers whose loans I had originally rejected!

As a result of my review I found that, of the four active loan officers, I was responsible for the least amount of bad loans for that year. As a matter of fact I was responsible for less than 3% of all the loans charged off during that year. Ninety seven percent of those charged off loans were attributable to the three other loan officers, and I was being singled out for poor performance! Again the work climate created by Norbert began causing me much anguish. It was through prayer that I would overcome rather than succumb to the evil which was to plague me. My prayer life increased

In discussing the work problems with one of my heart doctors, Dr. Streeter considered it urgent enough to write Norbert a letter. A copy of that letter is as follows:

Norbert responded to my Doctor's letter with more frequent abuses. One such abuse was that he had our secretary prepare a "Time Card" for me. As the bank's vice president and comptroller, I

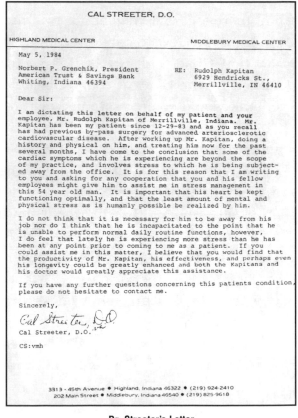

CAL STREETER, D.O.

HIGHLAND MEDICAL CENTER   MIDDLEBURY MEDICAL CENTER

May 5, 1984

Norbert P. Grenchik, President   RE: Rudolph Kapitan
American Trust & Savings Bank   6929 Hendricks St.,
Whiting, Indiana 46394   Merrillville, IN 46410

Dear Sir:

I am dictating this letter on behalf of my patient and your employee, Mr. Rudolph Kapitan of Merrillville, Indiana. Mr. Kapitan has been my patient since 12-29-83 and as you recall has had previous by-pass surgery for advanced arteriosclerotic cardiovascular disease. After working up Mr. Kapitan, doing a history and physical on him, and treating him now for the past several months, I have come to the conclusion that some of the cardiac symptoms which he is experiencing are beyond the scope of my practice, and involves stress to which he is being subjected away from the office. It is for this reason that I am writing to you and asking for any cooperation that you and his fellow employees might give him to assist me in stress management in this 54 year old man. It is important that his heart be kept functioning optimally, and that the least amount of mental and physical stress as is humanly possible be realized by him.

I do not think that it is necessary for him to be away from his job nor do I think that he is incapacitated to the point that he is unable to perform normal daily routine functions, however, I do feel that lately he is experiencing more stress than he has been at any point prior to coming to me as a patient. If you could assist me in this matter, I believe that you would find that the productivity of Mr. Kapitan, his effectiveness, and perhaps even his longevity could be greatly enhanced and both the Kapitans and his doctor would greatly appreciate this assistance.

If you have any further questions concerning this patients condition, please do not hesitate to contact me.

Sincerely,

Cal Streeter, D.O.

CS:vmh

3313 - 45th Avenue ● Highland, Indiana 46322 ● (219) 924-2410
202 Main Street ● Middlebury, Indiana 46540 ● (219) 825-9618

Dr. Streeter's Letter

228

was compelled to PUNCH THE CLOCK along with the secretaries and tellers. I had shed that symbol of serfdom back in 1957, some twenty-six years ago, when I was elected to an officer's position. Now, as a loyal and dedicated bank Vice President and Trust Officer with years of service, Norbert gleefully forced me to punch the clock! That alone was enough to break my heart all over again. What's more, the "Time Card" required an employee signature. So, being treated like a child, I signed the card with a childish signature.

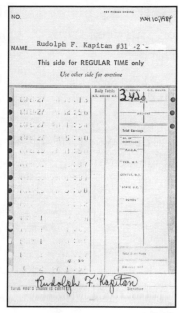

Norbert responded by returning the card with the following note:

Other fiascoes occurred as evi-

Signature does not correspond with one on file

denced by a travel voucher submitted just months prior to my retirement:

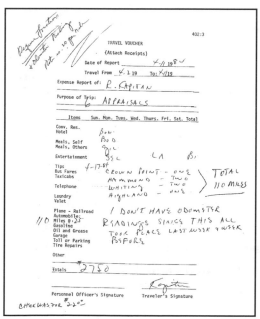

Take a look at Norbert's note at the upper left corner of that travel voucher. Even now my heart weakens as I recall Norbert's shameful and ignominious behavior. I came to realize that I could expect no mercy or justice from Norbert, a Dr. Jekyll and Mr. Hyde personification.

In days gone by I was often opposed to the Federal Government's intrusion into the affairs of the business world as they attempted to legislate morality. I now came to a sad realization that the government did not do enough to legislate the kind of morality that was often needed. But then, how could any body legislate morality!? Surely there were, and are, many workers suffering even more inhumane treatment than did I, and all at the hands of heartless and ruthless chief executives.

As my heart became weaker, my longevity became threatened. I couldn't seek employment elsewhere because of my severe health problem. I prayed that I live to see the day when, at age fifty-five, I would be able to take an early retirement. My prayers included requests that I live long enough to see my children happily married and to witness the birth of grandchildren. I knew that if I expected my prayers to be answered, it would be absolutely necessary for me to remove myself from the presence of Norbert Grenchik.

So, six months prior to August 16, 1984, I tendered a letter requesting my early retirement. When planning for my retirement I was under the assumption that the bank played by the same rules as did industry in our area. At age 55 with 32 years of service, my combined years of service plus age, gave me 87 points, more than enough for full retirement benefits! At the mills and the refinery 77 to 80 was the magic number for full retirement benefits. That was not to be the case for me. The bank calculated that I was taking an early retirement and therefore my retirement benefits would be minimal regardless of the number of points which I had accumulated.

As I sat in Norbert's office reviewing my retirement benefits, I was appalled to find out that my retirement check would be for **$226.94 with NO cost of living adjustments ever in the future**. I was also apprised of the fact that the cost of my family's health insurance, over $400.00 per month would become my sole responsibility. With a pre-existing health condition I could not shop around for a less expensive health insurance premium. It was necessary for me to stay with the bank's health insurance program for my wife and two dependent children. I was appalled that, after thirty-two years of dedicated and loyal service, my cash flow in retirement would be in the negative. I would be reduced to less than poverty level. With an existing heart condition employment elsewhere was unlikely.

As I drove home after work that day, thoughts of self-destruction came to mind. How could I lead my family into poverty when <u>life insurance benefits</u> were available to take care of the financial needs of my wife and children? On retirement I would become a hindrance to my family's financial stability. I continued to pray the rosary as I did each day while driving to and from work. The more I prayed the more obvious it became that self-destruction was certainly not the answer. The thought became repulsive and I set it aside.

That evening Mary and I sat in discussion long after the children went to bed. We concluded that all was not lost. Kapitan Motor's Inc. had become a six-year success story. We would apply for a 50% mortgage loan on our five-acre country estate. The loan proceeds would be used to pay off the insignificant mortgage balance at American Trust (we were in the 18th year of our 20-year mortgage loan). The remaining loan proceeds (some $90,000.00) would be used to purchase inventory (cars) at Kapitan Motors. With an infusion of those funds, we would add some thirty cars to our already forty-car inventory. We had a resolution to the problem created for me by the bank's retirement policy. We had solved our negative cash flow problem.

As a long time member of the bank's loan committee I knew what documentation would be required for our loan. There was no doubt that our 3000 square foot house and five plus acres would appraise for twice the amount of the loan request. To answer any questions regarding the ability to pay, I produced three years of Profit and Loss Statements and three years of Kapitan Motors, Inc. Financial Statements. I presented my loan application at the next loan committee meeting. To my utter dismay Norbert stated that the loan committee could not and would not act on my application. My application, he said, "Would have to go before the bank's full Board of

Directors." No one on that surprised loan committee dared challenge the CEO, the omnipotent "voice of authority".

Several days later Norbert Grenchik came into my office and threw my application onto my desk saying, "You will never get the loan at this bank! Your retirement pay will not be enough to make the loan payments." "Norbert," I said, "Look at the financial statements and the profit and loss statements of Kapitan Motors. The financial statements as presented more than justify the mortgage payment." He glared at me and repeated, "You will never get the loan here" as he stomped out of my office. The fact that I reminded him of the conservative approach I used in all of my dealings and investments in behalf of the bank did not change his mind. I was in a state of distress and my heart ached. In all my years I had never been late even one day with any loan payment. My credit was excellent as was the credit history of our corporation Kapitan Motors, Inc. The balance in our corporate checking account at the American Trust & Savings Bank was an average five figure balance. All our accounts, both financial and insurance, and all of our children's accounts both personal and corporate, were with the bank. How could it be that the bank, my thirty-two year employer, rejected my well documented and worthy loan request?

Recovering from my shock, I looked elsewhere for our real estate mortgage loan. Within the week I had secured a loan guarantee from Liberty Savings and Loan, one of our local competitors. Each of three lending institutions, whom I contacted regarding my loan request, tentatively approved a $100,000.00 loan over the phone. Bill Kennedy at Security Federal, John Babinec at Citizens Federal and Milan Kansky at Liberty all said they had no problem and would be happy to accommodate me with whatever the mortgage loan amount was to be. Since Liberty Savings and Loan had the best interest rate, we procured the loan from them. The rest is history. Kapitan Motors prospered and we grew by leaps and bounds. We overcame my banks injustices and God was good to us.

Several days prior to my retirement I inquired about my two hundred and fifty unused sick days. I expected that I would be reimbursed financially for my thirty two-year accumulation of unused sick time.

Rudolph F. Kapitan has retired as vice president, comptroller and trust officer of American Trust & Savings Bank in Whiting.

He began his career with the bank in 1952 as a teller. In 1958 he was elected assistant cashier. He was named assistant vice president and trust officer in 1963, vice president in 1971 and comptroller in 1978.

Kapitan was graduated from Dayton University in 1951 and has been a member of and served on the executive committee of Region Two of the Indiana Bankers Association.

He will devote his leisure time to his Merrillville tree nursery and to satisfying customers at Kapitan Motors, Inc., in Gary.   ▪

Hoos. Banker
MAB

From 1984 Fall Issue of Hoosier Banker.

With an insolent voice, one that I had become accustomed to, Norbert responded that my sick days would be forfeited on the day I retired. As he berated me I so wanted to tell him, as I had many times before, Norbert take your job and shove it!

It was especially difficult for me to reconcile Norbert Grenchik's inhuman treatment of me from several perspectives. We worshiped together at St. John's church and sang in the same choir. We receive Communion at the Masses that we attended with one another. Not only were we of the same religious persuasion but we were also of the same ethnic background. We were working buddies during his father Joseph Grenchik, Senior's tenure as bank president. We remained working buddies during the many years of his Uncle Stephen J. Kovacik's tenure as president. Both men, although I was not a family member, appreciated my work ethic as a result of which promotions and salary increases came easily. During their tenures I became involved in most every aspect of banking. Being employed by a small bank certainly had its rewards and I loved it. I was responsible for several innovative investment policies, which enhanced the bank's bottom line. Although I was tempted a few times to take positions offered me elsewhere, there was no reason for me to do that. I loved the small bank atmosphere and the opportunity it gave me to be involved in most every aspect of banking. And then I became Norbert's "whipping boy" and my heart problems precluded me from seeking employment elsewhere.

His ignominy followed me even into my retirement, and this is how that happened. Norbert denied me the customary retirement party. It was several months after my retirement that I received a check from the bank for $725.00. Norbert's cover letter explained that the check was in lieu of a retirement party. It was an unexpected gracious thought, and I appreciated the gesture. However, a tax problem ensued because of that check. Norbert sent the IRS a 1099 Misc Income Form advising them of the $725.00 cash payment. Since I did not receive a copy of that 1099 form, I did not report that as income on my tax return for that year. As a result I had problems with the Internal Revenue Service, problems which made it necessary for me to be interrogated and to file amended returns. I paid the penalties and the interest on the "in lieu of a retirement party" dollar amount. I should have suspected that there was a reprehensible motive behind Norbert's "generosity."

To conclude my reflections on my thirty-two years of employment at the American Trust & Savings Bank, I tender a copy of a letter I received from Mrs. Theresa Grenchik, Chairman of the Board. I received the letter on the twenty-fifth anniversary of my employment at the bank.

AMERICAN TRUST
& Savings Bank

1321-119TH STREET · WHITING, INDIANA 46394 · PHONES (219) 659-0850
(312) 734-7044

November 17, 1977

MR. RUDOLPH F. KAPITAN

TO OUR FELLOW ASSOCIATE:

The Board of Directors of the American Trust and Savings Bank in appreciation of your services as employee and officer from December 10, 1952 to the present--some twenty-five years, wish to acknowledge your valued participation in the conduct of our affairs and recognize your unfailing readiness to aid in our progress. Your efforts have contributed to our growth and enhanced our spirit and prestige.

We therefore extend to you our sincere gratitude.

Gratefully yours,

Theresa Grenchik
Theresa Grenchik
Chairman of the Board

Above is a copy of my monthly retirement check of $226.94, my reward for thirty-two years of loyal and dedicated service to the American Trust and Savings Bank of Whiting, Indiana.

It is interesting to note that the letter from the Chairman of the Board reflects on the many and valued contributions that I made during my thirty-two years of employment. Consider that in 1952, the year I began as a bank teller, the bank's Capital, Surplus and Undivided Profits accounts totaled about $300,000.00. When I retired those Capital Surplus and Profit accounts totaled $3,300,000.00 and the customer's deposits increased from $6,000,000.00 to over $40,000,000.00. I am proud to say that I played an important role in those significant increases. **It is unbelievable that my retirement check is $226.94!!**

Incidentally, Norbert was so gracious as to allow that, on my death, my wife, Mary will receive a ***whopping 50%*** of my bank pension amount, or $113.47 per month, for as long as she lives! When Norbert retired I wrote asking the bank to reconsider my ridiculous retirement benefit. I asked that since Norbert was the next to retire after me, my retirement compensation be adjusted based on a portion of Norbert's retirement benefits. In that letter I stated that if Norbert predeceased his wife, her benefit from her husband Norbert's retirement pension account would more than likely be a whole lot more than the measly $113.47 Mary will receive should I predecease her. I received no reply from the bank and knew that Norbert was still in control.

Chapter XXVIII - OUR SON RUDY

Although there is much that can be written about the achievements and successes of my six children, my life's narrative would be altogether incomplete without a brief reflection on the life and death of my dear son Rudy J. Kapitan. Rudy was our first born. He had a difficult time in being born. He was in a transverse lie. His mother labored for over twenty hours as she lay in the hospital's labor room waiting for Rudy to open her womb! I paced the waiting room floor for hours anxiously awaiting some news from the delivery room. He finally left the comfort of his mother's womb on Saturday, May 3, 1958 at 4:36 PM. Our first born son was baptized Rudolph Joseph a name that had been given to his father Rudolph and to his grandfathers, <u>Rudolph</u> Kapitan and <u>Joseph</u> Kasper. He was the third Rudolph in the Rudolph -Johanna-Kapitan-line.

Rudy was an outgoing child, quick to make friends. One day while in kindergarten he came home very disappointed. That was unusual for this friendly child. "Why doesn't Johnny like me," he asked his mother. Mary explained that not everyone would want to be his friend. It was so very difficult for Rudy to comprehend an unfriendly attitude. His life was a bowl of cherries and he wanted everyone to be as spirited and happy as he was.

While Rudy was in the first grade Mary gave birth to Carol, our fourth child. On that occasion Rudy wrote the following note:

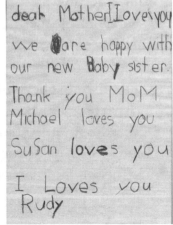

dear Mother I Love you
We are happy with
our new Baby sister.
Thank you MoM
Michael loves you
SuSan loves you
I Loves you
Rudy

One day shortly after Mary came home from the hospital with our newborn daughter Carol; Rudy came home from school with several boxes of candy. He explained that each child was asked to take one box home to sell. Enthusiastic six year-old Rudy, (confident that he could sell more than one box of candy) volunteered to take not one but several boxes. That was typical Rudy. His enthusiasm for selling began in the first grade and it continued during his entire life. That first selling experience was an educational adventure in salesmanship. What a valuable life experience he gained at so young an age.

It was several years later while selling homegrown sweet corn from door to door in Whiting, that many former neighbors and Whiting friends remembered that little Kapitan boy, trudging over the snow covered sidewalks on those cold December days, selling candy for St. John's School. Rudy was now a little more aggressive and a little more mature. It was difficult for anyone to refuse him a sale. Seldom would he accept "no" for an answer. He loved to use the word "please." People loved him for his enthusiastic approach to life. His every day life included whistling, laughter and joke telling. It was fun to have him around and he was fun to be with.

Living in the country offered many outdoor sporting opportunities for this energetic young man. He participated in most all of the sporting games, baseball, football, basketball and volleyball. He relished being a part of many other sporting activities such as biking, motocross, hockey, rollerblading, jet skiing, downhill skiing and snow mobiling. His sporting enthusiasm rubbed off onto his many friends and associates, as he shared his zest for life with them.

As Rudy grew in wisdom and age he cherished the faith and customs of his fathers. He especially relished the "*Vilia*" dinner on Christmas Eve at Grandma Kapitan's house. His prayer life included Slovak prayers that he learned at the feet of his parents. He was never one to be ashamed of his religious beliefs. On one occasion we were dining at Phil Schmidt's restaurant in Whiting, one of Rudy's favorite restaurants. As usual, prior to dining, Rudy blessed himself making a large sign of the cross. A passerby noticed that Rudy's sign of the cross was more demonstrative than ours and praised the young man for his religious conviction.

At the age of twenty-three Rudy decided that it was time for him to forge out on his own. His first house was located midway between his two loves, his "growing-up-home" and his "business home'" Kapitan Motors. As manager and Vice President of Kapitan Motors, Inc., and with his excellent credit history, he had no problem in obtaining a real estate mortgage loan. Shortly after he moved, his friends told him that he would no longer need to go to church every single Sunday to satisfy his parents. He told his friends that he did not go to church on Sunday to satisfy his parents but rather to thank God for all the blessings which he was receiving and which he had received.

Because of his level headedness Rudy's friends looked to him for advice in solving life's problems. When we were unavailable, Rudy's brother and sisters always looked to him for counsel and he didn't disappoint them. As the eldest of the Kapitan kids he shouldered that responsibility with the utmost of competence. He loved to tell the story of "The Wise Old Owl." It went like this:

"A wise old owl sat on an oak
The more he listened the less he spoke
The less he spoke the more he heard
Why can't we all be like that wise old bird!"

Even after Rudy moved into his own home he relished making visits back to the home of his youth. One such visit always happened on the 5th of December, the eve of the feast of St. Nicholas. On that visit Rudy would bring his tall "<u>engineer's boots</u>" to place near the fireplace alongside the shoes of his brother and sisters. Our custom, as was our parents, was to have the children put their shoes by the fireplace before they went to sleep. St. Nicholas came while they were asleep and filled those shoes with goodies. That happened each and every year in the Kapitan household. Although Rudy was no longer living at home, St. Nicholas made it a point to fill those engineer boots to the very top with all kinds of delights.

Rudy's celebration of life was especially noteworthy as he celebrated birthdays. One such special birthday happened on May 3, 1988, his 30th birthday. He was having a bash and everyone was invited. Mary and I could only be there later. Fr. John Lefko, C.PP.S., our former pastor and friend, was celebrating his 50th Priestly Ordination Anniversary. We were invited to the celebration of his Anniversary Mass and reception. We explained this to Rudy and he understood although Mary and I caught a hint of disappointment in his saying, "that's OK." Mary said, "Rudy, you will have so many more birthdays which we will help you celebrate, but Father Lefko will have only one 50th Ordination Anniversary." We came later and helped Rudy conclude the celebration of his 30th birthday party. It would be his <u>LAST</u> while Fr. Lefko went on to live for fourteen more years, celebrating his 55th and 60th and

64th ordination anniversaries!

It was Rudy's example in Christian living that prompted his fiancée, Tammy Bowen, to begin taking instructions in the Catholic Faith. Shortly before Rudy and Tammy were married Tammy was received into the Catholic Church. She was baptized a Catholic and received her First Holy Communion. Not long after, Tammy's mother Carol followed in Tammy's footsteps. Then again, thanks to Rudy's exemplary Christian living, Tammy's sister Jamie took instructions and was baptized a Catholic. What an accomplishment for that young son of ours!

Rudy and Tammy became active in their parish's activities. Fr. Jerry Schweitzer, pastor of St. Stephen the Martyr Church, asked Rudy and Tammy to become involved in the marriage preparation classes held at the church. Their leadership qualities, coupled with their devotion, served them very well as they gave freely of their time and talents.

THE MERRILLVILLE HERALD WSD JULY 13, 1988

A different kind of carnival ride

Amid the food and fun at the St. Stephen the Martyr Church Festival will be a chance to win this 1983 Chrysler E Class auto donated by Kapitan Motors. Pictured with the auto are (l to r) Rudy and Tammy Kapitan; festival chairman Donald Kovan; the Fr. Jerry Schweitzer, and May and Rudy Kapitan Sr. The festival runs from July 21 to July 24 and will feature home-cooked dinners. Hours are 5 p.m. to 11 p.m. Thursday through Saturday and 1 p.m. to 11 p.m. Sunday. All rides will go for a flat fee of $5 from 1 p.m. to 6 p.m. on Sunday.

Rudy, Tammy, Mary and I were all involved in the 1988 St. Stephen the Martyr Church Festival. I served as chairman of the finance committee while Rudy, Tammy and Mary served in the food and beer garden. It was during that festival that Rudy suggested we do something special for

243

our parish. That "something special" would be to donate the first prize for the festival raffle, a car. Rudy went out personally to look for that special car, one that would be a source of pride and joy for anyone to own. He located a 1983 Chrysler with only 28,000 miles. It was a real cream puff, a gold colored four-door model. Little did Rudy or any of us realize that the 1988 St. Stephen's church festival would be his last. What a proper and fitting way for so dedicated a young man to conclude his festival activities for the parish he loved so very much.

As mentioned earlier, we had set a rather lofty goal for Kapitan Motors, Inc. The goal was to sell a million dollars worth of cars in a year. Since the average sale price of cars sold at Kapitan Motors was about $2500.00, Rudy often wondered whether our goal would ever be attained. He said it would happen, using his favorite phrase: "being the good Lord willing!" We came very close, we almost did it. On Saturday, November 5th, 1988 our sales total was $942,600.00. With two months to go before year-end, we would have easily reached our goal of a million dollars in sales. We didn't, Rudy was tragically taken from us!

On the snowy Sunday morning of Nov. 6th, Rudy awakened early, eager to begin what was to have been an exciting day for him. He was going to a Chicago Bear's football game. But first, he had an obligation to fulfill. He would respond faithfully as was his custom, by attending Sunday Mass. He must have kissed his sleeping wife as he left home to participate in the 7:00 AM Sunday Mass. A dusting of light snow, the first snowfall of the year, greeted him as he drove to St. Peter and Paul Church.

His final act of worship began with a smile, typical of Rudy as he extended the "sign of peace" to the Tuckers and the Wolfs, parents of boys with whom he grew up. They especially remembered his firm handshake and warm greeting. Barbara Pawlicki, the Eucharistic Minister, remembered Rudy's warm smile and peaceful countenance as he received the body and blood of Jesus Christ. "Go in peace to love and serve the Lord" was Fr. Teles' final admonition. With a whistle on his lips Rudy hopped down the church steps and jumped into his car eager and willing "to love and serve the Lord."

He was now on his way to our house to pick up those Chicago Bear's tickets for the football game that afternoon. I had placed them on the kitchen table next to a poncho for Rudy to take along. The note said, "Enjoy the game Rudy and use the poncho in good health." Then, Mary and I left for church to attend the eight o'clock Mass at St. Stephens. When we came to the Grand Trunk Railroad crossing, a mile north of our house, a Grand Trunk freight train had just stopped, blocking the crossing. It was 7:45 AM. I suggested to my wife that we turn around and go another way, little knowing that the reason the train stopped was because our son Rudy lay dying on the other side of the tracks!

When we came to the Taft Street crossing, that too was blocked. Realizing that we were not going to cross the Grand Trunk crossings, we decided to go southward to St. Andrew's Church for the 8:30 Mass that morning. There were several St. Stephen parishioners at that Mass, all there because of the blocked Grand Trunk railroad crossings. After Mass one of them said that the reason why the railroad crossings were blocked was due to the fact that a car had been demolished at the Hendricks street crossing. I went numb knowing that Rudy was traveling that way. We hurried home only to see just one set of tire tracks on our snow-covered driveway. We had made those tracks earlier as we left for church. It was evident that Rudy had not driven onto our driveway! We entered the house and there, on the table, were the football tickets and the poncho. Mary and I were numb with fear and in a great state of shock. The telephone rang and we ran to answer it. It was Tammy. "Where is Rudy?" she asked. "Ron Bernachi and Dale Fieldhouse are both here waiting for Rudy to come with the tickets. Where is he, where is he?" she cried.

We called the hospitals. We called the police station. No one had any information for us. Horrifying moments ticked away as hope against hope dwindled. We waited for positive news. Then came the call, which we dreaded. It was from the coroner's office. "How serious were Rudy's injuries?" Mary asked. "Rudy did not survive the accident," came the voice over the phone. "The coroner's office representative is on the way to Rudy's house." We screamed in desperation. "Please God, No. It can't be!" We hurried to Rudy's house where his grief-stricken wife Tammy was being comforted by officers from the coroner's

office. As one of the officers handed Rudy's wallet to Tammy, we knew immediately that it was our dear son Rudy who had been killed at that infamous Hendricks Street railroad crossing. Barely able to speak, I made just one telephone call, to our second eldest son Mike. I announced the horror that had just befallen us. I asked

Rudy's death scene

Mike to call his sisters to tell them the most crushingly tragic news; "Rudy was dead!" Our life had been changed forever.

Rudy's brother and sisters all hastened to Rudy and Tammy's house. There we were comforted by the kind of love that can only flow from family. Tammy's mother and sisters comforted Tammy while my brothers and sisters comforted us in the darkest hour of our lives. Tears flowed freely and the sobbing was uncontrollable. Fr. Jack Winterlin, our pastor, offered support as he led Rudy's grieving family in prayer. I asked Fr. Jack if he had anointed Rudy's body and he said that he did.

For us the only solace of the moment was knowledge of the fact that Rudy's last food on this earth was the Body and Blood of Jesus Christ. Within twenty minutes of his reception of Holy Communion, Rudy would be in eternity with his Lord and Redeemer. Rudy's lips, soon to be sealed forever, were to remain unstained into eternity. The Body of Christ would nourish him on the most important journey of his young life. Unbeknownst to him, with Christ in his heart, he was on his way to eternity!

As the Coroner was removing Rudy's crushed and mangled body from the tracks, strains of "Be Not Afraid" could be heard coming from nearby St. Stephen's Church. The hymn, one of Rudy's favorites, continued, as Rudy's soul was homeward bound ascending heavenward.

"You shall wander far in safety, though you do not know the way....
You shall see the face of God and live...
Be not afraid, I go before you always, come follow me and I will give you rest...
If you stand before the power of hell and **DEATH IS AT YOUR SIDE**,
know that I am with you through it all.
Be not afraid, I go before you always, **come follow me and I will give you rest**!"

In life it was a hymn that Rudy sang with enthusiasm,

and now it accompanied him on his final journey into eternity.

The following day we gathered at our house where Father Sammie Maletta, a friend of ours and of Rudy's, extended himself to assuage our grief and to lead us in prayer. As I spoke I envisioned that the first to greet Rudy as he entered heaven were his grandparents Rudolph and Johanna (Trizna) Kapitan (born in Bobrovec, Okres Liptovky Sv. Mikulas, Slovakia) and Joseph and Anna (Wagner) Kasper (born in Zborov, Okres Bardejov, Slovakia.) Nearby stood a proud great Uncle, Father Ambrose Kapitan with whom Rudy, as a youngster, visited in McKeesport at the Vincentian Sisters of Charity Motherhouse. Rudy was the first grandchild to join his Kapitan-Kasper grandparents. Sts Cyril and Methodius, saints of the Slavs, probably stood by as he thanked both of his grandmothers and grandfathers for having nurtured the faith brought to the Slovak peoples by those two great Saints. What a reunion there must have been in Heaven!

As we sat memorializing Rudy, I voiced a silent prayer of thanksgiving for coming to recognize that my former evil-spirited employer, Norbert Grenchik, presented me with a golden opportunity. I calculated that had he not been such an obtuse person consumed by so evil a spirit to me, I would not have taken an early retirement. Hence I would not have been able to spend the last four years of my dear son Rudy's life with him on a day to day basis. Rudy and I hugged and shook hands hundreds of times as we enjoyed and complimented each other on the business successes which we achieved from day to day. I came to know that the ways of God are indeed inscrutable, and that God does permit bad things to happen to good people for reasons known only to Himself. In God's good time those reasons become apparent to us as they did for me on that first day of broken hearts.

Rudy's brother Mike was late in coming to that therapeutic meeting. Mike had gone to the railroad crossing, cup in hand, to pick up Rudy's brain parts which he had seen earlier at the tragic site. "I didn't want animals to eat any of Rudy's body parts," he said tearfully. "I want all of Rudy's brain and skull parts to have a proper burial." Mike scoured the entire area for over an hour gathering every speck of his brother's precious body parts.

The next day, tears streaming from our eyes, we respectfully buried that cup full of Rudy's parts on the hill of a tract of land where he had planned to build a new house on Harmo road in Merrillville. Rudy, Mike and Carol had just purchased that forty-acre tract two years earlier. Several days before his tragic death, Rudy had picked out a building site. He asked if I would make arrangements for Krull and Sons Surveyors to survey his building site. I made that appointment with the surveyor on Thursday Nov 3rd, three days prior to Rudy's tragic death. The day that we buried part of Rudy, on what was to have been his building site, was the same day on which I called the Surveyor to cancel Rudy's building site survey. Rudy would never build his dream house. He would never have any children to enjoy that house. Rudy and his wife Tammy were "just going to build a house and start a family." None of that would ever be; our beloved Rudy was dead!

It was a somber Wednesday morning as we gathered at Rendina's funeral home to begin our final farewell. I so wanted to shake Rudy's hand and give him a great big farewell hug just as we did so many times during our daily business life together. I couldn't. The doctor forbade my viewing Rudy's mangled body. Although his casket was closed, I could visualize Rudy all dressed up in the white suit that Tammy had purchased for him for their honeymoon. The funeral procession wended its way past Rudy's pride and joy, Kapitan Motors car lot. The building was shrouded in black bunting as it mourned his passing. The wording on the lit marquee was final: "Farewell Dearest Rudy, Rest In Peace." It was there that Rudy displayed an unselfish devotion for service to others. Our workshop and store were a ray of sunshine, a happy place to be. His management made life rewarding for customers and workers alike.

A cold mist fell as Rudy's casket was borne to St. Stephen's Church. There, as he began his last and final entrance, he was greeted by three priests, Fr. Sammie Maletta, a friend of ours, Fr. James Froelich, C.PP.S., a friend and classmate of mine from seminary days, and by Fr. Jack Winterlin, the pastor. As Rudy's white draped casket approached the altar, the congregation sang "The Strife Is O'er, the Battle Done...

Alleluja! Alleluja! Alleluja!
The strife is o'er, the battle done;
The victory of life is won;
The song of triumph has begun.
Alleluja! Alleluja! Alleluja!....
The powers of death have done their worst;
But Christ their legions has dispersed;
Let shouts of praise and joy outburst;
Alleluja!

The church was packed as the mass of Resurrection, celebrating Rudy's young life, began. After the Gospel reading Fr. Sammie Maletta had the homily in which he eulogized Rudy as a saint. Fr. Jack Winterlin, our pastor, then read my farewell letter to Rudy:

"Dearest Son Rudy. Usually I'm pretty good with words, but this morning I'm not! Whatever I say will be void because of the void which fills my broken heart. Throughout this final letter to you dearest son Rudy, whenever I say 'I' or 'my' or 'our,' I mean 'we' — all of us - your loving wife, Tammy; your Mom, your brother Mike and his wife Mary, your sister Sue and her husband, Richard; your sister Carol and her husband Joe; your sister Laura and her dear friend Dan; your sister Dorothy; your niece Jacqueline; your nephew Richard; your dear mother-in-law; your sisters-in-law Beth and Jamie; all your uncles and aunts, cousins and business associates, customers and all who loved you, Rudy, which includes most everyone whose life you touched in your all too brief thirty years of life among us.

Rudy, we loved you because you really were you. Our family philosophy was simple yet powerful - 'whatever you do is a reflection on your whole family.' You outdid yourself son, and our hearts, though very grieving, are full of pride...proud of you, proud of all your accomplishments, proud of the love and happiness and fun which you stirred up on the lives and hearts of all those who were privileged to be a part of your beautiful life. You accomplished in your all too short thirty years what most of us will not accomplish in a full life of sixty or seventy or more years.

You displayed all those admirable qualities, which reflect the essence of your innermost being - a true, sincere Christian spirit. Whatever you were called upon to do, you did it enthusiastically, unselfishly, lovingly, without complaint from the most demanding tasks to even the most menial - like picking up the dog poop at the car lot.

As our first-born, you shouldered the responsibilities placed upon you with a keen awareness of the importance of the moment being lived. And so, Rudy, you fulfilled this responsibility of leadership with wisdom, with love, with patience and always, ALWAYS with generosity.

As you sought to build a life for yourself, Rudy, you looked and were blessed to find a precious young lady, Tammy Bowen. As your courtship brought you two to marriage and you began to live the happy life wished for you on your wedding day just three years ago, I saw the glow of happiness and contentment blossom into a very special life. You and Tammy responded to the love of each other. I was privileged to see the expression of your love for one another as you worked together from day to day at the car lot. I liked what I saw and I considered myself a fortunate father. I prayed that your loving relationship be long and happy and fruitful. It is said that those who honor their father and mother will have a long life on earth. Well, dear soon Rudy, you should have had two hundred years and more of life to share with Tammy, to bring your dreams to fruition. You were the instrument of your wife, Tammy, being baptized into the true church established by Christ. Then her mother and her sister Jamie were baptized into the Catholic faith. What an accomplishment, Rudy —what an accomplishment!

You were the vessel of Christ that brought Mom and me into membership here at St. Stephen's. Thank you Rudy, for introducing us to this most loving community of St. Stephen's. Our lives have been enriched because of this beautiful community and because you brought us here.

In your business dealings, Rudy, you always displayed an unselfish devotion of service for others. This devotion was as much a part of you as the constant smile on your face. When duty called, you were first and foremost of all honest and then compassionate in your dealings with each and every one of your customers. It's no wonder that Kapitan Motors, your pride and joy, nourished by you for ten loving years, had come to exceed the goals and expectations that we placed on it. Our workshop and store were rays of sunshine - a happy place to be. Your management made life rewarding for all your workers and for all associated with Kapitan Motors.

And so, dearest son, your grandparents have met their first grandson, our first born, in the Kingdom of Heaven. You now know the source of the foundation upon which you so successfully built your Christian life. They are proud and we are proud!

We lay you to rest consoled by the knowledge that you received Jesus Christ in the Most Holy Eucharist just minutes before you came to your most tragic death. With Jesus still in your body, your soul was taken into the Kingdom of God.

If the wake service last evening was any indication of our fond farewell, what a tremendous reception you must have received when you arrived in heaven on the first Sunday of the month dedicated to the 'Souls of the Faithful Departed.' When my time comes to leave this world, dear Rudy, it will be easier for me knowing that you will be the first to greet me and I'll be looking for you.

So that your tragic death at the hands of the Grand Trunk Railroad, a federally protected killer, be not in vain, know that we who have loved you in life, vow that your killer will be brought to justice. We will pray to you Rudy, for inspiration. REST IN PEACE DEAREST, DEAREST RUDY."

During the Communion service of Rudy's funeral liturgy, Janet Pietrzak, my sister Mary (Kapitan) Germek's

Angels Wings

daughter, sang a memorial song which she composed especially in memory of her dearly departed cousin and friend. Janet and Rudy were very close throughout their childhood and even into their more mature years. They were like brother and sister. Rudy and Janet were inseparable as cousins.

The Mass of Resurrection, celebrating Rudy's life, was finished. Voices of the congregation permeated the church with the glorious sounds of the recessional hymn—"The Battle Hymn of the Republic." What a fitting conclusion to the church services as those assembled burst into so powerful a song.

"Mine eyes have seen the glory of the coming of the Lord,

He has trampled out the vintage where the grapes of wrath are stored,

He has loosed the fateful lightning of his terrible swift sword,

His truth is marching on....glory, glory Halleluja....his truth is marching on!"

Shivers ran up and down my spine. There was hardly a dry eye as tears streamed down many a check of those assembled. We sang our hearts out as we processed out of St. Stephen's church following Rudy's casket.

At the grave prepared for Rudy as his final resting place, Fr. Sammie Maletta eulogized Rudy as a saint. He concluded the graveside service by saying let us say the prayer that Rudy learned at his Mother's knee. Before Fr. Maletta could begin the Hail Mary, Mike, Rudy's brother began "Zdravas Maria milosti plna."

In unison we all continued the prayer "Pan s tebou;
ty si Pana požehnana medzi ženami
a požehnany je plod života tvojho svateho Ježiš.
Svata Maria Matko Božia,
pros za naš hriešnych
teraz I V HODINU SMRTI našej, Amen."

Rudy's Uncle John Kasper, a retired Air Force Colonel, commenting on Rudy's funeral said: "I've been to hundreds of funerals at Arlington National Cemetery; funerals of VIP's, Admirals and Generals and never have I attended so beautiful and inspiring a funeral as Rudy's. What a tremendous outpouring of love, the spirit of God was surely present."

The funeral director stated that never before had so many waited in line to pay their last respects. He also mentioned that never before had the funeral chapel been so overfilled with floral tributes. There were floral tributes from all of the family member's employers. Conspicuous in its absence was the fact that the American Trust & Savings Bank, my thirty two-year employer, sent no floral tribute or any expression of sympathy. It was difficult for family and friends to comprehend that Norbert Grenchik, the bank president, joined by his brother Philip, his Vice President, continued his abhorrent animosity and evil spiritedness even in the face of death! Dolores Grenchik Smolen, a member of the Board of Directors of the bank, was the

Thoughts

Life has not really ended,
It has only just begun,
For those who follow Jesus,
The victory's already been won.

We cannot understand His ways,
For all walk a different path.
But if we trust His mercy,
It will lead to joy not wrath.

Rudy was so very young
When suddenly — one snowy day,
His earthly life was over,
From loved ones he went away.

We must remember dear ones,
That today is here for a while.
Let us not waste precious moments,
Even when faced with this trial.

God has a way of healing
The wounded, broken heart.
Let Him enter yours now
And tender a fresh new start.

Lord teach us to love one another
Today, before it's too late.
We believe and trust in Your mercy,
That met Rudy at the gate.
                              Tillie Bryan

In Loving Memory ~ Rudy Kapitan Jr. ~ 11·6·88

only Grenchik to share in our grief by attending Rudy's wake and offering her condolences.

Besides the hundreds of Mass cards, floral tributes and other mementos, there were poems written in memory of Rudy. One such poem written by my sister Tillie (Kapitan) Bryan, is printed on previous page.

Of the many sympathy cards received, one especially is worthy of mention. It came from Randy Padol, a friend of Rudy's. Randy lives in Texas and wrote as follows: "This is what I will remember most about Rudy, his enthusiasm and determination for a challenge. Just a beginning skater and determined to master the terrain. His confidence made him explain his plans in detail like a teacher. He made every meeting feel like a special event from the road trips to Texas, the Indy 500, Redbud races, skateboarding in Lafayette, down to trips to South Park (Griffith), Sa-cha grinders, or looking at cars. These and more I will always remember. Please accept my love and condolences." Randy enclosed a photograph of Rudy skateboarding in 1978, ten years prior to his death. Note the determination

A study in "Intensity" - Rudy skateboarding at age 20.

on the face of 20 year old Rudy!

Within two week after Rudy's tragic death, the Grand Trunk railroad installed gates and lights at that infamous Hendricks Street crossing, thanks to the involvement of Governor Evan Bayh and U.S. Senators Richard Lugar and Dan Coats. Tim Sanders of their office was most helpful in this praiseworthy effort. These Senators joined the hundreds of voices in protest asking the Federal Highway Administration and INDOT for an immediate resolution to the safety problems that existed at this and other Indiana rail-highway crossings.

On Sunday November 5, 1989, a year to the Sunday of Rudy's death, I organized a Memorial Service and Dedication at the Hendricks Street's Grand Trunk Railroad crossing. The memorial service was for my son Rudy, killed at that crossing on Nov 6, 1988; for Julie Rothenberg, killed at that crossing on Oct. 4, 1987 and for Frank Razmus killed at that crossing on June 19, 1986. In an awful 29 month period, each of the trio was struck and killed by a train passing through the then-unmarked, unguarded crossing. Rudy's crumpled wreckage was made visible at that service. It was returned to the site on a flatbed.

Despite the gray skies and chilling drizzle, some two hundred tearful friends stood together at the death site to memorialize the three young lives lost at that infamous crossing. In their honor, Rudy's brother Mike constructed and erected two crucifixes, one for his brother Rudy, one for Frank Razmus and a Star of David for Julie Rothenberg.

WLTH radio personality John Jage presided over the hour-long service. Fr. Jack Winterlin prayed the invocation and the benediction. Lake County Corner Dr.

Mourn

From Page 1

Rudy Kapitan, Sr., holds wooden crosses bearing the names of two of the accident victims.

Photos by Joe Negrich

Mike Kapitan erects the wooden cross bearing the name of his brother.

stallation of the Hendricks Street crossing gates and lights, Rudy F. Kapitan Sr., said.

In his emotionally-charged speech, Kapitan implored the gathered citizens to become involved and voice complaints to politicians and railroad officials.

"You have the power, you do the voting," Kapitan exclaimed.

CARRS goals, Kapitan explained, are three-fold. First, the group will educate the public on the need for flashing lights at all crossings and, secondly, work toward establishing and enforcing alcohol and sub-

berg remarked. "But," she added later, "we will do everything in our power, through litigation and this organization (CARRS) to change what happens here."

CARRS is actively seeking members to keep its fight alive. Annual donations are $15 per individual and $50 for organizations and businesses.

Send checks to: CARRS Inc., 6929 Hendricks St., Merrillville, 46410. Checks should be made payable to CARRS, Inc.

Daniel Thomas addressed the crowd. Local and state political leaders were there to lend their support. At this memorial service I introduced our newly formed organization Citizens Against Rail Road Slaughter (CARRS). Quotes from my prepared text are as follows: "A year ago on this Sunday, my son Rudy J. Kapitan was killed at this crossing. Here is where the Grand Trunk caused a most terrible nightmare, changing our lives forever...His vehicle was crushed with a force similar to an automobile crushing a pop can! Several days prior to Rudy's death I spoke with Grand Trunk workers. I complimented them on what appeared to be the completion of a long overdue improvement to this sight. I asked when the gates and lights would be installed. They said not until next year. I responded, 'you cannot open this crossing to traffic without gates and lights, there's going to be another fatality here.' Little did I realize that in a few days my son Rudy would be the victim. We have lived on this road for some 23 years. Rudy knew this crossing like the back of his hand. We all did! Despite this, Rudy was killed and on more than one occasion members of my family including myself were almost killed here. There are some of you out there who have told me of your near death misses at this crossing....Now come the statistics published by the railroads and by Operation Lifesaver. They claim that over 50% of all fatalities occur when the victims go around lowered gates. <u>These statistics are not accurate</u>. They do not take into account irresponsible railroading or the ineffective and shoddy maintenance of gates and lights, or the callous disregard of the RR as they fail to provide safe trespasses.   Is the GT a responsible member of this community when it fails in its statutory obligation to maintain its crossings? To quote the statute: 'the RR's are responsible to afford security for life and property of persons and vehicles using the public highways.' Did they violate this statute allowing Rudy, Julie and Frank to be killed here? I submit that they did and they did so most flagrantly....Is the GT a good neighbor when they maintain their right-of-way as they do. Look east and on the south bank you will see a pile of rusting metal bandings laying there for almost a year. On the north side you will see rotting railroad ties strewn all about the right-of-way....Add to all this the fact that the GT is 4 years delinquent with payment of real estate taxes on property owned by them in this county....Statistics published by the US Dept. of Transportation Federal Railroad Administration paint a picture of carnage at railway crossings throughout the United States.   Of all the States in the Union, we in Indiana, according to these statistics, rank either first, second, or third in all the rail-highway crossing accidents and incidents. Consider that we rank 14th in population and 38th in land area; further, that of the 7744 RR crossings in Indiana only 967 are protected by gates and lights!....... I quote even more horrendous statistics: Indiana, with four and a half million registered vehicles ranks 14th in vehicle registrations of all the states. Yet, per 10,000 automobile registrations, Indiana ranks second in total accidents, third in fatalities and second in total injuries sustained at RR crossings....Given the extremely poor status regarding the protection and preservation of our rights at railroad crossings and the extremely well lobbied protection of what railroads claim to be their rights, it becomes incumbent upon us to organize in order to protect our rights. We now ask that you be supportive of those goals which we propose as worthy of your most serious consideration. We ask that each of you join us as members of CARRS....Our goal is to preserve your life by protecting your rights in favor of railroad rights We do not want any of you to suffer the kind of tragedy that we did, nor do we want you to endure the pain that we do when looking at a wreckage like this (pointing to Rudy's crushed vehicle)."

Because of my efforts in behalf of CARRS, I was honored and privileged to be named Merrillville Man of the year in 1989.

So that Rudy's death would not be in vain I continued in my efforts to promote safety at rail-highway crossings. A year later, I spoke at a State Chamber of Commerce meeting in Indianapolis. During that same year, at the invitation of Congressman Pete Visclosky, I was given the opportunity to address a congressional committee. I quote from that address as I made an impassioned plea: "In my hand I have a death certificate. It is a death certificate of my thirty-year-old son Rudy J. Kapitan. It specifies that his death occurred at the Grand Trunk's Hendricks Street crossing in Merrillville. Here in my other hand I hold a photograph of his crushed vehicle. If you look closely you will see his mangled body laying some 25 feet from the wreckage...Three fatalities in less than 29 months to say nothing of many other accidents at that infamous crossing. Dana Meulemans of Griffith is a survivor of one of those tragedies. His life was forever unmistakably altered there on July 22, 1981 by a speeding Grand Trunk freight train. To this day the nightmare of this 26 year old Dana haunts him as he continues to make attempts to recover from that crushing, near death experience......

Are we Hoosiers a reckless lot, hell bent on self-destruction? Is that what the FRA and Operation Lifesaver want us to believe? Do they believe that Hoosier's rights are adequately protected when only 967, or to put it more susicently, only 12% of the 7744 rail-highway crossings in Indiana are protected by gates and lights?.....I submit that when you or I fail to be 100% attentive to the demands placed on us as highway users, we're only human! Should we then be condemned to death because of our humanity, because of a momentary misdirection of attention? Should not the extreme hazard of a MEGA TON TRAIN, speeding along at up to a permitted 110 M.P.H., be unmistakably marked as EXTREMELY HAZARDOUS? Killers on death row are afforded more consideration than this!.....Ladies and gentlemen of this committee, we need your support at the Federal level to fund and implement safety programs in Indiana.....The primary objective of the organization, which I represent, is to promote safety at rail-highway crossings. To that end we outline five proposals as goals of our organization. 1) Flashing lights as a minimum protection at every crossing. 2) Require mandatory alcohol and substance abuse testing of all railroad personnel involved in any accident. 3) Set a time limit for a railroad to correct malfunctions, imposing meaningful penalties for delays. 4) Educate through media publicity in order to correct railroad abuses.   5) Promote legislation which would compel the railroads to pay their fair share for rail crossing improvements."

I concluded my address by saying: "The voice of my son Rudy cries out from his grave to correct the obscene and disgraceful state of railroad affairs in Indiana.   From hundreds of graves throughout Indiana, Rudy's lament is joined by the cries of hundreds to put an end to railroad abuses, an end to the kind of irresponsibility which denied them their constitutional guaranteed right to life, liberty and the pursuit of happiness. The nightmare caused by Rudy's tragic and violent death will never cease for us. It is with broken hearts that we consider the acts of omission and commission of those responsible for rail-highway safety.   Legislative bodies continue to be plagued by legislation geared to protect what the railroads claim to be their unjust and unfair rights, at our expense. Powerful lobby groups are positioned throughout this state and nation, concerned only with promoting the selfish demands of railroads.   CARRS, we "Citizens Against Railroad Slaughter" invite your individual and collective assistance in promoting legislation to correct the injustices caused by the negligent acts of so irresponsible a railroad system and the legislation which has allowed that. Thank you for asking me to participate in this Congressional Hearing."

Efforts to promote safety at rail-highway crossings continued while in a court of law Rudy's widow filed a lawsuit. Her attorney succeeded in obtaining a favorable decision in the case of Tamara Lee Kapitan, Special Administratrix, versus the Grand Trunk Western Railway Co. It took fourteen years of Railroad procrastination, of venuing the case from county to county, of continuances, of filing appeal after appeal until finally Rudy's case came to rest before the United States Supreme Court! There, the Association of American Railroads filed an Amicus Brief. Their contention was that this case was so important for the railroad industry that the entire Association of American Railroads needed to show its support for the

No. 01-1212

In The
Supreme Court of the United States

GRAND TRUNK WESTERN RAILWAY CO.,
Petitioner,

v.

TAMARA LEE KAPITAN, Special Administratrix
of the Estate of RUDOLPH J. KAPITAN,
Respondent.

On Petition for a Writ of Certiorari
to the Indiana Court of Appeals

RESPONDENT'S BRIEF IN OPPOSITION

KENNETH J. ALLEN
(Counsel of Record)
JAMES E. BRAMMER
KENNETH J. ALLEN & ASSOCIATES
Allen Law Building
1109 Glendale Boulevard
Valparaiso, IN 46383
(219) 465-6292

Counsel for Respondents

April 22, 2002

Grand Trunk's position.

Thanks to the diligence and the brilliant pursuit of Attorney Allen, the Supreme Court of the United States found in Rudy's favor. The multi-million dollar award to Tammy was upheld. The attorney wrote to us saying: "Most importantly, at least for now, the results achieved in your son's case will encourage the entire industry to be more vigilant in installing flashing lights and gates at railroad crossings—ultimately saving many other families from the terrible loss you have suffered and the grief which I know you continue to endure."

The landmark status of Rudy's case will live in legal annals forever. **Little Rudy, our David, had defeated Goliath!** Rudy was not ours to keep; we had to give him back! Was that why Rudy was born; to make his mark by becoming a martyr for the cause of safety? Perhaps it was. In any case, Rudy's death was not in vain and his family, although we continue to grieve, have closure. We whisper, "Thank you Rudy for all your marvelous accomplishments even in your death." Our thanks is from those whom you have already helped and from the unknown many who will benefit from your untimely and tragic death.

A Twin Miracle? - Just as he helped in life so does Rudy help from his celestial position. Rudy's brother Mike and his wife Mary wanted to start a family early in their marriage. Wanting to have immediate success, they began praying to Rudy. After all, Fr. Sammie Maletta eulogized Rudy as a saint, so why not ask him to place their petition at the feet of the Giver of all good gifts. My wife began praying, praying to her son Rudy, asking him to intercede in behalf of his brother Mike and his wife Mary.

One sunny spring day Mike invited us over for dinner. As we sat around the table on his deck, a deck which Rudy helped him build, we prayed a blessing "Bless us oh Lord and these gifts which we are about to receive from thy bounty through Christ our Lord, Amen." Then, Mike added excitedly "and bless the child which Mary is carrying." What a beautiful way Mike chose to announce Mary's pregnancy. We were overjoyed. Our prayers had been answered. The hugs, which were extended, had a very special meaning. On our way home that evening Mary said, "I'm not done praying, I'm going to pray for twins. I've always wanted twins and now I want Mary Kapitan 'Junior' to have twins."

Mary was having difficulty in keeping food down and so the doctor ordered an ultrasound. The ultrasound came back showing that Mary had conceived twins. Both Mary and Mike were ecstatic. When Mike called us to announce the good news, his Mother was out shopping. On her return I said, "call Mike, he has some good news." Mary said, "I'll bet that the good news is that Mary is pregnant with twins!" "How did you know that?" I asked. "Remember'" she said. "I've been praying to Rudy for twins and I knew that my mother's prayer would be answered!" "That is not the end of my praying," she said, "now I'm going to ask for twin boys, one for Mike and one to take Rudy's place."

Seven weeks before her due date Mary went into premature labor. Mike called from the hospital keeping us abreast of Mary's progress. We prayed for a healthy delivery as we drove over to the hospital. When we arrived, an exhausted but overjoyed Mike greeted us with the news that Mary had given birth to twin boys! As preemies one weighed in at 4 lbs and three oz., and the other 4 lbs and 6 oz. Although the doctors gave the boys a good survival rate, they were both weak and placed in incubators where they remained for four weeks. The first born was named Jacob Rudolph and his twin brother was named Brandon Michael.

Another Miracle? - At a meeting of St. Stephen's altar rosary sodality my wife Mary spoke of her success in praying to Rudy; first of all for a quick pregnancy, then for twins and finally for twin boys. Months later, one of the St. Stephen's parishioners came to us after Mass one Sunday morning and said, "Thanks to your son Rudy, we have a healthy grandson." As it happened she was at that altar rosary sodality meeting when Mary explained her success in praying to Rudy. Her daughter, a high school classmate of Rudy's, was having difficulty in becoming pregnant. She and her husband prayed to Rudy. Their prayers were answered and she delivered a healthy baby boy. The efficacy of intercessory prayer was made manifest.

On the Thursday after Rudy was killed, the altar rosary sodality of St. Stephen's had scheduled their annual Christmas party. Mary had tickets for that event which went unused. Several days after Rudy's funeral Jeannette Romischer, President of the lady's society, gave Mary six miniature porcelain Christmas bears. The four-inch porcelain bears were used in the centerpieces, which adorned each festive table. "Since you were not there," Jeannette said, "we gathered six of those porcelain bears for you, one for each of your children."

On her return home Mary placed the six miniature porcelain bears on the table and marked each with an indelible marker. The marks were the initials of each child's first name. The first miniature bear was marked R for Rudy; the second M for Mike; the third S for Sue; the fourth C for Carol; the fifth L for Laura and the sixth was marked D for Dorothy. Then she proceeded to stand each of them on the table. The R for Rudy bear would not stand up, it kept falling down. All the other bears stood upright on the table except for Rudy. Rudy kept on falling down. To this very day the bear marked R for Rudy keeps on falling down; it will not stand up because it died!

Chapter XXIX - Some Of Our Travels

In the year that followed Rudy's death, Mary and I decided to do some traveling just by ourselves. We purchased a motor home and began visiting states that we had not visited with our children. Then, to keep our minds off the horrible tragedy which had befallen us, we traveled to those sites and places that we had especially enjoyed while traveling with our children. It was during that year that Mary's sister Marge Dubczak wanted to ease our burden of having lost a son. She asked us to go on a cruise with her and her husband Ray. We so enjoyed that cruise that cruising became a part of our travel planning.

It was on a subsequent cruise, dubbed as a "Caribbean Valentine Cruise," that I responded to a contest held aboard the cruise ship on Valentine's Day. The rules of the contest were to write in two hundred words or less why your valentine should be chosen as "The Perfect Valentine of the Cruise." I wrote:

"Thirty two years later I would again marry the same gal that I recommend be chosen as 'The Perfect Valentine of the Cruise.' Because of her unselfish giving of self she made a home where love could always be found. Her husband and six children always came first. From early morning prayer, sitting around a well balanced breakfast table, to evening time when a sit down dinner always awaited her husband and children, to later helping with the children's homework, she daily found time to satisfy the needs of her family UNSELFISHLY. Her sacrifices flowed over to the children's school and church activities where she often volunteered.

And now, as President of two family-owned corporations she continues to provide the leadership and dedication which has prompted success for our five living children. The sixth child, our first born son Rudy, was tragically killed while returning home from church on a Sunday morning. It happened three months ago at an unguarded railroad crossing in our hometown of Merrillville, Indiana. Again at that most tragic time in our lives, she provided the love and comfort that were so desperately needed. I recommend Mary E. Kapitan as the Perfect Valentine of the Cruise."

Mary was chosen as "The Perfect Valentine of the Cruise." At a special recognition dinner we were invited to sit at the Captain's table. There she received some gifts and her award certificate. The Captain proposed a toast in tribute to Mary Elizabeth Kasper Kapitan, "The Perfect Valentine of the Cruise." I sat there proud as a peacock.

One of our later cruises was referred to as "The Cruise to Hell." This cruise was a Panama Canal Cruise taken during the end of March and the beginning of April. I wrote this summary of that infamous cruise to the Director of the Regency Cruise Lines. The detail, which may prove to be uninteresting reading, was left in so as to preserve the genuineness of that letter.

A 1999 APRIL FOOLS CRUISE - Fools that we were, we accepted after much protest, the air travel package for the March 28 Panama Canal Cruise prepared by Regency Cruises. We chose Regency because on three prior Regency cruises, we had direct, non-stop flights from Chicago to the cruise ship's port and because we thoroughly enjoyed the cruises. But not this time. We were to fly from Chicago to Atlanta, connect there for a flight to Miami and connect there for a flight to Montego Bay. After unsuccessful attempts to cancel the cruise, our travel agent upgraded our cabins two levels. She knew that the cruise was a special birthday present for my wife. I had just had angioplasty and prior open-heart surgery. Doctor's orders were okay to go but not to exert myself. The travel agent told us to relax and to prepare for a pleasant vacation aboard the Regency. What followed was anything but that. We, my wife and I, my brother Tony and my sister-in-law Marge Dubczak, experienced enough stress to last a lifetime! What follows is an abbreviated narrative of that tortuous experience. THE LETTER:

"Boarding for Delta flight 1696 departing from Chicago for Miami at 6:15 AM on 3-28-93 was as scheduled. Due to a mechanical failure we departed Chicago two hours later. As a result we missed Delta flight #15095 in Atlanta connecting for Miami. Red coats hurried us from terminal 5 to 33 where Delta flight #1207 was being held for the 150+ passengers bound for Miami. During that hurried and arduous hike, twenty-eight terminals in length, my wife Mary began to wheeze and her breathing became labored. When we finally arrived at the plane, an anxious stewardess helped seat my wife and relief came when Mary began to inhale Proventil.

We arrived in Miami at 1:05 PM and were told that 'Red Coats' awaited to assist with our connecting flight. There were no 'Red-Coats' and we were at the mercy of Miami airport personnel. Delta personnel advised that we hurry to the Air Jamaica terminal (from one end of the airport to the other) to make our connecting flight. Arriving at the AJ ticket counter, we rushed to the ticket agent for direction and were told to get in line behind some fifty people. We told the agent we could not wait in line because we were to be aboard SAJ #22 bound for Montego Bay. She advised that AJ #22 had just departed. We were frantic as we spoke to her of our dilemma—our cruise ship, Regent Star, was to sail from Montego Bay at 8:00 PM. That was not her problem, she advised in broken English. I felt like I was back in Prague, Czechoslovakia, where in 1985, we had a similarly sad experience with Communistic airport personnel — we were DIRTY AMERICANS!

After many hassles, we were 'confirmed stand byes' on the AJ 3:00 PM flight bound for Montego Bay. We had to be on this flight since the next AJ flight was at 8:00 PM and our cruise ship was sailing at 8:00 PM. A little over an hour prior to departure, we arrived at the departure gate. We spoke to the boarding personnel of our dilemma. We surrendered our tickets to an AJ lady agent who assured us that we would be on the flight. Boarding that flight were some sixty Jamaican 'migrant workers.' Each had a 'boom box' radio in hand. During the boarding we approached the attendant several times expressing our concern and anxiety. Not once did AJ announce an oversold position to ask ticket holders to exchange seats for a later flight. The AJ agent told us not to worry, she would call us. When the announcement came that the flight was to depart, we ran to her and asked for seating confirmation. She told us all seats were taken that she had six seats but gave them away because she 'forgot about us.' How could she forget about us when she had our tickets in her hands? The anxiety, which overcame all of, caused me especially to experience debilitating angina. My cardiologist agreed to a vacation without STRESS! It took several nitro tablets to relieve the angina. We made a hurried walk back to the AJ counter where, fortunately, we were not told to get back in line. Rather, the agent advised that an American flight was departing at 5:30 PM for Montego Bay. She said it would be necessary for us to personally return to the Delta ticket counter for a signed voucher authorizing flight on

American Airlines. Back across the entire airport to the Delta counter where we receive the necessary authorization with the admonition 'hope we don't see you again.' Then, we again hurried across the airport to AJ and the to American Airlines counter.

At American we were placed on 'confirmed' for flight #880 departing at 5:30 PM for Montego Bay. Just before scheduled boarding, personnel at American announced that flight #880 had been oversold and were asking for passengers to relinquish their seats. Frantically we asked American personnel what 'confirmed' meant. They assured us that although no seat numbers could be assigned us, we were confirmed to depart on flight #880. Once more, we felt like thieves trying to steal a flight. The boarding announcements began to leave us numb. Again we approached the counter and made known that if we were not on this flight, our cruise ship was sailing without us. Twenty minutes seemed like hours, until we were finally allowed to board. AA #880 would be departing at 5:30 PM and arriving in Montego Bay at 6:45 PM, just enough time to go through customs, immigration and jump aboard the bus taking us to the port where Regent Star was docked. At 5:35 PM the pilot announced that there would be a slight delay inasmuch as three flights were taking off ahead of us. The three flights turned out to be over fifteen flights taking off or landing! As minutes ticked away, anxiety was mounting for the four of us. At 6:00 PM our pilot announced that the air controllers had just changed shifts and we'd be leaving momentarily with arrival time in Montego Bay at 7:20 PM. We finally departed at 7:20 PM just forty minutes before our cruise ship was scheduled to depart. Upon landing we rushed off the plane and headed for the baggage claim area. Thank God our luggage was there. It had arrived earlier on the 3:00 PM AJ flight. We went through customs, immigrations and boarded a bus waiting to take us to the Regent Star. At 7:55 PM, some seventeen hours after leaving home, we exhaustedly walked up the gangplank to strains of 'When the Saints Come Marching In' which was being played by the cruise ship's band. Just as we boarded the ship, the gangplank was drawn up. The first day of our cruise vacation will never be forgotten. Never before had we been so totally drained both physically and emotionally.

Monday, March 29th was pleasantly spent at sea catching our breath trying to forget the nightmare we experienced in getting to Montego Bay from Chicago. On Tuesday we arrived at Costa Rica. The four of us decided to see the sights by hiring our own cab driver. We had done this many times before on other cruises at various ports of call. We were always pleased with the results. As we disembarked several drivers who promised worthwhile tours approached us. We hired Oscar and his red Nissan van. While shopping in San Jose, my sister-in-law Marge fell bruised both knees and sprained her ankle. The streets and sidewalks were in much disrepair and she had difficulty in walking, so we began our return to the van. As we walked, Oscar suggested that, for safety sake, I transfer my wallet from my rear pocket, which was double buttoned, to my front side pocket. I did exactly what he told me. Moments later my pocket was being picked by a passer-by. It was fortunate that I grabbed his hand as it came out of my pocket with my wallet. I was in shock as I yelled, 'You SOB, drop my wallet.' He dropped my wallet and began to run. Oscar our guide, a supposed famous Soccer player, stood there without making any effort to apprehend the thief.

When we returned to the dock, I paid Oscar the agreed upon fare. He began an argument increasing the original fare by one hundred dollars. I soon began to realize that the pocket picking episode was a 'set up,' and that Oscar must have been 'in on it.' I hurried for the ship's gangplank. Oscar followed me as I walked up the gangplank where the ship's personnel stopped him. I disappeared into the ship. I had successfully 'escaped' from Oscar. I reported the incident to several ships' crewmembers. So, on the third day my report is that misfortune befell us again. We were physically hurt and emotionally drained.

On Wednesday morning, the fourth day, our cruise ship arrived at the Panama Canal. Just prior to our return passage through the Canal, our cruise director announced that we would not be going to Aruba, the next port of call. The Canal passage took two hours longer than planned and, we were told, there was a shortage of fuel and water! Rumors circulated that the same thing happened earlier, on a prior cruise. It seemed that a mutiny was in the making. Petitions for an uninterrupted sailing to Aruba began to circulate. To compound the adversity of the fourth day, the vessel's air conditioning had failed entirely. We had absolutely no air conditioning and cabin temperatures were higher than the 90+ degrees outside temperature. The cruise director announced that the air conditioning would be repaired at Cartagena, which would be our next port of call.

On the fifth day we arrived at Cartagena. The repair parts were not available. The air conditioning was not repaired as promised. As we left Cartagena on that 'April Fools Day,' announcements were made that our cruise was being cut short and that the Captain was in contact with the New York office for further direction. We sailed for Jamaica. That fifth day was a disaster.

Plans were being made to fly all passengers home early. The cruise was 'kaput!' That evening half of the ships passengers were sleeping outside on deck chairs. Heat in the cabins was intense and unbearable. At about 2:00 AM we experienced extremely rough seas. Waves came crashing up onto the UP deck where we were 'bunked.' We were forced to return to our cabins. It was there with the intense, oppressive heat and the rough seas that I became deathly ill. I expected that I would die. When morning came all my bedding was drenched with perspiration. What happened in our cabin was being experienced, to more or less a degree, in many cabins. Ships' attendants told of passengers crying and trembling, unable to get out of their cabins. The sixth day was a disaster! Petitions were being circulated for a 'class action' lawsuit against the cruise line.

On Saturday, the seventh day, we docked at Montego Bay. After waiting for three and one half-hours we were transported by bus to Wyndham Rose Hall Resort. What a suprisingly pleasant experience that proved to be. They couldn't be more pleasant or cordial. We almost forgot what it was like to be human. The next day, Sunday, we arrived at Sangster Airport at 7:45 AM for AJ flight #57 to Miami leaving at 9:30 AM. We were in line with our luggage when, at 8:00 AM our flight was cancelled and the ETD was announced to be at 5:30 PM, eight hours later. AJ Personnel began attempts to book alternative flights for Atlanta to Chicago or for Miami to Chicago. I went to a water fountain seeking a refreshing drink. When I turned on the water out crawled a cockroach. Unbelievable, or was it? Needless to say I drank no water at that airport. After

276

an hour our agent had finally confirmed flights AJ #311 departing Montego Bay at 12:45 PM for Miami and from Miami to Chicago at 5:30 PM on United #437.

We arrived in Miami at 2:00 PM, claimed our luggage and discovered that one bag was missing. A lost bag report was filed with AJ and we went through customs. United baggage handler took our luggage to United #437, our connecting flight to Chicago. We called home to give our children the new flight arrival information. We arrived at the United terminal two hours before the scheduled departure. As soon as a ticket agent arrived we asked for seat confirmation. He checked and said our names were NOT on the list. We told him AJ personnel in Montego Bay confirmed four seats early that morning on United #437. He looked at us as if we had lost our minds and said the flight was sold out two days ago! What kind of idiots work for AJ who make such anxiety-causing mistakes? Again we called our children to tell them we would not be on United #437.

Back we went to AJ (half way across the airport) to make new arrangements for our flight home to Chicago. After about an hour, the AJ attendant said we were not flying home tonight. She confirmed flights on American #562 departing Monday morning at 8:59 AM. Again we called our children to tell them we would be arriving in Chicago at noon, on Monday, April 5. We were then sent to the Best Western (really it was the WORST Western) for the night. Dinner vouchers were provided by AJ. Those vouchers proved to be totally inadequate. We were not in the mood for hamburgers and so we ordered 'ordinary' rib dinners. Our receipts show that we were $55.53 out of pocket for those dinners. The next morning we were again 'out of pocket' for our breakfast meal. We departed Miami on American #562 not at 8:59 AM as scheduled, but at 9:30 AM and arrived in Chicago at 12:30 PM. The reason for the delay in departing was that the airline had double-booked some seats and there was a problem.

When we arrived in Chicago, our luggage was not on the American flight. After some delay and searching, we found it at the United baggage claim center where it had arrived the day before. A drained and weary foursome, exhausted from a week in hell, returned home late that afternoon. It was a day later than originally scheduled and from a cruise that had been cancelled three days prior to schedule. Two of our foursome missed work on that Monday. Also, it was the first time that any of us lost weight on a cruise!

Having cruised with Regency on three prior occasions, we find their compensatory offer (a partial cruise, sans airfare) altogether inappropriate. Instead of providing what had been contracted for (a cruise typically pleasant and relaxing) we were mired in a sea of trouble. Misfortune befell us day after day leaving us numb from anxiety and torment of heart.

Further we hold Air Jamaica responsible for the kind of careless and in human treatment that produced enough anxiety to last a lifetime. We look to them for compensation. Delta failed in their responsibility to provide the kind of passage, which they proclaim in their motto: 'we're ready when you are.' We suffered much because of their incompetence.

It has taken me several weeks since our return to compose myself to the point of being able to relive and write about the above nightmare. We look for an early resolution and compensation from the three above mentioned offenders." **End of letter.**

Other Travels - Needless to say the compensation was

altogether inadequate. We were, however, reimbursed with a cruise to Alaska. On that Alaskan cruise we did gain the weight we had lost on the disastrous Panama Canal cruise.

IRELAND - A memorable overseas trip was the one we took to Ireland during the month of February in 1998. When we arrived in Dublin, we rented a car. We rented the stick shift because the automatic rented out for twice the cost of a stick shift transmission car. Although the steering and shifting mechanisms were on the right side of the car and we drove on the opposite side of the street, my wife Mary did manage. Mary figured if the Irish can do it well, Mary Kapitan can do it. And do it she did as she drove some 1,300 miles during the next twelve days, as we traveled around the entire southern perimeter of that Irish Isle. One of the many interesting adventures of that trip was visiting the "Blarney Stone." Although

Mary kissing Blarney Stone is held firm by niece Nancy Dubczak.

she didn't need to, Mary walked up the hundred plus steps to kiss the Blarney Stone.

One Sunday as we exited a church in Waterford, several parishioners stopped to talk to us. In our conversation they suggested that we visit their cemetery located behind the church. There, they said, we would find monuments dating back to the eleventh century. As we began to walk towards the cemetery, there on the ground, near the church, was a shiny coin. It sparkled in the morning sunlight. Mary stooped down to pick it up. "Oh, my" she exclaimed, "I cannot believe this." "Look at this Irish penny, its dated 1988, the year Rudy was killed; and after all these years it is still in mint condition! It looks like it has never been used!" Mary looked towards the heavens and said, "Thank you Rudy; I know that you are watching over us. I know that we are going to have a great time in Ireland." We did. And we came to believe that the coin was a "penny from heaven."

During our stay the native people were exceptionally friendly and the "bed and breakfast" hosts were most accommodating. The weather was unusually mild and dry. Unlike a typical rainy February in Ireland where it rains every single day, it rained very briefly on only two days during our entire twelve-day stay. As we prepared to depart, the headlines on the newspaper stands at the airport in Dublin read "Get Ready For Winter's Blast." The front-page story said that Ireland had experienced the balmiest February in history! It went on to say that it couldn't be remembered when there ever was a week without rain! I looked at Mary with misty eyes and she at me. Our emotions were stirred as we recognized Rudy's presence with us.

HAWAII - When I write about the weather that we experienced in Ireland, I cannot help but recall the weather of another time and another place. On the day that we were to return to Chicago from a Hawaiian vacation, the temperature in Hawaii was a short-sleeved 86 degrees. When we arrived in Chicago, we hurriedly changed from our summer attire to winter clothing. It was a frigid January day in Chicago. The temperature was a bone chilling 23 degrees below zero! What a shocker for our bodies as we experienced a 109 degree temperature difference within an eight-hour period! Our car, which had been parked at the airport for some ten days, was non-responsive to our attempts to start it. It was frozen solid!

Courteous airport parking personnel assisted and stayed with us until we got it started and saw to it that we were on our way back home to Indiana.

ITALY - Another memorable vacation worth mentioning was a trip we took to Italy. We spent Holy Week in the Eternal City. On Holy Thursday we were privileged to be present at the Chrism Mass celebrated by Pope John Paul II in St. Peter's Cathedral. We were part of a multi national, multi lingual congregation most of whom were overwhelmed at being present for so solemn a celebration. At the conclusion of the Mass the Pope rode down the center isle, blessing us as he went by. Chills ran up and down our spines, as the Vicar of Christ passed by us, no more than fifteen feet from where we stood in this magnificent basilica.

Adding to the solemnity of our stay in Rome was a general audience with the Pope in St. Peter's Square. *"Viva La Papa"* and *"Sto Liet"* and *"Nech Žije Papež"* and "Long Live the Pope" shouted banner carrying youths representing many nations from throughout the world. Bishop and Cardinal Emissaries from different nations, speaking in their native languages, made special presentations to the Pope as he sat on his throne on a podium with St. Peter's Basilica as a backdrop. Was it through Rudy's intercession that we were so blessed to have tickets for so momentous an occasion? Mary and I couldn't answer that.

Easter Sunday morning was celebrated with parades and fireworks in Florence. We positioned ourselves on the parade route near the *Duomo*, the Cathedral Church in Florence. The parade ended in the cathedral square. We watched in awe as wagon upon wagon passed by decorated with fireworks of every kind. Some of those wagons were two and even three stories in height and loaded with fireworks. Festooned in colorful costumes were hundreds of flag carrying marchers performing flag waving acrobatic stunts. They tossed and twirled those multicolored silk flags with absolute precision. The firework wagons came to rest in front of the Cathedral. As the parade ended white doves were released from the church tower as a signal for the fireworks to begin. For about a half-hour that church square shook as earth shattering "varooms" announced the glorious Resurrection of "Jesus Christ who had been crucified and rose from the dead." We were privileged to witness an Easter celebration of epic proportions.

BAHAMAS - Nassau in the Bahamas was the scene of a very memorable New Year's Day celebration. At 2:00 AM, we hurried to Bay Street a short distance from our hotel. It appeared that the entire island population was lined up along the miles long parade route. The island was about to come alive with the sound of drumbeats pulsating to rhythmic steps of islanders as they marched in the annual "Junkanoo" parade. This annual parade is their Mardi Gras and they spare no efforts designing mysterious looking, full body costumes made from cardboard. Their floats were also made from cardboard adorned with sequins and plenty of glitter and crepe paper. It was explained that the reason for the cardboard construction was to keep the weight of the float at a minimum. The parade rules state that the floats cannot be motorized and that only <u>one individual</u> is allowed to carry or physically pull the float along the entire parade route.

Elaborately costumed dancers beat on drums, rang cowbells and blew whistles, as they produced sounds to mimic original African jungle music. The scene was an endless sea of color as one float after another passed in front of us. "Mama, bake your Johnny Cake, New Years is coming," shouted the performing dancers. Another recognizable chant was "We're rushin', we're rushin', we're rushin' through the crowd." Each family and each entered group, worked for weeks creating their theme floats, coordinating them with their costumes, their music and their dance routines. The competition was keen. Thousands of prize dollars were at stake. No efforts were spared to present the best of the best. This expression of Afro-Caribbean culture was a never to be forgotten explosion of color and rhythm. It truly was a royal feast for both eye and ear, and a grand way to begin the New Year.

AUSTRALIA - Just last year, we experienced the longest ever air flight. It took thirteen hours as we traveled from Los Angeles to Sydney, Australia. Our cruise ship was anchored near the Sydney Opera House, a sight we had often seen on picture post cards. The sights and sounds of that "Land Down Under'" were both enjoyable and intellectually stimulating. For instance we learned that there really is a Tasmania and that there really is an animal called the Tasmanian Devil. To prove the point we even brought back some stuffed animal Tasmanian Devils for the grandchildren.

As we cruised from Australia to ports of call in New Zealand we were fortunate to visit that island country during the Maori peoples "Freedom Day" celebration. Their "Freedom Day" is similar to our 4th of July. Dressed in colorful regalia the Maori people paraded with banners of every color and native insignias. They held boating contests and spear contests. They debated the "English Colonial" control in public and at length speaking both in English and Maori language. How fortunate we were to attend Mass, much of which was celebrated in the Maori language. We were enraptured as we listened to the choir chant the Entrance Antiphon in that rhythmic Polynesian language.

On one of our tours while in Christchurch our cabby pointed out the jailhouse building. He told us that it was the least used building in town. Violent crime was virtually non-existent. The majority of the jail occupants, he went on to say, were drunk drivers. During that tour we learned that the kiwi fruit grows on vines in arbors similar to grape arbors. We were fortunate to sample some "fresh" off the vine kiwi fruit.

Snakes In The River - Another vacation experience worth sharing is one that happened right here in the good old U.S.A. It was a vacation taken with our daughters. We had received an invitation to experience a "free four night's lodging" in a fully furnished log cabin in Hot Springs, Arkansas. All that was required was that we spend some time with the promoters listening to their presentations. We even received a fifty-dollar bill to pay for the gas used on the drive to that Arkansas resort. What a deal.

While relaxing at that resort we decided to take a canoe trip down one of the rivers as advertised in their local newspaper. We drove to the canoe rental station located at the starting point for the river trip. There we rented two canoes, one for the girls and one for us. The girls jumped into their canoe and a mild current set them off. Mary and I followed floating down the river right behind them. As we approached a bridge the girls ducked down and went right under it. Mary and I couldn't do that so we got out of the canoe and jumped into the knee high waters. I held the canoe while Mary walked around to the other side of the bridge. I then pushed the canoe under the bridge. Mary caught it and held it until I walked around the bridge. We both got into the canoe and continued our river trip. At the next bridge we did the same. We hurried back into the canoe when we noticed a snake sunning itself on the river's edge. When we arrived at the end of our canoe trip we asked the young man who retrieved the canoes whether the snake that we saw could have been poisonous. He said the river was full of poisonous snakes! We shuddered at the thought of us walking around in the waters of that river with those snakes swimming around us. Had we known about the poisonous snakes we would not have taken that canoe trip.

A Millennium Present - There is one more vacation worthy of mentioning and that was our 1999 vacation in Puerto Vallarta, Mexico. Mary and I so thoroughly enjoyed our all inclusive, eight day stay at Club Marival, an ocean side resort, that we decided to treat all of our children, their spouses and all of our grandchildren to an all-inclusive vacation at that resort. It would be a "millenium present" for all 23 of us in the year 2000! Indoor and outdoor restaurants catered to every gastronomical delight from early morning to midnight. The swimming pools were equipped with "swim-up" bars serving both alcoholic and non-alcoholic drinks. Ocean surfing and other water sports occupied some of our children's time, while the grandchildren were busy competing in sand castle building and other sponsored events on the beach. Residents of nearby villages hawked their wares. Corn-braiding of hair was an art form that the locals performed with perfection. Our girls enjoyed parading around with their newly acquired "hair-does." Viewing spectacular sunsets from our balconies, which overlooked the ocean, was a pleasure in which we delighted at the end of each day. It proved to be an excellent time for family bonding and a "FAMILY" vacation never to be forgotten.

Someone Always Has It Worst - There is an experience that I want to share regarding one of our gambling trips to the Indian Casinos in Wisconsin. I enjoy playing Black Jack and have improved substantially from my first attempts at that enjoyable game. It gives me a thrill and a special kind of "rush." One day while sitting in the third position at a blackjack table, I felt as though someone was staring at me. Out of the corner of my eye I confirmed that the lady sitting in the first position was looking squarely at me. The second position at the table was empty. It began to be uncomfortable and I asked her if anything was the matter; was I annoying her? "Oh, my goodness, no'" she responded. "I'm not looking at you; I'm looking at my husband sitting over there." She pointed him out. He was sitting in her line of view, playing a slot. "He has Alzheimer's," she said, "and I sit him down at a slot while I take a seat at the table so that I can keep an eye on him. We come once a week for a little relaxation and enjoyment."

I struck up a conversation with her as we played, asking if she had any children who could take care of him. Yes she had children, three of them. One had died from cancer and the second of her children had just died from ALS. "What about your third child?" I asked. The lady replied, "she is in her final stages of life, dying of kidney failure." Wow! And I thought I had problems! Thank you Dear Lord for placing this lady next to me, I said to myself. What more demonstrative proof can there be that, regardless of how difficult one may think their life is, there is always someone whose life is even more difficult. I experienced another of life's powerful lessons first hand: "Don't count your troubles, count your blessings!"

Chapter XXX - FIFTIETH ANNIVERSARY OF GRADE SCHOOL GRADUATION

In 1993 the St. John the Baptist Catholic grade school class of 1943 celebrated their golden graduation anniversary. The 50th class reunion began with a Mass at St. John's church followed by a gala reception held in St. John's Panel Room. The committee asked me to be the Toastmaster for the occasion. I considered it a privilege and was honored to oblige. I began by commenting as to how many of us fit into those same church pews back then as compared to now. Where the church pew easily accommodated six of us 8th graders, we now found ourselves rubbing shoulders with only four of us in a pew. Times have changed!

The text of my prepared address is as follows:

The Year was 1939 and we were in the 4th grade. Sister Finbar was our teacher. She told us of an exceptional event that was happening at St. John's that weekend in 1939. There was going to be a 50th grade school class reunion. That my fellow classmates was the class of 1889! Back then, as kids, we didn't think anyone could live to be that old! If that doesn't age us, I don't know what will. Now, some fifty years later here we are celebrating a golden anniversary of our 1943 gradeschool graduation. Let us go back in time and recall gradeschool memories of a lifetime ago.

A black draped church as Fr. Rajcany's remains were brought to lie in state in what was then the new church. Fr. Kostik became our new pastor and remained pastor during all of our grade school years. Frs. Stadtherr, Telegdy, Lefko and Lutkimeyer were some of the assistants. Sister Constance was our Superior. Pope Pius XII was the Pope, Franklin D. Roosevelt was the President and Ray J.

Madden was our congressman. It seemed as though those three were in office forever. I often wondered when they were going to pass away so that we could have a new pope or president or congressman. Our nuns were 1st grade girls—Sr. Frances Elizabeth and 1st grade boys—Sr. Mary Ann; 2nd grade girls—Sr. Ellen Marie and Sr. Mary Brandon; 2nd grade boys—Sr. St. Lawrence; 3rd grade was Sr. Mary Avelino for the boys and Sr. Jean Marie for the girls. 4th grade Sr. Finbar for the boys and Sr. Jean Therese for the girls. 5th grade was Sr. Bernardo for the boys and the girls had two nuns——Sr. Lauerente and Mary Regina. In 6th grade the boys had Sr. Bernardo for another year (how devastating for some of us) and the girls had Sr. Ann Joachim. In the 7th grade the boy's nun was Sr. Mary Edward and the girls had Sr. Philomene Marie. In our final year at St. John's, the girls had Sr. Bridget Therese and the boys had Sr. Mary DeLourdes. When I conclude my presentation I'm going to ask you to share special memories that you associate with a particular nun or grade or priest. So, as I'm talking, remember, if you will, those happenings that left a lasting impression on you. Some of those impressions could very well been left on our knuckles or our rear ends!

A typical school day or week from the year 1943 went something like this: We all walked to school, rain, snow or shine. For some of us that walk was a mile and more. How long it would take to get to school depended on how many cans we might find to crunch over our shoe heel. Tin cans on heels, our pace would slow down as we made enough clatter to be noticed. When we got to school we went straight to church for Mass. We sat in the pews with our classes. Occasionally some of us "misbehaving ones" would have to sit next to Sister! The girls wore a headdress and sat on the Blessed Mother's side and the boys sat on St. Joseph's side of church. If it were 1st Friday we received Holy Communion as we knelt at the Communion rail. Afterwards, at our desks in school, we got chocolate milk and donuts. What a breakfast treat that was.

Our class subjects were Religion, Reading, English, Spelling, Arithmetic, U.S. History, and Geography and on Fridays we had Drawing and Music. We were graded on each of these subjects plus grades for Home Work, Conduct, Effort and Order. Also noted on our report cards were daily Mass attendance, Days Absent and Tardiness. I've brought along some of my report cards. I often wondered why I saved them. Now I know. It must have been for an occasion such as this or perhaps to show my grandchildren that grandpa was no angel!

Morning recess found us playing "migs" or marbles. We had shooters, commies, pimpies and boulders. The girls played jacks and jumped rope. The older girls jumped double dutch rope. We played ball on the street between the old church and the rectory. Old man Job lurked in his yard waiting for a fly ball. I believe we voted him the best outfielder on 119th St.

Sometimes we would listen to Mr. Zabrecky's squirrel hunting stories. Occasionally Nick Martich would come around, banging one hand against the other as he held our attention with outlandish stories. During the winter we slid on the ice in the schoolyard. If the packing were good we would throw snowballs around. An 8th grade boy rang a handheld cowbell to signal that recess was over. We all lined up class by class. There was silence; a Victrola blared out a marching tune as we marched to our classrooms. Does anyone remember the tune?

At noontime the patrol boys were excused from classes

earlier to get to their assigned crossing stations. With our white canvas patrol belts on, we sure felt important. We were little policemen authorized to stop cars, and stop cars we did. Most of us went home for lunch except if it was below zero or a blizzard. Then we went to Benedict Hall, the basement of the new church, for some of Pat Wirtz's tomato soup which he served with oyster crackers. It cost a nickel for the hot lunch. If we didn't have the nickel it was OK, we could always pay later.

After school, if we were lucky enough to have a penny, we would go to Frenchik's or Novotny's candy store. What choices we had; Holloway suckers, Boston Banked Beans, Mary Janes, Jaw Breakers, Guess Whats, Snaps, Dots (stuck on that ribbon of paper all in neat rows) and a whole showcase of other favorites. In the evening, depending on the time of the year, we had Novenas which concluded with Benediction of the Blessed Sacrament. During the war years we had Victory Novenas. The Novena to St. Theresa of the Little Flower was Fr. Kostik's favorite novena. I believe she was his favorite saint. The hymn we sang at that novena was "O blessed Little Flower, your praises now we sing....with Jesus Christ our King." When a novena ended, Fr. Kostik would, on occasion, give nickels to the servers. That was a special treat. Now we could go to Frenchik's or Novotny's and get a whole bag of candy, or go to Condes Grocery, next to Schlater Ford and buy a bottle of that new pop, Dr. Pepper. Or, we might go to the Igloo, at the corner of the Illiana Hotel building to choose our ice cream cone from ten different flavors.

White Castle was at the next corner and we could get a hamburger for that nickel. If we walked past Banana Bill's fruit stand, located kitty corner from the Igloo, Banana Bill with umbrella in hand, and would chase us away. At times we saved up our nickels to go see a movie. The admission to see a movie was a dime. At the Hoosier Theater we saw feature movies like "The Song of Bernadette," "For Whom the Bells Toll," of "Bud Abbot and Lou Costello Meet Frankenstein." On Saturdays, during the intermission, the theatre manager threw peanuts from the stage. If we were lucky we caught a peanut with a "free admission" pass tucked in it. Across the street was the Capitol Theater where you could see a triple feature cowboy movie for a dime. Cowboy favorites were Gene Autry, Hop-A -Long Cassidy, Sunset Carson, The Lone Ranger and of course Tom Mix, the "All American Boy." Also, if we saved that nickel that Fr. Kostik gave us, we could buy the Sunday paper which was sold in front of church.

Our mothers were miracle workers as they prepared meals bought with ration stamps. They needed Red stamps to purchase meat and blue for canned goods. I have a book of them on display on the table over there. Our mothers stored their perishables in wooden iceboxes. The amount of ice that the iceman delivered depended on the position of the "ice card" in our front room window. If the number 50 appeared on top, he brought in a 50-pound block of ice. If 25 or 75 or 100 appeared as the top number, the iceman brought in a block of ice that weighed that much. Besides the rationing of meat and canned goods, sugar and coffee were also rationed. My family didn't have to worry about the "A," "B" or "C" gas rationing stickers, we didn't have a car. Shoes were also rationed and made from reclaimed rubber soles, the kind that left black marks on the gym floor.

After supper, around Halloween time, we would go to the Community Center parking lot behind Ciesar's Plymouth - Chrysler dealership for a bon fire. During that bon fire Tojo, Mussolini and Hitler were burned in effigy. On a more typical evening, after supper and after our homework was done, we listened to the radio. What a treat as we listened and let our imaginations go to work. "Who knows what evil lurks in the hearts of men? The Shadow knows." Or we would hear "With his faithful Indian companion, Tonto, the daring and resourceful masked rider of the plains led the fight for law and order in the early Western United States. Nowhere in the pages of history can one find a greater champion of justice! Return with us now to those thrilling days of yesteryear....From out of the past comes the thundering hoofbeats of the great horse Silver! The Lone Ranger rides again!"

During our gradeschool days we drank a lot of Ovaltine. We saved the Ovaltine container tops to get decoder rings or magic "glow-in-the-dark" belts and buckles. It was the golden age of radio with programs like Inner Sanctum, Captain Midnight, Gangbusters, Just Plain Bill, Amos & Andy, the Hit Parade and many others. We listened to a lot of cigarette commercials like "call for Phillip Morris," or "Luckies are kind to your throat," or "Old Golds - not a cough in a car load." Pepsi Cola sang its praises with the jingle "Pepsi Cola hits the spot, twelve full ounces, that's a lot, twice as much for a nickel too, too to ro, too, too, too, Pepsi is the drink for you."

The evening news began with "Good evening Mister and Missus American and all the ships at sea," followed by Morse code beeps. In 1943 Walter Winchel told us that the tide of war was turning against the Axis Powers - against Germany in North Africa and against Japan in the Pacific. United States forces had taken Guadalcanal and Munda in the Solomon Islands. Mussolini and his entire cabinet resigned. Allies began "round the clock" bombing of

Germany. The Allied Air Force began bombing the Ploesti Romanian oil fields. With these and other air strikes, the devastation of much of Europe began.

On the home front the "pay as you go" Tax Payment Act was adopted in late 1943. Employers were ordered to withhold taxes from salaries and wages. In medicine, Penicillin was applied for the first time in the treatment of chronic diseases. The "Pap" test was recognized and approved by the medical establishment. In men's fashions the "Zoot Suit" with its long chain became the popular dress of "hepcats." On the farm front DDT was introduced to fight insect pests resulting in increased farm crop yields. In Washington D.C, the year 1943 saw the completion of the Pentagon. The Jefferson Memorial was also dedicated in that year. If we didn't get the news by radio, we got it from the guy running down the street hawking newspapers and yelling "Extra, Extra, read all about it!"

Some local sporting announcements came from the church pulpit before the Sunday sermon. We listened intently to hear what baseball games would be played at the Whiting Park baseball field that afternoon. The priest made announcements something like this: "St. Johns vs. Sacred Heart at 1:00 PM. followed by SS Peter & Paul vs. St. Als." At six o'clock it would be St. Mary's vs. I.C. Concessions were sold in the stands. Vendors hawked Cracker Jack as they shouted out "Cracker Jack, a prize in each and every pack. Cracker Jack, a nickel a pack...." Special victories would rate a celebration at Roby Café in Roby, Indiana or at Lundgrens where our classmate, Joe Dolak, was a bus boy.

Among the songs that were popular in the year that we graduated from grade school were: "I'm Looking Over a four Leaf Clover," "Praise the Lord and Pass the Ammunition,"

"Good Night Irene," "Coming in on a Wing and a Prayer," "I'll Be Seeing You," "When the Lights Go On Again," "The Wiffenpoof Song" and, of course, "Mairzy Doats." We hear these 1943 hits as they were sung on Saturday's radio program "The Hit Parade." The "Hit Parade" stars who sang those songs were Dorothy Collins, Teresa Brewer and Snooky Lanson. Military favorites were "From the Halls of Montezuma," "Anchors Aweigh," "Off We Go Into the Wild Blue Yonder," and the Army Caisson Song.

There are some statistics from *then and now* that are worthy of mention. For instance: The World Population more than doubled from 2.3 billion to today's 5.3 billion. The population in the US alone doubled from 125 to 250 million. Life expectancy for women increased from 67 to 79 years, and, for men, from 63 to 72 years. Major league baseball attendance rose from eleven million to fifty-four million, to say nothing of the salaries of professional ballplayers. Attendance at professional football games rose from one million to seventeen million.

Food prices during our grade school days were: nine cents for a loaf of bread; twelve cents for a quart of milk; eighteen cents for a dozen of sweet rolls; butter twelve cents a pound, ham eighteen cents a pound, coffee fifteen cents a pound and ground beef was fifteen cents a pound. Pillsbury flour, for that delicious home made bread which our mothers made, was eighty-three cents for a twenty-five pound bag. Those were the days. Cigarettes for our dads were $1.10 a carton; soap was a nickel a bar; Carters Little Liver pills were nineteen cents for a pack; Bromo Quinine was twenty cents for a thirty-count pack. Our graduation suits, with two pair of pants cost $10.95. Girls Graduation dresses were priced at $5.95 and our shoes cost $1.97. So our parents were able to outfit us for graduation for less than $15.00. The average hourly rate, however, for the ordinary worker, was just under a dollar an hour. All in all the cost of living may have been a bit higher back then, as opposed to what it is now.

The changes, which have occurred in our lifetime, have been as never before. We have witnessed the rise and fall of the Communistic Empire. We have been part of a technological explosion the likes of which had never been experienced before. Ours has been a lifetime during which we have benefited in every conceivable way—in medicine, communication, education, transportation, and recreation; in food and consumer goods production and in every area of our daily lives. We even landed a man on the moon!

Without a doubt you and I, all of us, owe a debt of gratitude to the Precious Blood Fathers for sharing their lives with us as they ministered to our spiritual needs. We are further forever grateful to the Sisters of Providence who labored so unselfishly not only in providing for us an educational foundation but also gave nurture to our faith, the faith of our fathers! And last but not least of all we cannot forget our parents to whom we owe a debt of gratitude.

At this time it is only proper and fitting to recognize Helen Bencur who spearheaded this reunion and the committee who worked along with her - Mitzie Holman, Norb Duray and the four Joes - Dolak, Domasica, Gulvas and Tomko. Let us please give them a round of applause.

Now, with your permission, I would like to invite you to share your memories fond or otherwise, of your grade school days."

Many grade school stories were then shared. A delightful time was had by all as we reminisced about the "good old days" of fifty years ago!

Chapter XXXI - GRANDCHILDREN

Grandchildren do say the funniest things and often in an uninhibited way. What they say sometimes means one thing to them and another to us. For example: One day while baby-sitting our four year old grandson Sammy Sanders, we heard him bemoaning the fact that Dinah Shore died. In very solemn tones he repeated: "Dinah Shore died." "Yes', Sammy," we said, "Dinah Shore did die." Well, it was a fact, she died the night before, and the newspapers carried the story that morning. But how and why would this four year old know anything about Dinah Shore, we asked ourselves? Why would he feel so sad about her death? We reasoned that even his mother Carol, our daughter, would more than likely know very little if anything about Dinah Shore. What difference would it make to her in any case?

We called Carol to ask why Sammy was so sad about Dinah Shore dying and why did he keep on repeating that Dinah Shore died. Carol burst into uncontrollable laughter. She explained that as they drove past Carroll Chevrolet in Crown Point, on their way to our house, Sammy noticed that the larger than life, inflated **dinosaur** had collapsed and lay on the ground. Someone had let the air out. So, yes, the dinosaur indeed had died. What we thought we heard him say was not what he was saying.

When the grandkids come for a visit they often say, "Grandpa, let's go for a ride around the property." We hook the Christmas tree farm wagon to the John Deere 345 lawn and garden tractor, set a blanket in the wagon and out we go. One sunny summer day Sammy and Sophia Sanders were visiting along with their cousins Abi and Garret Small. "Let's go for a ride around the property," they said.

It was a perfect day for a leisurely ride as we rode around the Christmas tree farm. They said, "Grandpa let's have a picnic." "Great," I said, "but let's go ask Grandma to make a picnic lunch." Grandma made a delicious lunch. We placed the picnic basket in the wagon and off we went driving around looking for the perfect spot to have that picnic. It was a small clearing right in the center of some nicely shaped Douglas Fir Christmas trees. We spread the blanket and sat down to enjoy Grandma's fixings.

After lunch Sophia decided to treat me. She was going to do the dance that she and her cousin Abi had just learned in dancing school. Those two five year-old granddaughters often practiced their "One-two-three step, one-two-three step" dance. So, Sophia jumped on the seat of the tractor and made a motion as though she had turned on a knob. "What did you do," I asked. "I turned on the radio," Sophia answered. "And what are we listening to?" I asked. "Dancing music, Grandpa, and I'm going to dance for you." As she jumped off the tractor Abi jumped on and made the same kind of motion as Sophia had. "What did you do?" I asked Abi. Abi said,"I turned off the radio, I don't like that kind of music!" "You shouldn't have done that," I said sadly, "Sophia was going to dance to that music for me." Sophia said, "Grandpa, that's all right I can dance without music!" What a pleasure it was to experience this childish fantasy and to watch such beautiful imaginations at play.

Of Television fame was the baptism of our grandson Michael "Mick" Metcalf, son of Dorothy and Tommy Metcalf. The baby was brought to the baptismal font at St. Paul's Church in Valparaiso, covered only with a blanket, otherwise naked. During the baptism the priest dipped the entire backside of the baby into the baptismal font three times saying, "I baptize you in the name of the Father and of The Son and of the Holy Spirit." He then handed Mick to his godfather Michael Kapitan. Mike held the baby facing the baptismal font in an upright position. Just as the priest was about to anoint the forehead of the baby, Mick decided to take a leak. The stream was a perfect arch right into the center of the baptismal font. As the arch got smaller, and so that no pee fell to the floor, Mike edged his way right up to the baptismal font where Mick finished his duty. It was difficult to keep ourselves composed. As a matter of fact the priest, who had never seen anything like that before, joined us in laughter. All the while our daughter Laura was videotaping the Christening ceremony and captured the entire incident on tape.

Mick Goes To Hollywood - At the Christening party suggestions were being made to send the tape to the "America's Funniest Home Videos" TV program. Dorothy and Tommy did exactly that. Within two months the studio called to say that their video would be shown on national TV. During the following week the Hollywood studio sent a limo to transport the threesome to O'Hare. There they boarded a flight for Hollywood, bound for the studios of "America's Funniest Home Videos." During their four-day stay in Hollywood all expenses were paid, including a per diem allowance for baby Mick's diapers and baby food!

On the Sunday appointed for the television debut of our newly baptized grandson, we called everyone we knew to announce the good fortune that befell our daughter, son-in-law, and grandson. They were going to be on national TV and we had everyone watching. As the video progressed and Mick was shown peeing into the baptismal font, the studio audience went into an uproar. There was no question but that Mick would take the first prize. Back home, as in the studio, we were ecstatic when the announcement came that Mick Metcalf won the first prize of $10,000.00.

NOT-SO-HOLY WATER

GEOFFREY BLACK / THE TIMES

Tom and Dorothy Metcalf won $10,000 from America's Funniest Home Videos for their son Mick's baptism.

'Whiz Kid' The

Video of Mick Metcalf's baptism wins Valparaiso family $10,000 on America's Funniest Home Videos.

BY TAMARA L. O'SHAUGHNESSY
Times Staff Writer

VALPARAISO – Little Mick Metcalf really took a "shot" at fame July 27.

With a pout on his face and a godfather cradling him on his back, the tiny, naked 6-week-old started to pee – a perfect arch that landed smack in the center of the baptismal pond.

St. Paul Catholic Church, filled with about 50 family members who witnessed the baby's full immersion during the solemn ceremony, burst with "uproarious laughter," father Tom Metcalf says.

Mick's godmother Mary Kapitan clasped her hand to her mouth, godfather Mike Kapitan checked to make sure Mick didn't hit his shoes and Mick's mother, Dorothy (Kapitan) Metcalf, quickly diapered her boy.

Now, five seconds of Mick's baptism

On the air

Tom and Dorothy Metcalf's video clip will air at 7 p.m. Monday on America's Funniest Home Videos, on ABC.

– titled The Whiz Kid – have won his parents $10,000 from ABC's America's Funniest Home Videos. The show will air at 7 p.m. on Monday.

The studio audience voted the video clip as the best in the show, which was filmed Oct. 29 in Hollywood, Calif.

"It all happened so fast." Tom says. "... We really didn't have time to get excited, because the next thing you know, boom, we're on a plane to California."

At everyone's urging, Dorothy, a pharmacist at Community Hospital in Munster, sent the tape into the show at the end of August. The show's producers called in mid-October and five days

after they got the call to appear on the show, they were on a plane bound for Hollywood.

As they watched, Dorothy says she didn't think the audience really laughed very much. It turns out they were doing a lot of laughing; the Metcalfs were just intent on watching the video.

"I didn't know what to say, I kind of started crying," Dorothy says when they were announced as the winner.

They returned to Valparaiso the next day, only to have to rearrange work schedules to fly back to Hollywood the following week for the $100,000 grand prize show. They didn't win.

"I think it's more exciting now," Dorothy says about watching the video next week.

After taxes, though, Tom, a stay-at-home dad who works as a part-time bartender at the Radisson in Merrillville,

See VIDEO, A-2

Within a month Dorothy, Tommy and Mick Metcalf were invited to return to Hollywood to compete in the competition for the grand prize of $100,000.00. Again, all

299

expenses were paid. Daisy Fuentes, the co-host of the program, told Dorothy and Tommy that their Mick was a "shoe-in." We were disappointed that the judges did not think the way that most everyone who witnessed the competition did. Regardless, we now had a grandson who was a TV star, and, boy, were we one proud family.

Another Miracle? - It was just last year that Mike and Mary's boys were witnesses to the miraculous power of prayer. Mary and I drove to our summer home on Swan Lake in Allegan, Michigan, for a summer weekend. As we drove eastward along I 80 -94 we decided to stop for a sandwich. It was the midway point of our drive. Mary pulled into a Burger King facility and parked the car. We got out and she locked the car doors with her remote and we began walking towards the restaurant. I felt for my wallet. It wasn't there. When we travel, I will usually remove my wallet from my back pocket and place it in the glove compartment. I asked Mary to unlock the car, which she did with the remote, and I retrieved my wallet. As I did I noticed a ratty old van with some black people in it. They were eyeing our Lincoln Cartier and I thought very little about that.

Inside we ordered our sandwiches and I asked the "floor sweeper" if he could get me more mayonnaise. "Youuu stay rrright heere'" he said in a halting voice, "annd I'll get itt forr youu." As we left I gave him a dollar, thinking that he probably seldom if ever gets a tip. As I did that, a black man standing next to me said, "What did you do that for?" I explained and he patted me on the back saying, "You're a good man, mister." He followed us outside and again said, "You're really a good man mister." He went to that ratty old van and entered it.

An hour later we arrived at Swan Lake. As we got out,

Mary went for her purse. It wasn't there. She looked inside and outside the car just in case it fell out as she opened the door. It wasn't there. Just then our son Mike pulled up with his family. Mary explained that she was looking for her purse. The boys began helping her. They even searched the house thinking that perhaps she brought it in. It was nowhere to be found. Mary called our daughter Laura in Crown Point and asked her to go to our house in Merrillville to take a look. Perhaps the purse had been left on the kitchen table. It wasn't there.

Mary keeps her purse on the floor to the left of her as she drives. Once she gets to her destination she either takes the purse with her or she places it on the hump in the floor between the front seats. She was positive that she had placed the purse on the hump in the floor between the front seats. When she unlocked the door for me with her remote, I retrieved my wallet from the glove compartment and did not think to lock the car doors. Did the occupants of that ratty old van parked next to us, take the purse from the unlocked car?

Mary was distraught. All her important papers were in it with several hundred dollars in cash. Also there was several hundred dollars worth of "Trip Tickets" from St. Mary's Catholic School in Crown Point. They were negotiable by bearer. "The heck with the money and the tickets," Mary said, "Let's pray for a return of at least my wallet with all the important papers."

We decided to call the Burger King where we had stopped several hours before. Perhaps it might have fallen out of our parked car and lay there in the parking lot. But which Burger King was it? There are many of them along I 80-94. The local Burger King restaurant provided us with several telephone numbers. We were in luck; Mary located the restaurant on her first call. She told the manager of her plight and asked if they had a handicapped person who swept the floors. "Oh' yes," the manager replied, "that is Keith. He had a serious automobile accident that left him impaired." Mary knew that we had the right place. It was Keith who had brought me that extra packet of mayonnaise. She asked the manager if he would look around and told him where we had parked. He went out and looked around. When he came back to the phone he said, "Your purse is not here, and I've looked all around, even in the trash cans." He suggested that we call the State Police, which we did.

The responding officer said he would investigate and call us back. He did and the news was not good. He scoured the entire area and the purse was nowhere to be found. Mary decided to pray not only to Rudy but also to St. Anthony, the patron saint of lost objects. We all joined in the prayer of supplication. The following morning a Michigan State trooper called to say that the purse had been found. We were elated beyond belief. The trooper said that someone had brought it into the Burger King restaurant that morning. The manager didn't seem to know who brought it in. We hurried to Michigan Post 16 where Mary identified the contents of the purse. The police had logged in every item in that purse. To our utter amazement not a single object was missing from the purse, which had been missing for the better part of a second day. Were the occupants of that ratty old van involved? Did my act of kindness to that impaired floor sweeper have an impact on whomever? We'll never know for sure. What we, and especially our grandsons, came to know is that our prayers were answered

Christening Of Our Last (?) Grandchild - The

following is a letter that Mary and I wrote to my brother John and his wife Mary on the occasion of the baptism of our latest granddaughter:

Dear John and Mary: "This past Sunday, Maggie Ann Metcalf was baptized at St. Paul's church in Valparaiso. Maggie is the daughter of Dorothy, our youngest, and her husband Tommy. Maggie's four piece-christening outfit was the one purchased in 1958 for Rudolph Joseph Kapitan's christening by his godparents John and Mary Kapitan.

Her uncle Rudy was the first to wear that special christening outfit followed by his brother Michael and his sisters, Susan, Carol, Laura and Dorothy.

Jackie Scuderi, our first grandchild (Susan's daughter) was christened in that outfit in April of 1985 and then Richard Scuderi in Oct. of 1986 and Matthew Scuderi in May of 1990.

Naturally, in March of 1990, our *twins*, Jacob and Brandon Michael Kapitan (Michael's sons and the first to carry on our Kapitan name) wore their own *individual* christening outfits. In May of 1992 Sammy Sanders (Carol's son) was the tenth infant to wear that special christening outfit. In the next year, 1993, it was worn by Andrew Kapitan.

During the following year it was worn twice, by Abigael Small (Laura's daughter) in May of 1994 and by Sophia Sanders in June of 1994. Still in remarkably excellent condition, it was worn by Garret Small in August of 1996.

In September of 1997 Michael Metcalf (Dorothy's son) was presented for baptism in this family heirloom. Olivia Small wore the christening outfit for her christening in June of 2001. Now, in its' forty-fourth year and for the seventeenth time, Maggie Ann Metcalf was baptized into the faith of our fathers, wearing the christening outfit purchased by John and Mary Kapitan back in 1958 for our dearly departed Rudy. We believe the christening outfit will now be put to rest to be used again by our great grandchildren! We thought that you would like to know. With love, Rudy & Mary"

The final photo is that of our grandchildren taken on March 8, 2003 as they gathered to celebrate the seventieth birthday of their grandmother Mary Kasper Kapitan.

THE BEGINNING OF THE LAST CHAPTER

In the seventy-third year of my life and the forty sixth year of our marriage, I am truly blessed to have experience most all of life's emotions, trials, tribulations & happiness beyond imagination. After each storm of life a rainbow, invariably, appeared; evidence that GOD IS GOOD! I wish to recount the latest of my life's blessings which involves the Cardiac Rehab program at Broadway Methodist Hospital.

Three one-hour weekly sessions under the guidance of Norma, Jan, Judy, Jerry and Rachael make for a "heart pumping" experience. Devotion to duty is displayed by each of the afore-mentioned as they diligently monitor all of our activities. Under their watchful eyes we receive cardiopulmonary benefits unique to such a health filled experience. Their zeal and enthusiasm provide attainable goals. To achieve some of those goals we also receive beneficial lectures from our knowledgeable dietician Jerome Sabo. The dedication and devotion to duty as demonstrated by the Cardiac Rehab team contributes to the well-being of those of us who are fortunate to receive their undivided attention.

In summary, the presentation of my life story has truly been a wonderful adventure. From a meager two bedroom basement apartment as a pre teen lad in post depression and pre WWII Whiting, to a country home six decades later as the father of six and grandfather of thirteen, my wife of 46 years agrees with me that it has indeed been a blessed life.

AN ADDENDUM —

MOTHER'S RECIPES

Many of the readers of my earlier book, "Seasons of My Childhood," said that they hungered with me in my mother's kitchen. They asked that I include recipes for some of the delicious foods that were described in that book. One of my readers exclaimed, "If only I had your mother's recipes I would think that I died and went to heaven." So here are a few of those recipes for which many have hungered. The following are among my favorites from mother's kitchen:

SZEKELY GOULASH:

I tablespoon oil
1 medium onion chopped
1teaspoon caraway seed
2 tablespoons sour cream

1 to 2 lbs. cubed pork
1 quart drained sauerkraut
1/4 cup flour
pint water

Heat the oil in large frying pan. Add cubed pork and allow to brown. Add chopped onion. Simmer until brown. Add rinsed and drained sauerkraut, water to cover and caraway seed. Simmer about an hour with cover on the frying pan. In a separate container mix together 2 Tbs. sour cream, 1/4 cup flour, mix together. Add a little milk if too thick. Pour over the pork and sauerkraut mixture and simmer for about 5 minutes. Add salt and pepper to taste. Goes good with a thick slice of homemade bread; otherwise use some crusty rye bread. Your drink, if you are over 18, is a can of ice cold beer.

GRANDMA'S SLOVAK MEATLOAF:

1 lb ground beef

1/4 lb.ground pork

1/4 lb ground veal

1/2 cup breadcrumbs

1 tablespoon chopped parsley

1 can cream of mushroom soup

Several sliced potatoes and carrots

I medium onion, chopped

2 ribs chopped celery

1 egg

1/4 teaspoon oregano

salt and pepper to taste

2 cans of water

Mix beef, ground pork (bulk pork sausage can be used) and the ground veal. Add the chopped onion, celery, parsley and bread crumbs. Add the oregano, blend in the egg and add a bit of salt and pepper. Form into giant sized hamburger patty. Place patty into frying pan and allow to brown on both sides Flip patty back to original side and drain fat if necessary. In separate bowl mix 1 can cream of mushroom or cream of celery or potato or asparagus soup with two cans of water. Pour over meat loaf. Surround the meat loaf with plenty of sliced potatoes and carrots. Cover and simmer for one hour and enjoy grandma's meatloaf with all the vegetables and gravy you need for a perfect meal.

CHICKEN PAPRIKASH with DUMPLINGS

1chicken, 2 & 1/2 To 3 lbs.	1 medium onion
2 tablespoons butter	2 tablespoons flour
1 teaspoon sweet paprika	1 pint sour cream

THE CHICKEN: Sauté onion in melted butter. Add the paprika. Section and cut chicken into parts. Salt and pepper and place into melted butter, onion and paprika mixture. Allow to simmer for about an hour, until chicken is fork tender. Remove chicken and add the 2 tablespoons of flour to the sautéed onion and paprika mixture. Add the sour cream, mixing as you do. Place chicken into the gravey and sgtir. Simmer a few minutes and enjoy!

THE DUMPLINGS: 4 eggs, add 1/2 teaspoon salt, mix in 1 to 1&1/2 cups flour. (If too thick add some water.) With edge of teaspoon, spoon the mixture into pot of boiling water. When dumplings float to the top (in about 15 minutes) they are ready. Strain in colander under hot water to keep warm and serve with the chicken. Delicious all year long!

VEAL PAPRIKASH :
Same as above except use cubed veal instead of the chicken. Yum, Yum**!**

BUCHTY S KAPUSTOU:

8 medium potatoes cubed and pureed in blender. Add 2 eggs, 1 teaspoon salt and a dash of pepper. Place the mixture in mixing bowl and add 1/2 cup flour (if too loose add flour as necessary). Mix well. Spoon the mixture with the edge of a teaspoon into pot of boiling water. When potato dumplings float to the top (in about fifteen minutes) they are done. Drain in colander under hot water and keep warm. Fry 1 lb of bacon until crisp and remove bacon from frying pan. Crumble into bits. Remove some grease, leave @ 2 tablespoons. Add 1 quart of drained and chopped sauerkraut to the bacon grease and fry for about 1/2 hour. Add bacon bits to the fried sauerkraut and simmer for an additional 15 minutes. Add the dumplings and mix. You will need to fill a good sized soup bowl to properly enjoy grandma's delicious, ole European *buchty s kapustou.* ENJOY this Slovak favorite of mine.

BUCHTY S SYROM:

Prepare potato dumplings as above. Fry a stick of butter to a golden brown. Add cooked dumplings, 1 lb. of cubed American or cheddar cheese and 1 pint of cottage cheese. Mix well and enjoy. And, if it is not a meatless Friday during Lent, you may add crispy fried bacon bits to the *buchty* and cheese mixture.

RASCOVA POLIEVKA:

In a large sauce pan, sauté 1 tablespoon caraway seed in 1/2 stick of butter or margarine. Add 2 tablespoons flour to make a roux. Keep stirring so it does not burn. Add 1 quart of water and let simmer for 5 to 10 minutes. Prepare egg drop dumpling mixture as follows: Whip 2 eggs and add a dash of salt and 2 tablespoons of flour. Mix well. Keep mixture of pouring consistency. Gradually pour egg drop mixture into soup stirring the soup while pouring. This soup is affectionately called "sick soup." It will cure anything! I enjoyed breathing in the vapors of the aromatic caraway during the cold winter days of my youth!

CHICKEN SOUP with LIVER DUMPLINGS:

Make the chicken soup as you ordinarily would by boiling the whole chicken. Prepare the Liver Dumplings as follows: 1/2 lb beef liver or chicken livers. Remove the membrane from the beef liver. Chop liver in blender, add 1 egg, 2 tablespoons fresh (dry, if fresh is not available) parsley. Add salt and pepper to taste and blend. Place blended mixture into mixing bowl and add 2 tablespoons of flour and mix. Using the edge of a teaspoon, drop spoonfuls of mixture into boiling soup. When dumplings rise to the top, approximately 15 MINUTES, the liver dumpling chicken soup is ready to EAT! This sure was a great way to begin a Sunday noon meal. The memories of those Sunday noon meals remain as treats in themselves.

DROBY:

Droby is a potato sausage made especially for the Christmas holidays. Beef casings are filled with a potato, pork mixture. A much less time consuming way to make the droby is to omit the casings. The potato, pork mixture is oven baked. I will give you the recipe for the droby mixture:

10 lbs Idaho potatoes	1 lb bacon
2 lbs pork shoulder	2 tablespoons salt
2 onions boiled	2 onions chopped
2 teaspoons black pepper	2 tablespoons marjoram
6 tablespoons ground mint	

Peel and quarter potatoes (keep potatoes in cold water to keep from browning) Cook the pork with two onions in a soup pot until the pork is fork tender and reserve the liquid. Fry the bacon and sauté the 2 chopped onions in the bacon grease. Grind (using course grinder) all the above ingredients together except the marjoram and ground mint. Sprinkle the mint and marjoram over the ground mixture, mix well, add reserve liquid as needed and place into roasting pan and cover Bake in 350 degree oven for about one hour or until potatoes are soft. You may remove cover during the last ten minutes or so.

DROBY MIXTURE IS EXTRA TASTY AS LEFTOVERS: Brown in Teflon pan until crisp. Perfect for breakfast with a hot cup of coffee and a couple of "sunny side up" eggs.

DILL SAUCE:

2 tablespoons butter	1 cup chicken soup stock
2 tablespoons flour	Salt and pepper to taste
2 tablespoons fresh dill, chopped	4 tablespoons cream or half & half

Melt butter and sauté finely chopped dill. Blend in flour mixing well. Allow to brown, gradually adding chicken soup stock until thickened. Add cream and seasonings and simmer for three minutes. Goes well with boiled chicken meat (from the chicken soup). Can also be used over pot roast or soup meat.

BEET SAUCE:

Same ingredients as above except substitute pickled beets for the dill and beef soup stock for the chicken soup stock. Mash the beets with a fork and follow the same procedure as for the dill sauce. The beet sauce is delicious when spooned over beef soup meat and/or the potatoes which were boiled in the soup.

KNEDLIKY:

1 lb fresh plums. Remove pits and stuff with cinnamon sugar. Wrap stuffed plums with dough which is prepared in the same way as *pirohy* dough: The recipe for *pirohy* dough is as follows: Mix 4 cups flour, 2 eggs, 1/2 teaspoon salt, 1/2 cup cold milk or water and 4 oz cream cheese. Knead thoroughly; roll dough out thin and cut into 3" squares. Place a stuffed plum in the center of square, bring up ends, close all open parts by pinching the dough. Place the filled dough balls into boiling water. When they rise to the top the *knedliky* are ready to eat. We ate them garnished with hot butter fried breadcrumbs.

BUTTER FRIED BREADCRUMBS:

Melt 1/2 stick butter, add 1 cup bread crumbs, 1 tablespoon sugar and 1 teaspoon cinnamon. Mix well and fry until golden brown. Spoon or sprinkle the butter fried breadcrumbs over the *knedliky*.

A special treat when eating *pirohy* or *palacinkly* (crepes) is to sprinkle them with the butter fried breadcrumbs. Irresistible. You will want seconds!

And Now
From Grandma Anna Wagner Kasper's kitchen
To Mary Kasper Kapitan's kitchen
Their favorite filled steak recipe

FILLED STEAK:

I (Mary) cook this in a 6 quart pressure cooker. It cuts the cooking time more than one-half.

2-3# round steak	salt, 1 tsp.
1lb bacon, chopped	pepper, 1/2 tsp
2 onions. chopped	Water-1 1/2 cups
1 rib celery, chopped	Toothpicks

If bacon is fatty, fry until brown. Remove bacon and mix with onions and celery in a bowl. Add salt, pepper and whatever spices you want. If steak is about 3/4 inch thick, cut into 3"x3" squares; then slice through the squares but not all the way through, making pockets. If steak is thin, then cut into 3"x6" pieces and fold over. Place 1/2 cup of the onion-bacon mixture into the meat pocket and fasten with toothpicks. Brown both sides of the stuffed pockets in bacon grease. Add water, cover, set control and cook. After the pressure cooker control begins to jiggle, cook for 10 minutes more. Cool cooker normally for 20 minutes. Remove meat from cooker. Mix 1/4 cup flour and 1/2 cup water together and pour into cooker. Cook until thickened stirring constantly. Serve with mashed potatoes and green beans.

BIBLIOGRAPHY

Farrington, Tony. *Rescue in the Pacific.* New York, The McGraw-Hill Companies, 1996.

Hartman, Sylvester, C.PP.S *A Textbook of Logic.* New York, American Book Company, 1936.

Howard, Michael & Rogers, Louis. *The Oxford History of the Twentieth Century.* Oxford, N. Y., Oxford University Press, 1998.

Hodgson, Godfrey. *People's Century.* New York, Times Books, 1998.

Kurzman, Dan. *Left To Die.* New York, Pocket Books, 1994.

Liber Usualis. Typis Societatis S. Joannis Evang., Desclee et Socii, Parisiis, Tomaci, Romae

Manuel Of Prayers (For the Members of the Society of the Most Precious Blood) Carthagena, Ohio: Messenger Press, 1946

Nelson Derek. *The Ads That Won the War.* Osceola Wi. Motor Books International, 1992

NEWSPAPERS:

Hammond Times, The Hammond, In. Various dates 1942, 1948 and 1955

Merrillville, Herald. Merrillville, In. Various dates 1988 & 1989

Our Sunday Visitor. Gary, In. 1971

Whiting Times, The. Various dates 1940-1945

ORDERING PAGE:

Copies of this book may be ordered through Pay Pal by logging onto www.rumsclad.com

Copies may also be ordered by e-mail to:
www.rudykap@prodigy.net

Copies may be ordered by mail as follows:

Cost of one book . . . . $15.99 plus $4.00 postage.

Indiana residents add 6% sales tax ($0.96) for each book. Additional postage for multiple books ordered is $1.00 for each additional book.

Send Money Orders or Checks to:
RUMSCLAD PUBLISHING
P.O. Box 1434
Crown Point, In. 46308

Copies of my first book **SEASONS OF MY CHILDHOOD** may be ordered for 14.95 + $4.00 shipping. (Indiana residents add 90 cents for sales tax)

Send checks to:
RUMSCLAD PUBLISHING
P.O. Box 1434
Crown Point, In. 46308